To Sam Bruce

It has been a privilege to work with you.

I thank you for being a good colleague and a good friend.

I hope you enjoy reading this.

Len

2-26-2001

MANAGING
STRATEGIC
RELATIONSHIPS

THE KEY TO BUSINESS SUCCESS

LEONARD GREENHALGH

THE FREE PRESS
NEW YORK LONDON TORONTO SYDNEY SINGAPORE

*f*P

THE FREE PRESS
A Division of Simon & Schuster, Inc.
1230 Avenue of the Americas
New York, NY 10020

Designed by Lisa Chovnick
Manufactured in the United States of America

2   4   6   8   10   9   7   5   3   1

Library of Congress Cataloging-in-Publication Data
Greenhalgh, Leonard.
Managing strategic relationships: the key to business success/Leonard Greenhalgh.
p. cm.
Includes bibliographical references and index.
1. Strategic alliances (Business) 2. Business networks. 3. Decision making.
4. Success in business.   I. Title.
HD69.S8 G74 2001
658'.044—dc21   00-064641
ISBN 0-684-86769-9

To my father, who strove to understand

the world around him in depth, rather

than relying on conventional knowledge

CONTENTS

PREFACE AND
ACKNOWLEDGMENTS

I want you to read this book because it will make you think differently about management.

Countless books have been written about managing. The advice that most of them give stems from a common vision of what organizations are and how they ought to be run. Managing is usually thought of as "getting things done through the efforts of other people." So the books have focused on such things as creating the right structures, planning and organizing the unit being managed, hiring and molding the staff, delegating to them, and using control systems to make sure they get their tasks done according to plan. This common vision is what scholars call a paradigm.

I'm going to be referring to it as the old paradigm, because the business world has changed so radically that we are now in a new era. This book makes the case that managers need a new perspective if they're going to be effective in the new era. There's a lot to be learned from global competitors that have achieved market penetration nobody predicted, from organizations that gain competitive advantage from (rather than simply accommodating) a diverse workforce, from "maverick" business leaders whose instincts and vision carried them beyond orthodoxy, and from the striking attractiveness—to employees, investors, and customers—of the "dot-com" start-up companies.

The central thesis of this book is that *being effective as a manager requires you to be good at managing business relationships*—relationships with peers, workers, bosses, suppliers, customers, regulators, competitors, and various stakeholders. If you do this well, you will be able to create a sense of *commonwealth* (inclusion in a common quest) and *consensus* (commitment to an agreed-upon course of action). Getting people, groups, and the organization focused on a common goal—and strongly committed to achieving it—is the pathway to *competitive advantage*.

In practice, managing relationships within the organization has always been important, even though it hasn't been emphasized as a component of managerial effectiveness. Managing relationships beyond the organization's boundaries—particularly those within a value chain—is becoming increasingly important because the nature of competition has changed. In previous decades, conventional hierarchical organizations competed with similar organizations within domestic markets. In the new era, integrated value chains (alliances of organizations that add value as a product or service takes form) compete throughout global markets. The new era presents new challenges, which call for new understandings and skills. The old paradigm doesn't tell us enough of what we need to know, and in some cases, is misleading.

Like most of today's managers, I was trained in old-paradigm thinking. I was taught to think of organizations as mechanistic structures: top management established the strategy, and everyone *below* played a predefined role in implementing it. This view of management was simple, straightforward, and widely agreed upon. I found it particularly appealing because it resonated with my training in engineering and science. But I was disappointed when I went to work as a manager in both small and large corporations, and as a management consultant. Every organization I spent time in was running poorly, and most of what I had been taught about management seemed inadequate or irrelevant to the problems I encountered.

This sparked my interest in returning to graduate school: I wanted a greater depth of understanding. But the more I learned, the more concerned I became that management scholars had been missing the boat. Their perspective arose from studies of the homogeneous workforce of previous decades—dominated by Western white males. The organizations that had emerged from this way of thinking weren't very effective, adaptive, or fun to work in. That perspective seemed even less useful for the future, because it couldn't easily be adapted to the increasing diversity of the workforce and the globalization of business.

After completing my doctoral work in 1978, I took a faculty position at the Amos Tuck School at Dartmouth College rather than returning to life as a practitioner. My job involved teaching young managers and executives how to manage conventional organizations, how to use power to make things go their way, and how to negotiate in competitive interactions. Although the learning experience was well received, managers didn't know that they really needed to be learning something different, and I didn't know what it was I should have been teaching them. I was still a prisoner of the old paradigm.

Fortunately, teaching has been only part of my role as a professor in a graduate business school. I have also been involved in research and consulting. The research gave me a role in advancing knowledge, and the consulting kept me abreast of current management practice.

These activities exposed me to a wide variety of workers, managers, and organizational settings. But I soon learned that even the organizations most admired by the business press weren't being managed very well, and the advice academics had been offering wasn't helping them much. The best ideas were coming from forward-thinking practitioners—like Jack Welch of General Electric—who set aside conventional thinking. The nagging sense that something was missing from the basic paradigm intensified over time.

Insight about what exactly was missing came from doing some research on the effects of increasing workforce diversity. I learned that Western gender socialization tends to make women highly attuned to the strength and health of relationships. In contrast, it makes men highly attuned to dominance, exchange, and competition, but otherwise fairly oblivious to relationship quality and relational dynamics. Because men, rather than women, had usually been the ones who designed, studied, and ran organizations, it was hardly surprising that their theories, concepts, and models gave a stilted and inadequate picture of business relationships.

The research also made me aware of cultural differences in workplace relationships. While Western white males tend to be individualistic, other ethnic groups tend to be more communal. These differences lead them to form qualitatively different relationships at work, which need to be understood and, in some cases, used as models.

My thinking took a different direction. The relational view of organizations that comes naturally to many women and ethnic minorities provided a thought-provoking alternative to the mechanistic, hierarchical view that has dominated Western management thought. In fact, much richer insights can be gleaned from viewing the business world as primarily *a network of relationships,* rather than structures or transactions. The relationships that suddenly become highly visible range in complexity from interpersonal relationships with co-workers to the complex bonds that integrate value chains. These all need to be understood and managed well.

My growing understanding of the central importance of relationships changed the direction of my teaching and research. I redesigned my popular "Executive Power and Negotiation" course and renamed it "Managing Strategic Business Relationships." I still taught people to use power and negotiate; but by taking the relationship into account, they found new sources of power and new ways to settle differences through negotiation. The broader learning experience made them more effective in managing ongoing relationships, without impairing their ability to come out ahead in one-time transactions—if that's what the situation called for.

My research also evolved in a new direction. I stopped doing old-paradigm laboratory studies that investigated what tactics helped people come out ahead in negotiations. Instead, I started studying how negotiators experienced and managed relationships that were strained by conflict. I spent time getting inside managers' heads, learning what was going on for them when they dealt with people, groups, and organizations. In conjunction with Deborah Chapman, I developed a research instrument that allows scholars to systematically diagnose the strength and impact of multidimensional relationships. In my fieldwork, I studied organizations that were being run well, and others that were being run poorly, comparing the relationships that were prevalent in each. I discovered that feeling included, having a sense of commonwealth, and gaining consensus about what needs to be done are as important to understand as the old-paradigm core concepts, such as self-interest, domination, and competition.

This book is the product of that research stream, which began almost fifteen years ago. It aspires to break old-paradigm thinking about managerial effectiveness. It's written for current and future business leaders, including executives, managers, MBA students, and undergraduates preparing for a managerial career in the new era.

The book is grounded in contemporary management theory—drawing on the best of the social sciences and economics—but it's not an ivory tower treatise. It is written for you, the people whose best practices give rise to management theory and who put management theory into practice.

THE BOOK'S FOCUS

We'll see how important an understanding of relationships is when we look at how they have evolved in Western countries. We'll learn that for centuries, business relationships were generally positive. But the Industrial Revolution brought changes not only in technology and organizational forms, but also in the way people construed business relationships. Managerial thinking became dominated by economic and military theory—or, more precisely, misapplications of what those perspectives had to offer—with the result that *adversarial relationships* came to dominate business life. It will become obvious that this approach has impaired the competitive advantage of Western businesses, made managers' jobs more difficult than they need to be, and made organizations less attractive places to work.

Although *understanding* relationships is an important first step, it can't, by itself, turn you into a more effective manager. You also need to know *how to manage* them, so the focus will be practical rather than theoretical.

You won't find many books on managing relationships. In the past, managing relationships seemed less important because managers thought they could get the results they wanted through the use of power. Businesses had hierarchical structures that clearly denoted who should obey whom. They also had either market or contractual relationships that defined their power over suppliers and customers. So when managers thought about relationships, they tended to think in terms of who was calling the shots. Aspects of relationships beyond dominance were largely irrelevant. That is, managing was construed as a rather mechanistic process in which decision-makers implemented their plans through command-and-control mechanisms.

The world has changed. Hierarchies have become flattened, reengineered, delayered, decentralized, globalized, downsized—and populated with a new generation of young, diverse, knowledge workers who don't like to be controlled. Command and control mechanisms have given way to empowerment, while markets and contracts have given way to strategic alliances of various types. As a result, much of the power managers once had over people and organizations has eroded. The new forms of influence available to managers are based on the relationships that they develop and manage.

Specifically, power is no longer the best mechanism for coordination, because the use of power tends to strain relationships. In its place, negotiation has emerged as the primary means of achieving managerial objectives. This presents a new perspective on what a manager is. *In the new era, a manager is a negotiator who operates in hybrid organizational structures by forming and managing relationships.* Said another way, the manager is someone who gets things done by securing commitment to the courses of action that will implement strategy.

After explaining the spectrum of relationships that managers must deal with effectively, we'll discuss negotiation as the primary means of getting things accomplished. You'll notice that this book is quite different from other writings on management and negotiation. I believe the principal differences are as follows:

- The book presents the most comprehensive explanation—based on up-to-date empirical research—of managers' relationships.

- The book is focused on managerial problems, rather than a particular disciplinary perspective. Most other books that address the same issues are rooted in decision science, economics, or social psychology. This book is rooted in practice. It focuses on what managers need to know—and do—to be effective in their daily lives.

- The book is eclectic. Multiple perspectives are brought to bear in understanding the role of the manager. These include strategy, clinical psychology, economics, social psychology, anthropology, political science, organizational behavior, business history, sociology, legal studies, industrial psychology, labor studies, feminist studies, organization theory, and marketing.

- The book presents negotiation in a management context. Most texts treat negotiation in the transactional context—as if it doesn't matter where you're negotiating, or who you're negotiating with. Those texts offer some universal principles that will supposedly bring managers success, whatever the context. But you'll see that negotiating as a manager is very different from negotiating as a used-car salesperson—and requires great flexibility in approaches.

- The book covers everything that other texts tell you about transactional negotiations, but in so doing, uses a more comprehensive seven-phase model to help managers understand the proper sequence. Then it goes beyond standard texts to cover *relational negotiations*, which are crucial to managerial effectiveness.

- The book looks at group decision-making from the perspective of creative consensus, rather than classical social psychology.

- The book is based on cutting edge theory and research, yet is not pedantic in its presentation.

The book is therefore very different, as you'll see. If it's successful, the book will explain, provoke, and inspire, but also provide practical advice about how to adapt and evolve as a manager and leader.

ACKNOWLEDGMENTS

But before we get into the details of creating competitive advantage through commonwealth motivation and a strong consensus that commits people to achieving their shared goals, I'd like to acknowledge an intellectual debt that's owed to a number of people.

Debbie Chapman has been my closest colleague during the last ten years. She has been a coauthor of numerous articles and a coinstructor at the Amos Tuck School at Dartmouth College and at the Graduate School of Business at Stanford University. Trained in psychology and philosophy, she has challenged, nourished, and guided my thinking about organizations, groups, and people, and how we manage them. This book is the result of a Socratic dialog—she has been Socrates, I the student—spanning a decade. If there are shortcomings in the book, they are no doubt due to my not understanding where she was leading me.

Blair Sheppard has had a great impact on how I think about organizations and their environments. Bob McKersie has had an equal impact on how I think about managing relationship strains and managing a workforce. Martin Davidson has helped me think through how emotion and race play out in conflicts. John Slocum has been a superb colleague, who gave me valuable feedback on the first draft. Roy Lewicki got me started teaching negotiation. Ray Miles got me thinking about how network organizations operate and why they are successful. Karl Weick taught me how to think outside the box in a disciplined way.

Numerous other colleagues have shaped my thinking in important ways—among them, Scott Neslin, Roxanne Okun, Rick Gilkey, Joanne Martin, Max Bazerman, Lucy Axtell, Tom Kochan, Susan Pufahl, Bob Sutton, Zehava Rosenblatt, Rod Kramer, and Gretchen Spreitzer. There are undoubtedly others I should be including here.

Although it is now impossible to remember every practitioner who shaped my thinking, some individuals stand out: Nick Scheele and David Hudson from Jaguar Cars, Shane Flynn and Gretchen Arey from MBNA, Carlos Mazzorin from Ford, Steve Schiller from Smith Barney, and Don Ephlin from the United Auto Workers. My thinking also benefited considerably from a discussion with a different kind of executive, Jimmy Carter.

Dialogues with managers and executives during executive education programs have also given me insights. Their organizations include ABB, Andersen Consulting, Baxter Healthcare, Blue Cross/Blue Shield, Boeing, Caterpillar, Chiron Vaccines, Chrysler, Coca-Cola, DEC, Deutsche Bank,

Dynavax, Ernst & Young, Ford, General Electric, General Motors, Goldman Sachs, GTE, Harnischfeger, Harris Corporation, Hoechst, IBM, ITT, Jaguar, John Deere, Koç Holdings, Lafarge, LG Electronics, MBNA, Merrill Lynch, Miles Pharmaceuticals, The Nature Conservancy, NEC, Nissho Iwai, Rolls-Royce, Rover, Sara Lee, Siemens, Smith Barney, Sterling Pharmaceuticals, Syntex, Timken, Travelers, U.S. Postal Service, Varian, Warner-Lambert, and Williams Holdings. My thinking has also benefited from the exchange of ideas with students and faculty at Dartmouth, Oxford, Stanford, Duke, MIT, and Cornell.

The intellectual debt dates back much further than conversations with academics, practitioners, and bright students. My father, Bill Greenhalgh, taught me how to think, and my mother, Wynne Greenhalgh, taught me how to write. Vera and Avard Fuller got me started on an academic career.

Others helped, too. Bob Wallace, Senior Editor at The Free Press, guided the development of the book from its crude beginnings. Anne-Marie Sheedy and Cornelia Faifar ensured that the publication process stayed on track. Karen Lander kept me supplied with materials. Vanessa Liu got me musing about how legal thinking intersects with management thinking. Undoubtedly—and regrettably—I am overlooking others' contributions.

So this book is the result of a journey I took—an intellectual journey into the future of organizational life. Giving credit to these people reflects the fact that I didn't take this journey alone. Many of the good ideas were nurtured by others; whatever errors or misunderstandings remain are not for lack of wise counsel.

Writing the book has been a fun endeavor for me. I hope you have just as much fun reading it.

St. George, Maine
April 9, 2000

CHAPTER 1

MANAGING IN THE NEW ERA

Gaining competitive advantage has become more difficult than ever before; and sustaining it, almost impossible. This is the result of several emerging trends. Agile competitors have sped up their time-to-market, and can quickly nullify a first-mover advantage. New technology is usually available to anyone smart enough to adopt it. Consulting companies identify industry best practices and soon "clone" them within competing organizations. And quality levels have become so uniformly high that people can't tell the difference between good and best. Meanwhile, markets have become crowded with competitors from all over the globe, major industries have more capacity than demand, and few market niches remain unexploited.

Managers describe it as a new era for business. And it is. Old pathways to success lead only to mediocrity in an arena that won't tolerate it.

Being good at some things is no longer good enough. In fact, being good at everything doesn't assure success if the organizational elements being managed aren't properly aligned. Thus, the organizations that will make out best in the new era are those that really have their act together—those that can successfully integrate strategy, processes, business arrangements, resources, systems, and empowered workforces. We'll learn that this can't be accomplished unless managers do a good job of creating, shaping, and sustaining business relationships.

But before we get too far ahead of ourselves, let's briefly contrast two companies to see the competitive disadvantages that arise when relationships aren't managed well.

TWO DIFFERENT ORGANIZATIONS

Joe and Josephine are twins, now in their late twenties. They live in the same city, but work in different organizations. The different organizations are pursuing sound strategies, have been reengineered to have good business processes, are dealing with the best available suppliers, are not lacking resources, have fully developed systems in place (such as state-of-the-art management information systems), and have a workforce trained well enough that they can do their jobs without being micromanaged. Nevertheless, the two organizations produce very different experiences, and very different outcomes. Let's look at a day in the life of each of the twins.

Joe arrives at the office a few minutes late, as usual. He nods a courteous but unfeeling greeting to his co-workers and boss as he walks through the office, then sits down at his desk and begins the day's work. He checks his voice mail and e-mail, organizes his paperwork, and then begins his first task.

He calls a supplier to try to expedite a late delivery of components. He listens to the reasons why the delivery is late, applying pressure by implying that the supplier might lose future business. When this fails to improve the delivery date, he calls alternative suppliers to see if they can do any better. (They can't.) Then he calls his own customer who is expecting delivery of the finished product, and explains the problem with the supplier not delivering components on time. He assures the customer that he has called alternative suppliers and can't get a better delivery date, and concludes the conversation by saying, "I'm sorry if this causes you inconvenience. But this is beyond our control."

The supplier senses that despite Joe's polite expression of regret, Joe doesn't really care whether the late delivery causes inconvenience, or whether the customer does business with someone else in the future. This impression is, in fact, accurate. Joe and his co-workers agree that "this is just a job. There'll be other customers if we lose this one. There'll be other hassles. The boss will always be breathing down our necks, looking for opportunities to write us up. But everyone has bills to pay, so we have to put in our time on the job." Their cooperation with each other is limited to keeping the boss in the dark. There's an unstated agreement that they will "cover" for each other.

Joe's twin, Josephine, has a very different day at the office. She arrives there early, and interrupts reading her e-mail to greet arriving co-workers with genuine affection. Their caring is communicated by their touching. When the boss arrives, she pauses at Josephine's desk to exchange stories about unruly kittens. Then they review the day's priorities.

At 10 A.M., Josephine patches together a conference call so that her customer can speak directly with the components supplier who's causing a production delay, and the three of them engage in earnest problem solving. The customer learns that he'll have to adapt to the delay, but his commitment to continue buying from Josephine is strengthened as a result of the interaction.

Josephine's organization is functioning more effectively than Joe's. It's more efficient and more innovative. It creates greater value for customers and is increasing its market share as a consequence. It has low employee turnover, and attracts good people as it grows. It's very adaptable, with employees responding quickly to the need to change, which happens a lot in their volatile industry.

Josephine and her co-workers work hard, yet they look forward to going to work each day. Their tasks aren't always fun, but their camaraderie gets them through difficult times. This is a stark contrast to Joe's work situation, which is drab and gray, and operates far below its potential.

Joe's boss is as frustrated with the state of affairs as Joe is. But he doesn't really understand what's wrong. He followed the consultants' advice about installing a tougher control system and providing more training. He tightened up the performance appraisal system and began providing incentives for good results and penalties for poor outcomes. He even singled out the best performers for recognition as Employee of the Month. But nothing has made a real difference, and he has become discouraged. At this point, he, too, dislikes coming into work each day.

Many of us—in fact, most of us—have worked in underperforming organizations like Joe's. And all of us have had the misery of dealing with someone who has developed an attitude like Joe's: a store cashier, an airline ticket agent, a motor vehicle registration clerk, or a hotel telephone operator. It's easy to attribute the bad attitude to personality, but you know from your own experience that some situations bring out the worst in you, and others bring out the best.

TWO DIFFERENT SETS OF RELATIONSHIPS

Joe's company is organized conventionally—that is, according to the economic principles espoused by Adam Smith and the economists who extended and elaborated his writings. These principles include individualism, self-interest, power, control, and competition. All of these involve *adversarial relationships.* To the old-school economist, adversarial relationships are seen as a positive factor, because they are the means of survival and prosperity in a dog-eat-dog world. But they are also the relational dynamics that *create* a dog-eat-dog world. The success of Josephine's organization shows that *it doesn't have to be that way.* After all, dogs are by nature pack animals with genetic predispositions to live their lives cooperatively rather than individualistically.[1] We'll learn that this is also true of *Homo sapiens* as a species.

In relational terms, Josephine's organization is a *community.* The people who work together form the same bonds they might form outside of work. From 8 to 5, they function as if they were close neighbors engaged in a common project. Their primary focus is on their shared task, but comradeship and social support are integral to getting the work done. Of course, they like some co-workers more than others, and they experience intermittent strains in relationships that need to be healed. This system is, after all, a human one, displaying all the friction, misunderstandings, and emotional reactions that arise when humans interact.

Josephine's boss is not an outsider to the group: she's a member with a specialized role. Neither are suppliers and customers seen as outsiders: they're part of the community, too—they're viewed as value-chain *partners.* Interestingly, even competitors aren't viewed as archenemies. Josephine realizes that they can be allies when her organization needs to take on a project that's too big or too risky for her organization to take on alone. Maintaining a positive relationship with her counterpart in the competitor organization also comes in handy when she needs to outsource work, such as when production problems in her own organization are causing delays. But even when competitors can't help her at all, she doesn't want them to have animosity toward her organization. Ill will could motivate them to undermine her organization in their advertising, or embroil the two businesses in a crippling price war.

Two primary relationship principles determine how strong a sense of community Josephine and her co-workers will experience: inclusion and commonwealth. *Inclusion* gives Josephine a sense of belonging—the belief that she's an insider rather than an outsider. *Commonwealth* involves the sense of having a common fate—the notion that success is everyone's success, and failure is everyone's problem.

Inclusion and commonwealth are the building blocks of collaborative business relationships, and are vital for business success in the new era. We need to understand them in detail, because they're a source of competitive advantage that's largely overlooked.

We also need to understand why Joe's organization is such a failure. Even though the organization is still economically viable, nobody wants to work there, customers and suppliers don't like doing business with it, and it's neither efficient nor adaptive. Its failure is attributable to opposite relationship dimensions—exclusion, and a culture of self-interest.

While Josephine's organization is a *communal* form, Joe's is a conventional *hierarchy*—a vertically layered structure with power and privilege at the top, and subordination and deference at the bottom. Its designers had envisioned an entity that functioned more like a machine than a social system. When the human element was taken into account at all, the design was guided by misapplied economic assumptions about human nature: that self-interest is the ultimate determinant of behavior, and is maximized when employees earn as much as possible from contributing as little as possible. Managing such people involves setting up constraints, controls, rewards, and punishments to overcome these supposedly "natural" inclinations.

There's a cost to being wrong about human nature. The down side of managing this way is evident in Joe's response to the work culture in which he spends his days, and his response is both understandable and predictable. If he's viewed and treated as a cog in the machine—the current occupant of a role programmed to carry out a job description—psychological withdrawal is an adaptive reaction to the circumstances. Being sullen and reserved is appropriate and healthy behavior within the relationships he experiences. How else could he react?

Furthermore, if customers and suppliers are viewed as simply pursuing their own self-interests, then it makes sense to limit the relationship to arms-length contractual arrangements, and deal with each other as adversaries. If the economic bargain is attractive enough, they'll take the deal. If it isn't, then Joe has to put more on the table, or find others who are hungrier for the business. He doesn't need to think about relationship factors other than roles in an economic transaction: any other considerations are irrelevant.

From this perspective, Joe is a model employee: he sticks to business and doesn't get involved in distractions. In contrast, Josephine wastes a lot of time engaged in "touchy-feely stuff." She needs retraining and close supervision. Yet she's bringing in twice as much business as Joe, and at a higher profit margin; she retains customers while increasing market penetration; and, she gets suppliers to contribute ideas and information that increase her company's competitive advantage.

Something is obviously wrong with conventional models that visualize mechanistic structures and promote adversarial relationships. If managers don't fully understand *why* Josephine is more successful than Joe, they won't be very competent in the coaching role. And if they don't fully understand why Josephine's organization is more successful than Joe's, they won't be competent in designing organizations that create and sustain competitive advantage. Note that if you were to transfer Josephine into Joe's organization, before long, she'd start acting just like Joe—if she didn't quit first.

A NEW APPROACH FOR THE NEW ERA

The themes of this book outline an approach to designing and managing businesses that differs sharply from the one that prevailed throughout most of the twentieth century. The old approach is not well suited to the changing business environment. Look closely, for example, at the new generation of "subordinates." They consider themselves autonomous—as independent professionals who can be given a general goal and left to accomplish it without any micromanagement. They look to the manager to *facilitate* their achievement rather than to direct and control their work. They want to be supported rather than supervised as they strive to provide increasing value to the client or customer.

The Old-Paradigm Hierarchical Organization

Despite the changes and our growing awareness of them, Joe's plight is not unusual today. Many managers' understanding of organizations is seriously outdated. It's easy to see why. The management books written during most of the twentieth century were based on Western experience with traditional businesses competing with other traditional businesses. Their struggle for dominance took place in a domestic marketplace sheltered from global competition. A business didn't have to be well managed to survive and prosper in this environment: it only needed to be managed better than its domestic competitors.

This situation led to a lot of false learning by managers and by the scholars who studied them. Managers figured that if their business was doing well, then they must be doing things right. A more accurate conclusion would have been that if their business was doing well, then they must not yet have faced world-class competition.

Scholars fell into the same trap. They studied organizations that were apparently "successful" and wrote about what seemed to account for the success. What they didn't do was look at what it would take for organizations that had been successful in the past to hold their ground against the new generation of competitors.

Another impediment to the development of our knowledge has come from the overemphasis on (and misapplication of) economic theory. Economics is extremely useful in certain domains—especially in understanding how markets should operate—but not very helpful when applied to a particular organization or its employees. An organization is a dynamic system of complex human relationships, most of which fall outside the scope of economic understanding. As a result, there remains a lot of misunderstanding of how to achieve organizational effectiveness as well as plenty of bad advice about how to manage people.

Economic theory isn't the only body of knowledge that's been used inappropriately. We can trace much of the problem with twentieth-century thinking to the inappropriate use of imagery from the physical sciences. When an organization is productive and well coordinated, Westerners tend to describe it as "running like a well-oiled machine." But machine imagery has serious drawbacks. All the parts of a machine carry out unvarying tasks, and these are coordinated by control systems to optimize efficiency. The machine is impersonal, highly adapted to its current role, and has only one way of doing things.

When this metaphor is applied to organizations, workers like Joe are seen as cogs in the machine, each carrying out specific tasks. It doesn't matter *who* carries out a task, but it's very important that the task be carried out exactly as prescribed. Thus, each organizational role is carefully designed so as to optimize efficiency, and workers are interchangeable so long as they're proficient at the task. This creates the role of "worker-as-robot."

Managers' roles in this system are almost as constrained. Their primary mission is to provide machine maintenance—to ensure that work continues according to plan. To accomplish this, managers are organized into a hierarchy with the most comprehensive responsibilities at the top and the most task-specific at the bottom. Each manager's job is to assure that the machine runs smoothly, with no interruptions, departures from design parameters, coordination problems, or disharmony.

The problem with a machine, of course, is that once it's designed and built, it stays fixed in form. It doesn't adapt its basic structure as everything around it changes. And the machine can never be better than its design. Yet in reality, *organizations are relational systems* that don't operate according to the laws of physics or mechanics. It's empowered workers, not hierarchical system designers (such as industrial engineers), who are in the best position to achieve continuous improvement, responsiveness to customers, quality, and efficiency. They make these efforts when they feel included as members of an organizational community (as Josephine does)—but not when they feel like cogs in an impersonal machine.

The shortcomings of the old paradigm are evident when we consider that *few conventional organizations ever achieved greatness, and those that did usually excelled in spite of their structure* rather than because of it. These shortcomings are also evident when you ask Americans to provide examples of high-performing systems—situations in which they were drawn into the excitement of a group operating at the outer limits of achievement.[2] They almost invariably pick examples *outside* of business—the crew of a racing sailboat, a set of strangers striving to cope with a disaster, a surgical team, a race-car pit crew, or a group of neighbors helping to raise a barn.

This isn't surprising: there's a lot of evidence that conventional Western businesses don't bring out the best in people. A song that had the title "Take This Job and Shove It" became very popular in the United States, because it conveyed a sentiment that most U.S. workers could relate to. As further evidence, bosses are usually portrayed as oppressors in U.S. folklore. And many workers who have the potential to be good managers recoil at the thought of taking on the role: the social status doesn't compensate for the bad relationships they expect will develop with the people they now work with.

It's important to note that the only time businesses are described as high-performing systems is in the case of certain start-up companies. In these examples, egalitarian groups exert their maximum effort and can achieve astonishing results. The people may be working harder than they would in the worst nineteenth-century sweatshop, but the work isn't drudgery: it's exhilarating. But start-up companies aren't organized according to old-paradigm principles. The workers tend to have strong inclusion bonds, high commitment, unstructured roles, and a sense of commonwealth—if the enterprise prospers, it's to everyone's credit and to everyone's advantage. You don't hear these people humming "Take This Job and Shove It" as they watch the clock creep slowly toward quitting time; you're more likely to hear them saying that they work 80-hour weeks because they can't manage to work *even longer* hours.

Clearly, something's wrong with the conventional Western body of knowledge about organizing a business. What's wrong is that scholars haven't given enough attention to business relationships—relationships between people, within and between groups, and within and between organizations. Economic theorists assume that relationships are basically adversarial as people pursue their self-interests. Organization theorists have looked primarily at structural relationships in machine-like systems, deriving a rather sterile view of the interconnections in organizations. Yet you know from your own experience that in reality, people form much more complex relationships than scholars have given them credit for.

We'll explore what's wrong with the way Western managerial thought developed, and show that naturally occurring human systems—such as those that form in the best start-up companies—have the greatest potential to be high-performing organizations. When we remove the distorting lens of the old paradigm, we'll recognize that people have an instinctual drive to form communities rather than hierarchies. That's why managerially naive people (like many successful entrepreneurs) create communal forms of organizations, which consist of networks of relationships rather than layers of hierarchy.

The New-Era Commonwealth Organization

When organizations are communal rather than hierarchical, managers have very different roles. Their primary objective is to preserve the cohesion and stability of their work group. They need to make people feel fully included, foster a strong sense of commonwealth, and prevent cohesive coalitions within the organization ("ingroups") from destructively excluding nonmembers ("outgroups"). This book explains how they can accomplish this.

New era managers also need an understanding of how webs of relationships take shape and operate. We'll explore why the new organizational forms do a better job of creating value for customers and clients, and why they're able to compete successfully against the less-adaptive conventional organizations.

We'll also develop an understanding of how managers can evolve their own units to operate less like an outdated hierarchy and more like a state-of-the-art communal form. Most managers aren't given a "green field" organization—one with no structure already in place. Those who are lucky enough to have them—such as those involved in start-ups—encounter pressures to turn them into conventional organizations when they grow to a size that's difficult to manage informally. So, in practice, the majority of Western managers find themselves saddled with a suboptimal organization. They need to understand why it's suboptimal, and how it can be improved—and positioned to succeed in the new era.

Said another way, new-era managers need to develop an alternative view of what an organization *is*. They need to visualize a network of business relationships that radiate throughout their own organization, and extend beyond its boundaries to other organizations in its value chain. These business relationships enable the organization to achieve strategic consensus, to implement strategy, to tie in strategic partners, and to achieve strategic dominance in the marketplace. Thus, managers in the new era don't establish, maintain, and manage relationships just to be nice. They do it because the strategic success of the business depends on it.

In fact, the most successful organizational forms of the twenty-first century will be extended enterprises. These aren't freestanding organizations, but rather sets of companies that each contribute value according to their distinctive competency. The participating organizations form a loose but enduring association of value-chain partners (i.e., associated businesses in supplier and customer roles). This network can even include competitors in domains where it makes more sense to collaborate than to compete.

The extended enterprise can create a level of value (quality, low price, fast time-to-market, and customer responsiveness) that no single company can attain. It achieves this high level of performance by taking the best that each participating company has to offer (for example, one contributing organization may be the best at research and development, another best at manufacturing, and a third best at distributing the products or services). In effect, an extended enterprise has all of the advantages of Japanese *keiretsus*.[3] It may, indeed, be the only business form that can prosper in a global economy that is increasingly dominated by this interorganizational form.

THE CENTRAL IMPORTANCE OF RELATIONSHIPS

If organizations are to be construed as networks of relationships, we'll obviously need to develop a sophisticated understanding of what relationships are. Conventional organizational theory hasn't paid enough attention to relationships. This neglect is an understandable consequence of having relied on mechanical metaphors. A machine designer cares only about the *instrumental* relationships between each component—such as which driveshaft causes which gear to turn. But we need to go beyond this and understand the broader and stronger cohesive ties between individuals as these constitute the *real* organizational structure.

More specifically, we need to understand the ties that bind individuals to the organization, their work groups, and their peers. We need to understand the ties that bind groups together to operate cross-functional processes (such as how a customer order is handled on its way to becoming a completed delivery). And we need to understand the ties that bind organizations together in strategic alliances, value-chain partnerships, and competitive détente.

We also need to understand the divisive dynamics that undermine relationships. Some of these dynamics are inherent in the concepts Western managers use when they think about relationships. Many Western managers take for granted that the basic structural elements of organizational systems are hierarchies, markets, and contracts. This needs rethinking, because these concepts embody relationships that are inherently adversarial. Hierarchy is a power structure based on ownership rights. It exists as a means of control, enabling managers to force subordinates to obey. A boss, in this context, is an adversary to any subordinate who cherishes autonomy. Similarly, markets involve buyers and sellers striving to maximize their self-interest at the other's expense, which seems inconsistent with the notion of a value chain *partnership.* And *contracts are adversarial in the sense that they're only useful in forcing the other party to accept a bad deal.* (If it's a good deal, you don't need a contract to enforce the agreement!)

Many Western managers have accepted these adversarial relationships as "given." This is surprising because the same managers would view such relationships as pathological outside of a business context. That's no way to treat neighbors or family members, if you want to get along with them. Yet Western business education has taught generations of managers that such relationships are not only inevitable, but also desirable. Competition is revered as the central force in the free-enterprise system, yet competition is inherently adversarial.

In this book, we'll consider an alternative view—that it's collaboration rather than competition that's central to any enterprise system, free or otherwise. Even if adversarial relationships can be a useful self-regulatory dynamic in markets, this doesn't mean they're useful elsewhere in business, as many Asian companies have found. The most familiar adversarial relationships—hierarchy, markets, and contracts—are usually an *impediment* to business success. In other words, Western businesses have prospered *despite* these dynamics.

NEGOTIATION AS A KEY MANAGERIAL SKILL

But even strong collaborative relationships are strained by conflict. As you know from your own experience, people don't simply form a relationship and live happily ever after. Strains arise whenever people have dissimilar views or interests. Because people aren't clones perceiving situations in an identical way, there'll always be strains in relationships. But this isn't much of a problem if they're managed well.

There are three basic alternatives for managing relationship strains: negotiation, conflict management, and power. Of these, negotiation seems to be the manager's best approach, using power the worst. Therefore, negotiation is a core managerial skill and is the one we will focus on in this book. In traditional hierarchical organizations, managers were able to use power as the primary means of resolving differences. But new-era organizations are flatter, they have empowered workers and they depend on cross-functional collaboration as a means of internal coordination. Managers have little authority over the people they're dealing with; therefore, they often have no choice but to negotiate. We'll see that negotiation is the process of gaining agreement on—and, more importantly, commitment to—the desired course of action.

Most of what's been written about negotiation emphasizes what people should do in one-time transactions with strangers. But think about it: this isn't what managers do. Managers usually interact with people they know well, and few situations requiring negotiation are one-time transactions. As a result, much of what you read is bad advice. The kind of negotiation managers really need to be good at—relational negotiation—is very different from transactional negotiation (which is epitomized by haggling over the price of a rug in a Middle Eastern bazaar). Relational negotiation involves working out agreements in an ongoing relationship, rather than maximizing one's outcome in a one-shot deal.

We'll also spend some time looking at how agreements are negotiated within groups. Twentieth-century organizations were designed as hierar-chical arrangements of *individuals*. But people don't lead their lives as iso-lated individuals, on or off the job. People naturally form groups. Look at what you, yourself, do in a new social setting: a new school, a new work-place, or a new neighborhood. You join a group, or perhaps several groups.

In addition to having instinctual appeal to workers, groups are useful to management. Groups provide the collective expertise to make wise deci-sions that no person could make alone. Look at the examples in everyday corporate life. Task forces take on special analysis and decision-making assignments that can't be done effectively by hierarchical managers. Cross-functional groups achieve levels of coordination that elude managers rely-ing on traditional command-and-control structures. Informal groups coalesce at every opportunity and can enhance—or inhibit—organiza-tional functioning. I could go on, but you no doubt get the point. Because groups are all-pervasive, managers need to know how to influence their processes so as to maximize their benefit to the organization.

MANAGING IN THE NEW ERA

The ability to manage relationships is essential for carrying out the man-ager's primary function, *integration.* Let's see how. Managerial effectiveness involves integrating a set of factors that determine the organization's ability to adapt to an endless stream of new challenges. These factors are shown in Figure 1-1. But before we explore the importance of each factor, let's review how the notion of the manager as integrator evolved.

During the latter half of the twentieth century, several scholars devel-oped models for how to *align* the various factors that managers need to pay attention to. Alignment is important. Systems of all types need to be in bal-ance. Scholars recognized early on that strategy and structure needed to be aligned. That is, some structures won't let you achieve your strategy. Suppose, for example, that your company makes a simple product that will absorb food odor in a refrigerator. The product is simple because all you really need is a package filled with a highly absorbent substance—baking soda or charcoal. You need to produce the item cheaply, which requires large quantities. And you need to sell it at such a low price that other com-petitors will figure it's not worth entering the market. This is a strategy. A conventional hierarchical structure is probably appropriate to achieve this

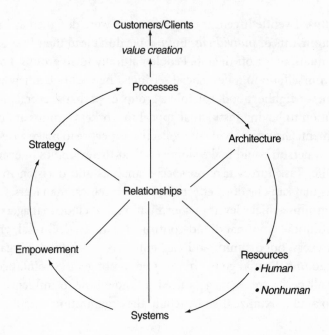

FIGURE 1-1 The SPARSE Organization: Managerial Integration in the New Era

strategy. There's little need for innovation, so managers need to give primary attention to controlling—making sure that everything comes out according to plan. The strategy calls for "a machine" that'll turn out identical products, year in, year out.

But suppose instead that you're operating a hospital emergency room, and your strategy is to give priority service to patients with the most-urgent needs. A hierarchical structure won't help you because priorities can change within minutes, each situation is unique, staff need to be instantly redeployed as new patients come through the door, and being effective at saving lives may mean being inefficient in serving particular patients' needs. The structure is amorphous and flexible—and it needs to be, given the strategy.

The need to align structure with strategy was so intuitively appealing that scholars soon identified other organizational arrangements that needed to be "in sync." Many managers are familiar with the 7-S framework, for example. The seven elements that need to be integrated are strategy, structure, systems, style, staff, skills, and shared values.[4] Other scholars have questioned whether these are the most important elements, but no one has doubted that the various factors—whatever they are—need to be *aligned* with one another. If parts of a system are badly mismatched, then the system as a whole won't work as well as it could.

The 7-S model needs to be updated. The organizational success stories that gave rise to the 7-S model were stories of the 1970s. The world has changed radically since those days, so managers need to align a somewhat different set of elements. Figure 1-1 shows the set of elements that most need to be integrated.

Notice that *customers* are given their rightful place at the very top of the figure. They're given such prominence because, ultimately, the organization's survival and prosperity depend on how well it meets customers' needs. You, yourself, will stop doing business with organizations that fail to meet your needs. You'll avoid flying on poorly run airlines, you'll switch doctors, you'll decide not to take particular courses, and you'll stop shopping in stores with low value or bad service. If enough customers respond the same way when the organization does a poor job of meeting their needs, it will go out of business. That's how market mechanisms operate.

Organizations lose customers when they fail at *creating value.* The basic plan for how to create value is a central element in the organization's *strategy.* Managers need to agree on things like whether the organization is positioned as the low-cost producer, the technology leader, the most dependable supplier, or the firm that caters to a specialized clientele that nobody else is serving adequately.

In practice, what actually creates value for customers is a set of *processes.* Traditionally, scholars have focused on the products and services that organizations provide when evaluating market appeal. But it's more insightful to focus on processes. Suppose, for example, you need a hotel room for business travel. Objectively, you're renting a bed. But you don't experience the bed most of the time you're using it, because you're asleep. What creates value is efficient processes. You want to go to your room as soon as possible: you don't want to stand in line waiting to register. The same is true at checkout time. And you want room-service meals to arrive at the time you asked for them, not within a half-hour "window" that maximizes the hotel's convenience. Processes create value.

Processes are now recognized as being so important that most organizations have gone through "reengineering." This involves systematically analyzing key business processes, then figuring out how to improve them. Done properly, a reengineering program aligns processes with strategy. An organization can't achieve its strategy unless the right processes are in place. And organizations gain competitive advantage when their processes create greater value for their customers than do those of competitors. For example, Saturn Corporation gained great market penetration in the United States when it offered customers a better *process* of buying or leasing a car.

Next, the manager needs to have the right organizational *architecture* in place. Architecture is similar to what twentieth-century theorists called "structure," but its meaning is broader. Structure focuses attention on a single organization. The term "architecture" encompasses all of the organizational arrangements needed to carry out the processes that create value. This may involve several groups, several departments, or even several companies.

For example, people in the United States used to go to hospitals, clinics, or doctors' offices to take care of their medical needs. These were independent organizations. Now they're more likely to be dealing with an HMO (a health maintenance organization), which has very different architecture. To manage an HMO you have to coordinate the processes, products, and services of insurance companies, pharmaceutical companies, the federal government, employers, and networks of hospitals, clinics, and doctors—with the needs of patients. The lack of integration in the old system of health care delivery made it too expensive for the value received. The HMO, when it works well, makes health care more affordable.

When processes and architecture are in place to carry out the strategy, the manager's attention can turn to securing the right *resources.* These fall into two basic categories—human and nonhuman. Human resources consist of enough people with the appropriate skills to do the organization's tasks—working effectively in groups (it's groups, rather than individuals, that carry out processes). Nonhuman resources include such things as the budget, physical facilities, time available, and the raw materials and tools needed to do the job. Coordination involves ensuring that enough of these resources are available to carry out value-creating processes that will implement the strategy.

Systems need to be in place to ensure that strategy is being implemented on time, efficiently, and according to plan. Perhaps managers' most important system is the control system—the mechanism for determining whether specific objectives are being accomplished. Performance appraisal, quality control, budget compliance, environmental monitoring, and financial audits are all control systems. They tell managers when things are going well, and alert managers to problems that are developing. Additional systems need to be in place, such as management information systems and communication systems.

It's especially important for the manager to make sure that systems are tailored to processes. For example, if strategy implementation requires a collaborative process between managers, but systems reward each manager individualistically, then the misalignment of systems and processes will undermine cooperation. Surprisingly, such misalignment is fairly common in Western businesses, even though it puts these organizations at a competitive disadvantage.

Finally, managers need latitude to make the decisions that they're in the best position to make. They also need to be able to delegate decisions to their workers when subordinates are in a better position to make these decisions. Such latitude is known as *empowerment.*

I know it sounds obvious that decisions ought to be made by the people in the best position to make them. But for the last century and a half, decisions have been made at the highest—rather than the lowest—levels, reflecting a belief that a manager who isn't "calling the shots" is either out of control, irrelevant, or a wimp. None of these characterizations is necessarily accurate. Managers are doing a good job when there's continuous improvement. It turns out that the people who are actually doing the work are in the best position to know how to improve things. So if workers aren't allowed to make decisions, the only improvements that'll be made are those that somehow come to the attention of higher-level managers. Thus, empowerment is a source of competitive advantage because it's the key to continuous improvement.

The circle of arrows in Figure 1-1 shows integration of these factors. Integration, in practice, involves working sequentially through the model. It starts with strategy, shown at ten o'clock in the figure. The organization's strategy will determine what processes are necessary to create value for customers. The processes will drive architectural form: they'll tell you who needs to be involved, and how. The resulting organization will have to be properly staffed and supplied with the other resources it needs. Systems will have to be put in place to ensure that the strategy is being implemented efficiently. And the people involved will have to be empowered to achieve the continuous improvement needed to stay ahead of competitors—which is a key objective of an organization's strategy.

The arrows that show the sequence of coordination depict a *cycle.*

Integration isn't something a manager does once and for all, as in the case of designing a machine. Each element in the cycle needs to be constantly monitored and adjusted because businesses operate in a constantly changing environment. The competitive landscape shifts, new processes are introduced, architecture evolves as better suppliers replace mediocre suppliers, resources become scarce or abundant, new systems are made possible due to technological evolution (bar codes and embedded smart chips might be good examples), and empowered workers make adaptive changes. Managers may need to compensate for the change in any element by appropriate changes in other elements, so as to restore alignment.

Managers must pay close attention to alignment since it's the organization's ultimate source of competitive advantage. Doing well isn't enough in today's global marketplace: you always need to do better. Competitors monitor a company that's doing well (they call it "benchmarking"), and they try to copy whatever's creating competitive advantage. If you're constantly optimizing and realigning each factor, by the time competitors have caught up with what your company used to be doing, you'll have become even better. So then they have to reach for the higher standard you've set. If you do a good enough job of staying ahead of the competition, they'll get discouraged and shift their efforts to another market niche. Thus, excellence and continuous improvement are great "barriers to entry" into any company's domain, and perhaps the *only* source of competitive advantage these days.

Relationships and Alignment

Relationships are at the center of the model. This surprises most Western businessmen, who are more used to focusing on structures, controls, and economic variables. It doesn't usually surprise Asians: they'd be surprised if relationships *weren't* at the center of the model. Nor does it surprise most Western women, who tend to be more like Asian managers than like Western businessmen. We'll discuss this gender difference later in the book, because it's an important one. For now, we'll focus on which relationships are important, and how they shape the way managers achieve alignment of the key factors we just discussed.

The most familiar relationships are those between individuals. But individuals also have a relationship to the group, and to the organization. Think about loyalty, for example: a manager can be loyal to the organization, to his or her work group, and to another manager. Groups have relationships with other groups: they can be allies or rivals. Groups also have relationships to the organization: they can be strong contributors—as in the case of high-performing teams; or an internal opposition—as in the case of a sullen work group that conspires to hold down production. And organizations can have relationships with each other: they can be archcompetitors, arm's-length buyers and sellers, or strategic allies. All of these relationships need to be created and maintained if the manager is going to be effective at integrating the various factors in the model. Here's why.

Relationships are important in achieving strategic consensus. *Strategy* is relatively easy to formulate. What's tricky is getting other managers fully committed to achieving the strategic objectives. If they "buy into" the strategy, they'll be more likely to "go the extra mile" to ensure that it gets implemented. They're unlikely to exert extraordinary effort if they have no sense of "ownership"—such as when they feel others made the decision and their input wasn't even sought.

Commitment has its deepest roots in relationships. People need to experience a sense of inclusion and commonwealth if they are to become committed to a course of action. You can't expect much commitment from them if they feel like cogs in a machine, or like "outsiders" paid to carry out someone else's directives. Neither of these will generate the enthusiasm and ingenuity needed to overcome the obstacles that inevitably arise in implementation. So, if relationships are exclusive rather than inclusive—such as when an elite group makes strategic decisions—top managers will have to depend on power and control to get the strategy implemented. That's a costly way to execute a strategy. And it's usually ineffective.

In Western businesses—particularly those based in the United States—exclusion is the rule rather than the exception. A common rationale for excluding people is that if word leaks out and competitors learn what the strategy is, they'll counter it. In some cases, this is a real risk, and full participation would require the kind of relationship that would ensure confidentiality. In many cases, however, the risk of leakage is just an excuse, because the strategy has already been announced to the world in the company's annual report. The real reason top managers don't want broad participation is oldthink. They were socialized during an era when management made all the decisions and workers were kept in the dark. It's macho—as well as ego enhancing—to be calling the shots. But even when the strategy must be kept secret, people can participate in decisions about how best to *implement* it. Meaningful participation is valuable because of the relationships it generates.

Processes are carried out by groups. The groupings may be simple or complex. A simple group is involved in the process of getting your car serviced at the local dealership. It involves a service manager scheduling the appointment, a mechanic working on the car, a cashier collecting your payment, and a data-processing person entering information relevant to the car's warranty. If group relationships are good, everyone works together, and your car gets serviced efficiently. If group relationships are poor, and employees don't work well together, you'll spend a lot of time waiting unnecessarily.

A complex group may involve people from different departments, or even different companies. Look at the process of getting an aircraft ready for takeoff after it has just arrived from another city. On-time departure requires close coordination between gate agents moving passengers off and on the aircraft, the cleaning service, the refueling service, the catering service, pilots, flight attendants, baggage handlers, air-traffic controllers, maintenance mechanics, and possibly deicing crews. If relationships with any of these groups are bad, the people involved have the ability to delay departure. All they have to do is follow their job descriptions to the letter, refusing to make adjustments to accommodate other groups' tasks. That's enough to disrupt air service and snarl busy airports that already have problems keeping planes flying on schedule. The all-important cooperation depends on the relationships with the groups involved in the process.

The importance of relationships is fairly obvious in the case of organizational *architecture.* In new-era organizations, a network of contributors—rather than a machine-like structure—delivers value. As a result, relationships are vital. In conventional hierarchies, coordination comes from bossing people around. Conventional boss-subordinate role relationships were adequate for doing this, but they didn't have any effect beyond the organizations' boundaries. Today, managerial coordination may need to extend beyond the conventional organization chart, so different kinds of relationships are important. Competitive advantage often comes from strategic alliance as well as from excellence and continuous improvement.

We'll see that the value-chain partnership is one of the most important of these new-era relationships: networks of organizations and their suppliers create competitive advantage when they jointly strive to outperform rival value chains. For example, the casual observer might perceive competition between Ford and Toyota. In reality, the competition is between the Toyota value chain and the Ford value chain. The source of competitive advantage may not lie within either Ford or Toyota, but rather in the contributions of their suppliers. Thus, a collaborative relationship between the networked companies is absolutely vital to success. For these reasons, it's not an overstatement to say that *relationships are the most crucial element of organizational architecture.*

It should be obvious that relationships are important in managing *human resources.* This is where many Western businesses fail miserably. Look at how management and unions deal with each other in most Western countries. Managers see—and treat—their own workers as the enemy. These workers, in turn, behave like an enemy, shutting the manufacturing facilities down through strikes, and creating bad publicity intended to turn customers away from their employers. Both parties are usually at fault for this bad relationship, which saps competitive advantage and leaves the workers, as well as the employer, worse off.

Relationships are also important in managing nonhuman resources. Managers have to give people the resources they need—such as time to do the job and the funds they need to do it. But how these resources get used depends on the relationships involved. Two bad relationships, from an organizational standpoint, are exchange and entitlement. An exchange mentality leads managers to put in extra time only if they get extra money, or compensatory time off. An entitlement mentality leads managers to argue for the same resource allocation that other managers are getting, irrespective of their managerial need. In the context of these bad relationships, when resources become scarce, unit performance becomes depressed: managers say, "I did what I could with what you gave me." If the relationship were stronger, they'd respond with resourcefulness and extra effort. Despite this dynamic, Western reward systems tend to foster exchange and entitlement.

Relationships also determine the effectiveness of *systems.* Control systems, for example, are designed to ensure that objectives are being achieved. But the relationship between the people doing the controlling and the people being controlled determines the effectiveness of control systems. If the relationship is adversarial, the control system will be seen as a policing mechanism imposed by managers who don't trust their own people to do the job properly. Because the relationship determines how the system is experienced, it will determine peoples' motives in responding to it. *When the relationship is adversarial, people will be motivated to outwit the control system.* It's all part of the game when subordinates distort the inputs to the control system—such as by "burying" true costs by manipulating accounts, falsifying time cards, and enlisting the support of co-workers in undermining the system. These tactics would be unconscionable if the relationship were different—if there were a strong sense of inclusion and commonwealth.

Empowerment is very obviously a relationship-driven factor. Managers empower people because they want them to make their own decisions about how best to contribute to organizational success. The relationship with their manager determines workers' motive to make contributions beyond their job descriptions. Empowered workers with positive motives can improve the organization immensely. But empowered workers with negative motives don't want latitude to make their own decisions. They want to do the minimum, with no extra responsibility. As a customer, you've run into disaffected workers, who were obviously "just going through the motions."

When empowerment initiatives fail, there's a tendency for managers to blame worker personalities when the real problem lies in the relationship. You hear, "You can't expect much from the kind of people we have working here. They just want to put in their time and do nothing more." In response to this misattribution, managers reduce empowerment and increase control. This makes the relationship worse, and further diminishes competitive advantage.

The SPARSE Organization

The title of Figure 1-1 is "The SPARSE Organization." The term "sparse" is chosen for two reasons. First and foremost, it extends the notion of a lean organization to the value-chain level. A lean organization—like a marathon runner—has little excess to carry around. There's low overhead, which allows the value chain to be profitable while offering high-value (low-price, high-quality) goods and services. And there are few encumbrances that would inhibit fast response. As a result, the value chain is very agile, and able to seize new opportunities and move quickly to counteract competitive threats.

For comparison, a wolf pack is sparse: at any moment, it may be spread out, but its members are lean and fast, and they can swiftly come together to concentrate their efforts. The pack can move around within vast territory, uninhibited by borders, seizing whatever opportunities arise. In the face of a threat, the pack either drives off the challenger—or vanishes, only to reappear as a formidable hunting unit somewhere else.

The term "SPARSE" is also a mental checklist for you. To be an effective manager, you'll need to understand the Strategy; optimize Processes; manage the Architecture, both within your own organization and within the network of value-chain partners; ensure that the right Resources are in place; operate and evolve the Systems that facilitate strategy implementation: and Empower the people who will actually make the value chain run, adapt, and improve on a day-to-day basis. If one of these elements doesn't get enough attention, then the organization as a whole will be less effective; the same is true if the elements are misaligned. You'll also have to create, improve, and heal relationships within and beyond your organization's boundary.

The chapters in this book will provide you with key information on each of the elements of the sparse organization model, with particular emphasis on the relationships that underlie organizational functioning. Understanding the model and knowing how to align the elements can be your keys to success as a manager in the new era.

NOTES

1. And they're not, in fact, cannibalistic: dogs don't eat other dogs.
2. For an elaboration of this concept, see the article by Peter Vaill, "Toward a Behavioral Description of High Performing Systems," in Morgan W. McCall, Jr., and Michael M. Lombardo (Eds.), *Leadership* (Durham: Duke University Press, 1978), pp. 103–125.
3. A *keiretsu* is a Japanese industrial grouping that involves long-term relationships and interlocking ownership. It is organized according to commonwealth principles.
4. See, for example, Peters and Waterman, *In Search of Excellence: Lessons from America's Best-Run Companies* (New York: Harper & Row, 1982).

CHAPTER 2

RELATIONSHIPS BETWEEN PEOPLE IN ORGANIZATIONS

The old way of thinking led Western managers to create organizations that were basically mechanistic. Managers didn't have an adequate theory of relationships, so they didn't have good alternatives when designing organizations. In this section of the book, we'll explore relationships in detail. We'll begin this by thinking about relationships between people. Then, in Chapter 3, we'll look at relationships within and between groups, and in Chapter 4, we'll consider relationships within and between organizations.

RELATIONSHIPS BETWEEN INDIVIDUALS

The most obvious relationships between people in an organization are their *role* relationships. Suppose you're a banker. Someone is your boss. Other people are your clients. Still others are in support roles—such as accounting, human resources, security, auditing, and information technology. Role relationships tell you how the cogs in the machine are supposed to mesh.

Even though role relationships are the most obvious, this doesn't mean they're the most important relationships. People form complex interpersonal relationships whenever they interact, and these relationships are largely independent of what organization charts and job descriptions prescribe. For example, let's continue to imagine that you're a banker, and look at your relationship with a particular bank client. The client may be a classmate from the same MBA program, which (depending on the business school) could evoke a rich set of interpersonal bonds. Maybe you don't fully trust this client, due to something that happened in the past. But there's also a sense of indebtedness and loyalty: the client spared you embarrassment in front of your boss when you made a mistake last year. Finally, you may be strongly attracted to this person.

The hierarchical model assumes you leave all these interpersonal relationship dimensions behind when you step into your organizational role. But that's not human nature. Real people form complex relationships that don't vanish when someone—you or your boss—tells them to. To the contrary, such relationships need to be *assessed accurately* and then *managed well.*

Moreover, the relationship dimensions emphasized in economics-based models—dominance, superiority, roles, exchange, and competition—aren't the ones foremost in people's minds when they think about their interconnectedness with others. Figure 2-1 shows what they *do* think about. We'll begin our work on relationships by exploring these dimensions and then move on to look at their implications for managers.

The relationship dimensions can be grouped into four areas. They are *rapport* (people's comfort in dealing with each other), *bonding* (the robustness of the relationship when it encounters strain), *breadth* (how far the relationship extends beyond organizational roles and the immediate transaction), and *affinity* (how appealing the person is). We'll try to understand each dimension in detail, because all of them can be important to managers.

Rapport Dimensions

The first group of dimensions involves the comfort people have in dealing with each other. Included in this grouping are trust, disclosure, empathy, acceptance, and respect. Let's examine each of these dimensions.

Trust. Trust is often viewed as the most fundamental dimension of interpersonal relationships. We all use the term and recognize its importance. However, in order to fully appreciate the implications of trust for managing business relationships, we need to begin with a clear idea about what trust is.

If you're trying to figure out whether you can trust me, the first thing you're likely to consider is whether I'll divulge things that you want me to keep confidential. The closer we work together, the greater the chance that I'll learn something about you that you'll wish I'd keep to myself. Maybe it's

RELATIONSHIP DIMENSION	RELATIONSHIP-WEAKENING POLE	RELATIONSHIP-STRENGTHENING POLE
Rapport Dimensions		
Trust	Distrust	Full trust
Interpersonal disclosure	Social distance	Vulnerability
Empathy	No empathy	Strong empathy
Acceptance	Rejection	Unconditional positive regard
Respect	Disrespect	High respect
Bonding Dimensions		
Alliance	Enemies	Allies
Competing	Competition	Collaboration
Economic exchange	No benefit	Great benefit
Breadth Dimensions		
Scope	Narrow	Unlimited
Time-horizon	Transactional	Continuous
Affinity Dimensions		
Stimulation	Boring	Interesting
Sharing things in common	Nothing in common	A lot in common
Liking	Dislike	Strong affection
Romantic interest	Repulsion	Attraction

FIGURE 2-1 The Dimensions of Interpersonal Relationships

something you told me, or something I overheard or observed. In trusting me, you have to be confident that I won't tell others.

Now, my motive in telling others might not be to do you harm. It might simply be to gain people's approval. Many people have strong curiosity about what others would prefer to keep to themselves. Think about it. There's a whole exposé industry—tabloids and TV gossip shows—that thrives on people's curiosity. I can ingratiate myself with others by disclosing things about you.

This is where trust comes in. Trust in relationships is a loyalty bond that makes it more important for me to keep your secret than to gain others' favor by disclosing it. If the bond is strong, I'll act as your agent, putting myself into your shoes, and not saying anything about you that *you* haven't already disclosed. If you trust me, this means you're assured that I won't make the disclosure decision *for* you: it's up to you to decide what you want others to know and not know.

The broader sense of trust involves being able to rely on me to take your best interests into account. Said another way, in trusting me, you want to be assured I won't knowingly or carelessly harm you. At the extreme, i.e., in trusting me absolutely, you know with certainty that I will give priority to your needs even when doing so means a loss of some kind to me. As a result, trust is a reflection of how much and how well one person cares for the other.

This caring involves two separate but related considerations: Do I *have your best interests at heart* and Am I *reliable?* Whether I have your best interests at heart is an important aspect of relationship strength. I have my own interests to take care of, as well as those of others I care about. The trust question centers on where your interests fall within my priority list. If the relationship involves indifference, only my basic sense of altruism or decency toward others will encourage me to make decisions in a way that benefits you. But as our relationship bonds become stronger, my concern for your well-being will become greater. In an extremely strong relationship, such as a mother's bond to her infant, concern for the other is so powerful as to motivate considerable self-sacrifice. These extremes—from indifference to mothers' nurturing of infants—define the continuum of having another's best interests at heart.

Even if you know that my predispositions toward you are well intentioned, you'll still wonder whether I'll *act* on them. This is where the reliability dimension comes in. Deep trust requires a response that can be counted on—irrespective of mood, whims, forgetfulness, or context. In making this assessment, you'll tune in to my past behavior and the general comments I make about trust situations. Your initial impression will be amended over time as new information gets factored into your opinion. At some point, you'll have achieved a fairly robust view of my reliability, one that isn't affected by further evidence one way or the other.

Your ability to predict what I'll do is influenced by my ability to rationalize letting you down. Rationalization is a psychological defense mechanism. It's a means of dealing with the discomfort that arises when there is dissonance. Dissonance occurs when I'm behaving in a way that's inconsistent with what my relationship partner expects of me. Let's consider an example.

Suppose that two young men, Andy and Zeke, are close friends. Andy has a very attractive girlfriend, Peg. Zeke is currently unattached. When Andy travels on business, Zeke and Peg keep each other company. Now, Zeke is obviously attracted to Peg so Andy wonders whether he can trust Zeke not to "hit on" (i.e., try to seduce) Peg while he's out of town. In making his trust assessment, Andy will factor in Zeke's general ability to avert guilt and shame by erecting a mental defense. He'll remember stories Zeke has told him about other breaches of trust and how he came up with self-serving explanations of this conduct. If Zeke has offered explanations like "Hey, I figured that if he never found out, there'd be no harm done," Andy's trust level will reflect this.

The development of trust is an extremely volatile process. People make initial assessments of the other's trustworthiness and then react very strongly if the other person doesn't live up to their expectations. The sense of betrayal arises because when people have made an initial assessment, they communicate their level of trust—usually indirectly, by symbolic acts such as sharing confidences. But, as you know from your own experience, indirect communication has enormous potential for being misunderstood. So the second person may not realize the level of trust being expected of her or him. Then, when she or he does something that violates these expectations, the first person gets very angry and is likely to attribute sinister motives. It's very typical, for example, for a person to say, "I have ZERO trust in that rat" after an early disappointment.

With more experience in a relationship, people are likely to make fine distinctions in their trust assessments, rather than making all-or-nothing judgments. They may say something like "I can trust this guy with confidences, and he means me no harm. But he seems to get sucked into competitive situations and treats them as a game. When he's out to win, I have to watch out for myself."

Distinctions like these define the *domain* in which the person can be trusted. For example, you might be able to trust a co-worker not to steal money from your desk, but not be surprised to learn that she undermined you by saying things behind your back. Or you may be able to trust a subordinate not to lie if you ask him a direct question, but not expect him to tell you things you need to know if you don't ask the right question. An important aspect of "getting to know someone" includes an assessment of the domain of trustworthiness. And "strengthening the relationship" with someone involves broadening that domain.

Interpersonal Disclosure. The closer our relationship, the more willing you are to disclose things to me. The issue here is whether I get to know "the real you," or have to settle for whatever façade you present to me.

The most obvious and familiar façade is the organizational role. Someone who's described as "all business" interacts in a way that carries out the role assignment prescribed by the organization chart, but "gives you nothing else to relate to." At the end of the day, you don't know that person any better than when the day started. The person remains a stranger carrying out a role.

Some people prefer pure role relationships at work. If they feel excluded, for example, they may have withdrawn psychologically and are now putting in their time as if they were human robots. Or, if they were raised in a culture that emphasizes social distance, they may be uncomfortable with disclosure. And sometimes the absence of disclosure is purely tactical, such as when a person "plays his cards close to his vest."

But most people want to feel "connected" with those they deal with at work. A sense of *inclusion* is very important to them. They spend half their waking hours on the job, and can find it a lonely experience if they have to spend this time in a relational vacuum. A certain amount of openness is necessary for them to feel connected. They offer openness by being forthcoming about their own lives outside of work, and expect other people to reciprocate. The people who initiate the openness are likely to be "put off" by people maintaining social distance, which is experienced as rejection: "She acts like she's superior." Or, "He doesn't consider me worth talking to."

As noted above, the closer the relationship the more likely it is that there will be mutual disclosure between the people; at the same time, the more disclosure there is, the closer the relationship becomes. Bonds are strengthened the most when disclosure leaves the person feeling vulnerable. Vulnerability involves the risk of being hurt—rejected, embarrassed, or betrayed, for example. Thus, exposing oneself to being hurt is a powerful signaling device: it takes a lot of faith in the other person to do it.

Disclosure obviously depends on the level of trust. You wouldn't risk disclosing much if you feared that the information might be shared carelessly—or manipulatively—with others. In contrast, if you believed that the person has your best interests at heart, you might disclose more. A trusted person may be strongly motivated to help with your situation, for example, but can't do so if she or he is unaware of "what's going on for you."

Empathy. Any situation looks different if you look at it from someone else's perspective. Consider the example of the husband who goes deer hunting. He sees killing as a "sport." His wife, by contrast, sees his hunting trips as a selfish choice that excludes her and the children. His young daughter sees "killing Bambi" as incomprehensible behavior from a father she knows as gentle and caring. The taxidermist sees his hunting as an opportunity to make money. Empathy is the ability to see a situation from the other person's perspective, and is very important in relationships. The hunter's wife resents being deserted, and she experiences revulsion every time she looks at deer heads mounted on the wall. But she's empathic in understanding how *he* experiences deer hunting. It's an opportunity for him to do some "male bonding." He's socially inept at expressing attachment to other men, but he's able to make connections by joining them hunting.

The scenario illustrates some important features of empathy that are relevant to business relationships. People differ in their ability to put themselves in other people's shoes. But at least one person in the relationship needs to be good at it. Without this, differences and misunderstandings will almost certainly escalate.

Even in the old days, when the workplace was fairly homogeneous, there were enormous differences in points of view. Managers didn't see situations the same way their subordinates (or superiors) did; sales people didn't see situations the same way that production superintendents (or financial controllers) did; and stockholders didn't see situations the same way managers (or union leaders) did. Today, workforce diversity makes empathy even more of a managerial challenge. Added to role differences are the differences in perspective that arise from very different racial, gender, class, or cultural backgrounds. As a result, there's never been a stronger need for people to understand each other.

Understanding needs to happen at both the thinking and the feeling levels. Empathy for how a relationship partner *thinks* involves perspective-taking ability. A test of this might be "Could he explain the situation the same way I would tell the story?" Active listening is a common technique used to foster perspective taking. In active listening, the listener has to restate the message to the speaker's satisfaction. Since empathy is as much a skill as a trait, people who start out with low perspective-taking ability can improve considerably.

The emotional counterpart of perspective-taking ability is sympathy.

This involves understanding how the other person *feels*. At the extreme, sympathizers are deeply affected by the other's moods: they feel the other's pain and share their joy. Some degree of sympathy seems necessary for strong relationships. For example, you wouldn't expect a colleague to be indifferent to your embarrassment, mirth, disappointment, surprise, or frustration. We call such people cold, heartless, or insensitive. It's a sign of closeness if another's mood affects you greatly, a sign of distance if it doesn't.

Acceptance. Blind dates, changing jobs, and new clients have a lot in common. They make you worry about whether you'll be accepted as a relationship partner. These situations bring to light a dimension of all relationships: whether the other person seems to accept you just as you are. Most of us experience some level of anxiety that people meeting us for the first time will find us lacking. That creates the need to put on a façade. We're careful to look our best on a blind date: usually, we look *very* different from the way we looked when we got up that morning. We prepare a résumé that stresses all the positives and leaves out the negatives when we're looking for a new job. And we roll out the red carpet for new clients, giving them a lot more attention than they'll get if they sign on. It's called "impression management." We manage impressions because we care about others' acceptance of us and think we know how to generate it.

Acceptance is important in relationships because that's where people get a fundamental need met. Psychologists note that people seek unconditional positive regard. They want other people to think they're OK irrespective of how they're presenting themselves in the moment. People's strong appetite for unconditional positive regard gets established early in life. A mother expresses adoration of her infant even though the baby has kept her up half the night, frayed her nerves with incessant crying, thrown up on her shoulder after breakfast, and soiled yet another diaper. In subsequent relationships, the baby in us yearns to recapture this feeling of nirvana, but we never even come close.

Lack of acceptance can take two forms. The most obvious is *rejection*. The other person wants as little contact with us as possible and we sense it in his or her behavior. This is never pleasant. Even if we care nothing about—or even detest—the person, *we* would prefer to be the ones doing the rejecting. The second form is feeling *judged*. It's hard to relax and be yourself when you feel constantly monitored and evaluated. Feeling judged also produces the impression that the relationship depends on the outcome of the ongoing assessment. That isn't the unconditional positive regard we seek.

People's natural dislike for feeling judged strains business relationships. Yet part of a boss's job is to judge subordinates and suppliers. And, in work situations that use "360-degree evaluation," managers may have to judge other people, too—their peers, their own boss, and people they interact closely with. This creates the need to make it very clear that approving (or disapproving) of specific work *behaviors* is different from accepting *the person*. The manager who is careless about differentiating these two judgments risks relationship problems. People often respond constructively when criticism of their performance is presented in the context of strong approval of them as a person. Don't you?

Respect. The final element of rapport is respect. Two factors determine your respect for a relationship partner: evidence of a strong value system, and the will to live up to it. We infer a strong value system when the person is leading a thoughtful life, making decisions conscientiously—that is, with reference to those values. Thus, it's a sign of respect when we describe someone as "having strong principles" or "a person of integrity."

Note that people garner little respect when their decisions are dominated by economic thinking. Take, for example, the classical "Economic Man"—someone who's primarily focused on maximizing utility and minimizing disutility. Unbridled self-interest is not an admirable value system.

Similarly, we don't respect corporate leaders who simply maximize shareholder wealth. Indeed, the corporate world is shifting away from this unidimensional view toward a "balanced scorecard" approach to evaluating business success. In addition to generating profit, the corporate leader must create value for customers, help employees grow and prosper, foster innovation and the application of technology, and serve the community that gives the organization its home.

Also note that the other person's value system doesn't have to be identical to our own in order for us to extend respect. When values differ strongly, the ones held by the other person are respected if that person appears to have arrived at them through careful deliberation. Someone who's simply parroting a creed (such as an unexamined political ideology or religious dogma) is unlikely to be respected: adopting someone else's values is accorded less respect than developing your own.

The second element of respect is whether people *act on* their beliefs and obligations. We describe those who do as people of integrity and when they do so in the face of costs or risks, as having courage. In contrast, we view those who "talk the talk but don't walk the walk" as unprincipled at best and as moral cowards at worst. While we might "respect *their right*" to live as they choose, it would be impossible to respect *them* in the sense described here.

Respect is surprisingly independent of other relationship dimensions. For example, people are as comfortable saying, "I like him but I don't respect him" as they are saying, "I respect him greatly but I also dislike him intensely." You can even trust people you don't respect, as when someone says: "He doesn't stand for much, but he always looks out for me. I can always depend on him."

Finally, respect is rarely symmetrical. One person in a relationship usually "looks up to" the other. Over time, however, the difference becomes less pronounced in close relationships because the strong-value person becomes a role model, making the other more respectable.

Bonding Dimensions

The second group of dimensions concerns how robust the relationship is. We refer to some relationships as "strong" and others as more "casual." Strong bonds allow the relationship to remain intact when it encounters strains. The relationship dimensions that determine robustness are the sense of alliance, the competitive dynamics, and the nature and balance of economic exchange.

Alliance. Most people can be placed on a continuum that ranges from ally to enemy. Strong bonds arise when the other person is an ally. This means he or she feels loyalty to you. Loyalty shows itself in three different circumstances. The first test is whether he or she will abandon the relationship for short-term gain. We refer to people who fail that test as "fair-weather friends." They can't be relied on "to be there for you" when they see an opportunity to take care of themselves instead. The second test is whether the person will take your side when you're not there to observe. Most people will be nice to your face, but what do they say behind your back? Strong allies are unwavering in their support. The third test involves public commitment to the relationship. Strong alliances are visible to others because the loyal person takes a supportive stance. The support is often nonverbal and symbolic—such as when allies stand alongside you when you're announcing an unpopular decision.

At the opposite end of this continuum are enemies, people who wish you harm. Their motive may be jealousy, revenge, resentment, or other emotions that lead them to take pleasure in your misfortunes. In practice, it's often difficult to detect this relationship dynamic because enmity is often masked. It's one thing for a person to feel like your enemy and another thing altogether to openly declare it. The masking is greatest when your enemy has low power because there are risks to declaring oneself an enemy. The first is the risk of attack. If you know a person is out to hurt you (i.e., is your enemy), you have a motive to attack first, as a deterrent. The second is the risk of organizational reproach. Organizations are supposed to be harmonious places where everyone gets along with everyone else. Of course, in reality, this can never be the case because conflict is an inevitable part of human interaction in organizations. Nevertheless, the myth survives, and this means people have to hide their enmity.

The midpoint of the continuum between ally and enemy is *either* neutrality or ambivalence. Neutrality means that you don't have strong feelings for or against the other person. Ambivalence means you do have strong feelings but they conflict with one another: you experience *both* loyalty and enmity. This often happens when two family members are fighting and you feel caught in the middle: their dispute generates conflicting feelings of fondness and resentment in you.

The alliance dimension is almost purely bilateral. If someone makes it obvious that you're considered an enemy, you'll view that person as your own enemy. It's hard not to reciprocate: you have to be in strong denial to remain neutral once you find out that someone wishes you ill. Conversely, if one party treats the other as an ally, social norms make it hard to respond with exploitation or rebuff without enduring guilt and shame; so there's a tendency to accept and reciprocate offers of alliance when these are viewed as sincere.

You've probably noticed that people tend to pay close attention to where every relationship falls on the ally-enemy continuum. In fact, it's a primary topic of gossip within and outside the workplace. Most organizations have a formal structure shown on an organization chart. But this only describes role relationships. The "informal organization" is a network of alliances and schisms. While this chart is never explicitly drawn, people are highly attuned to it. They want to know where they—and their allies—fall within the organization's power structure.

People seldom ask explicit questions about alliance networks. They ask indirect questions about people, then make inferences from the answers. They might ask, for example, "What's Dennis like to work with?" If the response is strongly positive, they will infer a strong alliance between Dennis and the person responding. They don't expect to hear a strongly negative response because they realize the hazards of openly declaring someone an enemy. So enmity usually brings an initial noncommittal response, such as "Dennis has his good points and bad points." If the person asking the question also comments on Dennis's negative qualities, the two may soon sense that Dennis is mutually disliked. Having a common enemy strengthens their own bond. Thus, gossip is not simply idle conversation: it's a mechanism for establishing and maintaining relationships within alliance networks.

The alliance dimension is important to understand because it underlies "organizational politics." An organization is supposed to be a meritocracy in which people make decisions that optimize attainment of the organization's goals. The term "organizational politics" indicates that something else is happening. Often, a subgroup makes decisions that serve ingroup members' interests rather than the organization's goals. The schemers "consolidate their power" by surrounding themselves with allies. To do this, they purge people from positions of influence who may be loyal to the organization rather than to the ingroup. The result is not a meritocracy, but a system that creates cynicism and apathy, which together undermine organizational effectiveness.

Alliance also takes the form of commitment to the relationship. This is easiest to understand in the context of marriage. If one partner is on a business trip and gets the opportunity to cheat on the spouse, the impulse may be restrained by his or her commitment to the relationship itself. The loyal person, though tempted, may think, "This could be an opportunity for a great adventure if I were single, but it's unthinkable in the context of my marriage." Business analogs of this situation abound. A consultant may be better off economically by starting a new consulting firm—pirating away key staff members and current clients. If the consultant's alliance with the firm is strong enough (i.e., is a dominant dimension), she or he will likely not even *think about* defecting. In this case, there would be no weighing of the costs and benefits of leaving versus staying.

Alliance explains a lot of behavior that seems *economically* irrational. In the examples we considered, taking advantage of the more-attractive opportunity was economically rational but *relationally* irrational. We'll return to the alternative forms of rationality later in the book.

Competing. This relationship dimension is best described in terms of its negative pole. Competing is negative because it's always divisive and always weakens bonds. Some people find this hard to accept: they argue that they compete in some of their strongest relationships. But when they describe these relationships in detail, it usually turns out that their strongest relationships aren't very strong, and whatever strength exists is *in spite of* the competing that goes on. That is, other relationship characteristics are needed to compensate for the destructive effects of competing.

Competition strains relationships because *if there's a winner, there has to be a loser.* The loser experiences some degree of shame and resentment. The fact that many people deny having these feelings isn't surprising. In Western cultures, it's hard to own up to feeling bad about losing. Social norms constrain what you can express. You're supposed to be a "good loser" if you participate in competitions. In this myth, the good loser rejoices in the other's victory and vows to try harder next time. In the real world, the loser mourns the loss, and resents the winner for causing misery and embarrassment. These feelings erode relationship strength, even when the feelings do not reach conscious awareness.[1]

Competitive impulses arise from our early life experiences when vying with siblings for parental attention. These formative experiences can be so potent that they give us the impulse to compete in any situation involving peers striving for the attention of an authority figure.[2] For example, consulting companies hire young analysts straight out of college and assign them to groups working for a high-status manager. The competition that develops between analysts often undermines the group's effectiveness.

Similarly, when a young, highly capable employee is added to an established group, older peers feel threatened. They fear they won't be able to compete with this more-recently-educated, technologically sophisticated person who doesn't yet have a life outside work and is therefore willing to put in 80-hour work weeks. The boss unwittingly makes the competition more intense by spending more time coaching the newcomer. Typically, the newcomer is unaware of the relationship strains this situation creates. And the older workers can't own up to feeling threatened for fear that the boss may question their adequacy and maturity. Nevertheless, the divisiveness inherent in this situation makes the group less effective.

In sum, interpersonal competition is so obviously harmful that it's hard to believe we tolerate it in Western organizations, much less encourage it. But cultural myths prevent us from treating it as pathology, and instead we revere competition as a positive interpersonal dynamic.

Managers need to be aware of the risks of deliberately setting employees in competition with one another. Even when the objective is to motivate subordinates to excel, there's a good chance it won't work out that way. Competing involves doing your best to win, which also means doing your best to make sure the other person loses. In tennis, for example, you make it as difficult as possible for your opponent to return the ball. In poker, you deceive your opponents—by bluffing—to get them to concede the hand to you. You're free to try whatever tactic will give you an advantage, so long as you don't violate the rules of the game.

Sometimes managers create competitive relationship dynamics without realizing it. For example, control systems facilitate accountability for the individual manager. But they also invite comparisons between managers to see which one is doing better. This induces managers to compete with one another. All the precipitating conditions are present: measurable outcomes (the ability to "keep score"), someone to compete with, and the presence of an authority figure who'll decide the winner. These systems tend to discourage the joint effort that's required for cross-functional collaboration—a necessity in the new era.

At the opposite pole from competing is *collaborating*. This involves working jointly with your relationship partner so that both of you will benefit from the outcomes. There isn't a winner and a loser: instead, there's a sense of *commonwealth*. The collaboration can be focused on pursuing opportunities for joint gain, or working together to solve joint problems. There's less of an emphasis on "my success" and "your success," and more of a sense that "we're in this together."

In the case of most other dimensions, the two poles are connected by a continuum; here the situation is different. Competing tends to be an all-or-nothing phenomenon. If you're competing, you're out to win and you'll do what it takes to win. You don't compete half-heartedly—not if you're a good sport. What does vary is the number of areas in which you're competing.

Suppose, for example, that the only time you compete with your life partner is when you're playing chess. The competition in your relationship may be strong within the domain of chess, and completely absent in other domains of your shared life. Competition doesn't get out of hand because couples invest a lot of energy in preserving the relationship—or at least one partner does. The onset of serious strain brings on the intervention that makes many men cringe: "It's time for us to work on our relationship."

Relationships with workplace peers don't have the same stabilizing mechanisms, however. So it's possible to end up competing in every area you share with these peers—who leads meetings, who gets the best results, who's next in line for a promotion, who drives what kind of car, who's faring better in the dating scene, and other areas related to status. In new-era organizations, which depend heavily on collaboration, such competition is a liability.

Economic Exchange. Sometimes people care most about the practical benefits they get out of the relationship. This is especially true in one-time transactions. For example, when you need to buy a used car, you enter into a temporary relationship with the seller. Meeting your needs is the dominant feature of this relationship: that is, if you didn't need a car, you probably wouldn't interact with this person at all.

In addition, a person might focus on personal benefit in the early stage of relationship formation, especially if the initial interactions arise in connection with a specific purpose. For example, a young account executive visits a clerk in the controller's office because she needs specific information about sales cyclicality. While there, she notices that he has a picture of an eagle on his desk. They discover that they both like wilderness, and exchange tales of hiking trips. Soon, they're eating lunch together and enjoying a broader friendship, both on and off the job. The personal benefit is still there—she still needs information to do her job well—but this instrumental motive recedes in importance as stronger forces bond the two together.

Personal benefit—or, more formally, utility gain through exchange—has received a lot of attention from economists and sociologists as the primary bond in relationships. But this is only true in the case of transactions. Indeed, the strongest relationships may have negative personal benefit. Remember Mom? Motherhood involves endless sacrifices, as she'll tell you. She has children *in spite of* her self-interest.

The exchange continuum goes from great personal benefit to great personal sacrifice. The midpoint could be neutrality in which there's neither gain nor sacrifice: this is typical in the case of most relationships with close friends, where the intent and the language are far removed from a balance-sheet mentality. When something of value is offered and accepted, it is done in a spirit of caring, a mutual process of meeting each other's needs—and simple sharing—with no thoughts of getting or sacrificing anything.[3]

Alternatively, the midpoint could involve a balance between gains and sacrifices. Many business relationships are of this second type. In fact, in stable relationships of this sort, both parties will be concerned with maintaining this balance. In general, the weaker the other relationship dimensions, the more prominent net personal benefit becomes in a person's assessment of the relationship's value.

In support of this last point, a study of relationship characteristics showed personal benefit to be a relatively minor consideration in most relationships that people considered important.[4] Indeed, a preoccupation with exchange balance in a primary relationship may be an indicator of poor relationship health. For example, when a marriage counselor hears one partner asking, "What have you done for me lately?" it's often a sign that other aspects of the relationship have deteriorated.

A preoccupation with net personal benefit can also signal problems in managers' relationships with others—such as subordinates, peers, bosses, suppliers, customers, and strategic alliance partners. It's hard, for example, for subordinates and peers to be loyal to a manager who sees them only as a means of accomplishing his personal objectives. They may "feel used" and resent it. Old-paradigm thinking stresses people's roles and their instrumental value: it assumes people don't mind feeling used. After all, they took a job in a system that's set up to do just that—a machine uses cogs. Yet, in reality, feeling used (that is, valued only for your utility) is a very negative experience, which makes it difficult for relationships to deepen if one or both people are preoccupied with personal benefits.

The conventional thinking that viewed relationships primarily as a source of net benefit missed an important point. Only in the shallowest of relationships do people evaluate benefits and sacrifices in economic terms. In deeper relationships, they evaluate the *meaning* of benefits received and sacrifices made.

Let's take a ten-dollar expenditure as an example. Suppose you give it as a birthday present to your 3-year-old son. He's happy, imagining the toys he'll be able to buy. You're happy, too. If you gave him one dollar, he might have been happy, but you would have felt cheap. If you'd given him a hundred dollars, he wouldn't have been any happier and you would have felt guilty about spoiling the child. Now let's suppose instead you gave that same ten dollars to your 21-year-old daughter as a wedding present. She'd be furious. It would signal to her that you didn't approve of her new husband, or that you gave cash because you didn't care about her enough to shop for a gift. Let's suppose instead that you gave the ten dollars as a tip in a restaurant. The server was extremely attractive and your light snack cost only three dollars. The server would try to figure out what you were signaling.

The economic value of the ten dollars was the same in each situation.

But the assessment of the expenditure on the benefits-sacrifices continuum was very different. What differed was *the relationship* that formed the context of the expenditure. *People assign meaning to benefits given and received, and meanings are always relationship-specific.* Imagine different relationships and see if the meaning changes. For example, what if the attractive server in the restaurant is your grandchild rather than a complete stranger? Does the ten-dollar tip for a three-dollar meal mean the same thing?

Economic thinking has limited applicability when it considers costs and benefits without taking into account the relationship context. Thus, net personal benefit is very difficult to assess unless you know a lot about other aspects of the relationship.

Breadth-of-the-Relationship Dimensions

The next set of dimensions reflects differences in how relationships are experienced in terms of scope and time. Some relationships are strictly role-determined, such as your interaction with telephone operators. They're trained to be only "a voice carrying out tasks following a prescribed routine." Other relationships are broader in scope. Some are limited to a single transaction, such as when you drive through a tollbooth. You can exchange pleasantries and ask for a receipt, but after that, the contact is over. Other relationships are experienced as ongoing. We'll see that it isn't just the objective situation that determines how relationships are experienced. It's what people focus on.

Scope. Some relationships are simple; others are complicated. What usually makes them complicated is broad scope. Think of what it means to be naked. You're probably quite comfortable being naked when you're taking a shower at home, but a little less comfortable in front of your doctor during a physical exam. The discomfort is manageable if there's a narrow-scope relationship. The doctor is a professional doing a job, and thinking of nothing except how to maintain your health. If the doctor is more than that—for example, your future father-in-law—you're likely to be much less comfortable. Thus the same situation can be experienced very differently depending on how broad the relationship scope is.

The old paradigm prescribed narrow-scope relationships. Middle managers designed organizational relationships, emphasizing roles. But *Homo sapiens* is a social animal, which makes sticking to pure role relationships a challenge for most people. We tend to bond with the people we deal with, but even when we don't want to get closer to them, we react to them—such as by competing—in ways that take us beyond the simple role relationship. So narrow-scope relationships have a natural tendency to broaden. It's worth pausing to consider whether this tendency ought to be resisted or encouraged.

Many organizations have policies forbidding nepotism. That is, you're not supposed to be working with a family member as a boss, subordinate, or peer. When you ask managers what are the advantages of this policy, they offer a variety of reasons. It's hard to discipline a member of your own family when you need to. Nepotism creates discontent because other workers allege favoritism. Workers' loyalty to family is stronger than to the company. Or, you can't trust managers to keep confidences when they're gossiping with subordinates at the kitchen table.

Thus, the case against nepotism has some logical basis. But family businesses *thrive* on nepotism, and can be very successful as a result. The relationships between family members are a positive force because they're broad in scope. The people involved in the business aren't just co-workers performing tasks: they're deeply concerned with each other's success on and off the job, and have a strong sense of commonwealth. In contrast, conventional organizational design prescribes narrow relationships between workers. They're limited to interdependent job descriptions—cogs in a machine. The message is "The only thing we care about is whether you get the task done as prescribed." But this message induces workers to react by *only doing* what's explicitly required. They respond to requests for nonroutine contributions by saying, "It's not in my job description."

The challenges of the new era require organizations to constantly adapt to changing conditions. Narrow-scope hierarchical relationships emphasize roles and rules. But organizational adaptability—continuous improvement in its broadest sense—requires flexibility in contributions, processes, and organizational architecture. Managers need broad-scope relationships to evoke broad-scope contributions.

Time-Horizon. Suppose you're a real-estate developer and you get the opportunity to obtain a commercial property in an auction. Your relationship with the auctioneer is truly episodic. The history and future of your relationship are irrelevant. The auction is a single transaction. Either you outbid others, or you don't. You and the auctioneer are indifferent to each other as people. You're simply a bidder and the auctioneer is simply a professional in charge of a process.

Now suppose instead that you're buying that same property from a local builder who has done work for you in the past, and relies on you for future business. You, in turn, need the builder to put up new buildings and remodel properties you already own. The builder is reliable, provides high value, and goes out of his way to meet your deadlines when it's important to you. Purchasing the property from the builder is very different from buying it from the auctioneer because the deal is taking place within the context of a continuous relationship. You'll learn important things, such as how much he has invested in the property and how soon he needs cash. The two of you can then work out a deal that's advantageous and fair to both of you.

How people *perceive* the situation can be more important than what's objectively true. Some people are predisposed to see situations as transactional, and others to see them as events within long-term relationships. That is, different personalities visualize different relationships, even when the objective situation is identical.

Some people tend to view all situations as transactions—as a deal that's decided on its own merits. They believe that anything that happened in the past is "a done deal" that doesn't need to be taken into account because it has no bearing on the current transaction. Similarly, they believe there's no point trying to build goodwill because future deals will be decided on their merits: if a viable deal is on the table, people will put aside "their personal feelings" and do what makes economic sense. This transactional perspective on relationships conforms to the ideal model economists have assumed, and is true of the way some people think—especially people in business. But it's not the way the *average* person thinks.[5]

Other people treat most relationships as if they were continuous, even when an objective observer would rate the probability of future contact as extremely unlikely. For some, this approach is purposeful and calculated. They figure, "You never know when you're going to run into this person again." Or, "If you treat people well, they'll respond by treating you well." For others, the notion of continuity of relationships is more abstract. They see themselves in a continuous relationship with *other people in general*; therefore, they need to behave at all times as if the relationship and the other person's welfare matter. One version of this is "The Golden Rule," which tells us to treat other people as we would like to be treated.

So there are really two determinants of whether a person will see a particular relationship as episodic or continuous. The first is the *objective situation;* the second is *their predisposition in relating to other people.* It's important to understand these subtleties because perceived time-horizon makes a big difference in how people approach business situations. The most serious problem arises when there's asymmetry of views: that is, the first person visualizes a business interaction as episodic, while the second sees it as an event in an ongoing relationship. The resulting misunderstandings can destroy trust and other aspects of rapport.

Asymmetries in perceived time-horizon most frequently arise in cross-cultural and cross-gender interactions, but people must always be conscious of the potential for misunderstandings. Even when both people view the relationship as continuous, they may have different views concerning whether the current situation should be considered a transaction. It's obvious that even if two attorneys are friends outside of work, when they show up in court on opposing sides, each needs to treat the case as a transaction. It's less obvious how the friendship between a purchasing agent and a sales representative should play out when a purchase contract needs to be negotiated. What's important is that the parties have a mutual understanding of how they will approach the negotiations.

Affinity Dimensions

This set of relationship dimensions concerns the degree to which the people find each other intrinsically interesting. Included are how stimulating the other person is, how much the relationship partners have in common, how well they like each other, and whether there's romantic interest. These dimensions tend to be correlated.

Stimulation. We find some people interesting and others boring. Stimulation involves the amount of psychological energy the other person arouses in you. Interesting people make you think, or inspire you to act. Boring people don't: if they give you any inspiration at all, it's to avoid them. These two end points define the continuum of this relationship dimension.

What makes someone interesting? Often, it's the element of surprise. Interesting people make you wonder. You had a particular way of viewing a situation, and the other person has surprised you by giving you a different way to think about it.

Sometimes you consider people interesting because they talk about things *you* find interesting. A good example is when people want to talk about you. You've probably heard the joke about the person describing someone he met at a cocktail party: "She was a really interesting person and a great conversationalist. We talked about *me* all night." This story, presented as ironic humor, reflects a perfectly understandable psychological dynamic. A good conversationalist must be a good listener (otherwise the person is an orator, not a conversationalist). A good listener is empathic and asks probing questions. So what the person telling the story found interesting was the insights he gained about himself as a result of her probing questions.

Sometimes people are interesting because of their personal characteristics. For example, some people have charisma. Something about their manner holds your attention. Usually it's something you admire: you wish you had their voice, their accent, their looks, or their presence. At other times, however, it's something negative that holds your attention: you can't believe their arrogance, their outspokenness, their insensitivity, or their unconventional appearance. Perhaps there's underlying admiration here, too. There are times when most of us would like to be freed of the need to gain social approval: we're fascinated by people who seem able to shrug it off.

When you experience someone as boring, this may tell you something about yourself, or it may tell you something about the other person. It probably tells you more about yourself if you're the kind of person who is "easily bored." Easily bored people have a need for strong external stimuli, and so it takes a lot to hold their interest. They may not be able to depend on a relationship partner to keep them amused all the time. Indeed, the kind of relationship partner that would never bore them would drive most of us crazy. Their partners might be risk seekers, people who reject social conventions, or "oppositional" personalities with particular antagonism toward authority figures. Such people are interesting, but they're also exhausting because they keep your anxiety level high. So it's not necessarily bad if your primary relationship partner isn't very interesting. If the relationship is strong in other ways, you can find other sources of stimulation (such as skydiving, watching scary movies, or putting a pit bull on a diet).

The sense of boredom occasionally tells you something about the other person. Sometimes, *you* feel bored because *they're* bored with themselves. This may reflect a psychological state such as low self-esteem, or certain forms of depression. Or their emotions are so heavily controlled that your own mood becomes apathetic or even depressed. They drain your energy.

Sometimes others are boring because of their extreme risk aversion. They want to avoid standing out in any way, so they become ultraconventional and invisible. They try so hard to avoid offending or provoking anyone that they provide almost zero stimulus in their relationships with others. They give you so little of themselves that there's not much to react to.

Sharing Things in Common. There are two sayings in the common wisdom that seem totally contradictory: "Birds of a feather flock together" and "Opposites attract." In fact, there's no contradiction because they refer to different relationship dimensions.

Opposites attract because they're more interesting. People need to be different from you if they're going to surprise you and to stimulate your thinking. Birds of a feather—people who are very much alike—flock together because we feel comfortable associating with people who are just like us. Even if they aren't as interesting.

People who are just like us are the most comfortable to be with. It's easier to interact with someone who has the same views and interests: we don't have to manage the tensions that arise from incompatible viewpoints. There are fewer misunderstandings because we think alike. We use the same expressions, tell the same kinds of jokes, and probably live in the same neighborhoods. We're likely to form broad-scope relationships with similar people because it's more probable we'll have things to share outside of work.

At a deep psychological level, we tend to seek out people who have much in common because they're a source of affirmation. *Many of us have a tendency—especially if we're high-achievers—to be self-critical.* We need affirmation that we're OK because we tend to constantly question whether we're living up to our potential, and whether we're worthy of others' approval. Our subconscious fears that we may not be good enough are eased when we associate with people who are no different from us. No different means no better.

Another psychological dynamic—the preference for avoiding dissonance—motivates people to seek out others who are similar. Dissonance is the psychological discomfort that arises when one thought is at odds with another. It creates a feeling of malaise—the sense that something isn't right. It gives you the urge to make some mental adjustments to restore balance to how you view your world. Let's consider an example of dissonance in a relationship.

Suppose one of your co-workers has become a good friend. The two of you see eye to eye on most things, but have very different views of political correctness. Your friend is very scornful of "PC" and makes insensitive jokes about women and people of other races. You have to compensate for this lack of commonality in your views. This is feasible because relationships are multifaceted. You can think to yourself, "He's a good friend despite his insensitivity. People come in complicated packages, and there are things about them that you like and things you can't stand. In his case, the good things outweigh the bad."

This way of *rationalizing* the dissonant thoughts minimizes the strain arising from them. But it doesn't eliminate it completely. Thus, there's a natural tendency to seek out relationship partners with whom you have a lot in common. That way, you minimize dissonance at the outset.

The affinity that comes from having a lot in common with the other person also arises because of its effect on other relationship dimensions. For example, it's easier to trust a person who is very much like you. He or she will be more *predictable,* doing what you would do under the same circumstances.

Finding things in common is especially important in the early stages of relationship formation. Time and energy are scarce for all of us, and we can't develop strong relationships with everyone we encounter. So we get close to some people and hold others at a distance. This means that we have to make choices at early relationship stages. Some people seem worth getting to know a little better, others don't. One of the earliest criteria used is how much you share in common with the other person. You've probably had the experience of meeting with someone briefly and quickly deciding that "I can relate to her." What you usually mean by that is that you've discovered that the two of you have enough in common that a broader-scope relationship seems feasible. Thus it's worth investing in this relationship, rather than in some others.

Sometimes people broadcast things about themselves to a group to speed up relationship formation. For example, in the opening ceremonies of many group meetings, people are asked to introduce themselves and "say a little about themselves." This is a formal opportunity to tell about your values, interests, hobbies, family situation, or whatever. You do this in the hope that others will discover something in common with you and you can use this as a basis for building the relationship.

The reason these ceremonies are important is that a substantial proportion of the population is shy. Shyness is a feeling of social discomfort in early relationship stages. A test for shyness is to imagine walking into a roomful of strangers, such as a cocktail party. "Outgoing" people view this as an all-positive experience—an opportunity to meet new people and learn new things. But shy people view this same situation as an ordeal. They're anxious about whether they'll hit it off with the new people, whether they'll feel at a loss as to what to say, or whether others will resent the intrusion when the shy person joins groups that are already conversing. Shyness occurs among sociable people—such individuals have a desire to connect with others, but are uncomfortable until the relationship is established. Having a lot in common with others makes the relationship-development process much easier.

Liking. Liking is a positive emotional reaction to other people. Being around them makes you happy. Smiling reveals affection across cultures.

Because it's an emotional reaction, liking is quite independent of other relationship dimensions. You can like someone you don't respect, don't trust, or have little in common with.

At the opposite end of this continuum is disliking. This happens when the other person evokes negative emotions in you. At the extreme, you'd experience revulsion. The expression "I can't stand the sight of him" indicates that negative feelings well up in his presence.[6] In either case, the midpoint of the continuum is indifference. Indifference means that the person creates no emotional reaction in you.

Liking is the relationship dimension most likely to be reciprocal. It's hard to like someone who doesn't like you: your positive emotion gets extinguished. Learning that someone doesn't like you also mobilizes your defense mechanisms. It doesn't take long for you to think of a dozen negative qualities in the other person. There's less dissonance if you can portray the person as unlikable.

Even children recognize the reciprocity. When they get old enough to begin exploring boyfriend-girlfriend pairings, they send messages—via third parties—to those they have an interest in. The typical form of these messages is "Tell Molly I like her if she likes me." The conditional clause is at one level a defense against rejection, but at another level, it's recognition that if Molly doesn't like him, his liking her is not viable. It won't last beyond the news that his affection is unrequited.

We describe some people as "likable," as if this were some sort of personality dimension. As often as not, people are likable because they like you. They may like a lot of people, or even people in general (i.e., they may be sociable). But the litmus test for likability is almost always whether they like you. Isn't this true of people *you* like?

Most of us have had the experience of "instantly liking" (or instantly disliking) someone. Psychologists would assume that this is the result of transference. That is, the person somehow reminds you of someone else, and you react before getting to know the person you just met. Transference is typically at the unconscious level, but sometimes the person is fully aware of the displaced reaction, as in the comment: "I can't stand her: she reminds me too much of my ex-wife."

Organizations are officially indifferent as to whether employees like each other. Nevertheless, managers sometimes need to intervene when workers dislike each other strongly. Norms of professionalism emphasize that employees have a job to do, and that their responsibility to the job must come ahead of their personal feelings. True professionals are able to resist the impulse to be mean or passive-aggressive when there's a job to be done. But when spiteful employees don't want to work with people they dislike, bosses have a responsibility[7] to intervene.

Romantic Interest. Some people are physically attractive to us, others aren't. We're drawn to the ones we find attractive because we can imagine romantic possibilities in the relationship. Romantic interest is similar to liking in that it's an emotional affinity; it differs in that it has a strong sexual component. Because romantic interest is an emotional reaction, you have no control over whether you experience it or not. All you control is how you act on your impulses. At work, you're paid to engage in the role relationships the organization prescribes for you. Acting on your romantic impulses is seen as inappropriate workplace behavior and is usually frowned upon.

Romantic interest can be unilateral or reciprocal. Unilateral romantic interest can—but doesn't necessarily—destabilize relationships. Unreciprocated interest can strain relationships when it generates feelings of rejection and resentment, but it can also strengthen relationships when properly managed. Most people find unilateral romantic interest in them to be ego-enhancing, so long as the person "respects the boundaries" that you set up and is not being an interpersonal nuisance.

In certain situations, however, if the romantic interest is unilateral, there's a risk of *sexual harassment.* In the workplace, harassment occurs when the attracted person makes it difficult or unpleasant for the disinterested person to carry out an organizational role. For example, it's difficult for people to do their job properly when the boss is pressuring them to have sex. Such pressure is an abuse of the authority the organization has granted the boss. But even when there's no power difference, it may be very unpleasant for someone to receive unwanted sexual attention from a co-worker. It can distract both workers from the job.

Even if the romantic interest is bilateral, there may be problems for the organization. Romantically bonded co-workers usually have primary loyalty to each other. This results in a coalition that others might resent. In departmental meetings, for example, the romantically involved person is seen as having two votes rather than one. Co-workers tend to overlook the point that the two are probably voting similarly because they have a lot in common, and therefore tend to approach issues the same way: instead, the identical vote is seen as a gesture of relational affirmation. There's also the fear that one romantic partner will share confidential information with the other, due to the high disclosure that's typical of intimate couples. Thus, couples need to be scrupulous in managing others' perceptions of their involvement. It seems to work best when there's zero on-the-job evidence of their off-the-job romance.

Reshaping Interpersonal Relationships

We've identified the different dimensions of relationships between individuals that have emerged from empirical research on the topic. Learning to diagnose what's going on in relationships is crucial because managers need to foster productive relationships with their workers, peers, bosses, value-chain partners, and competitors. Being aware of the different dimensions of relationships is a prerequisite for figuring out what's working well and what needs improvement.

In addition, understanding relationships between people is a stepping-stone to understanding relationships involving groups and organizations—the topics of the next two chapters. Groups and organizations are made up of people; therefore, much of what we've discussed already is applicable at these broader levels.

Let's briefly review two key points about interpersonal relationships before looking at how they can be shaped. First, relationships are multidimensional. Different relationships may be equally strong for very different reasons. One person may be someone you deeply respect and trust, you find very interesting, and is a source of net personal benefit. Another may be someone you like, who is empathic, and who makes you feel fully accepted even when you're confessing things you're a little ashamed of. You may find a third person so attractive that all other aspects of the relationship fade in importance: you figure you could adapt to whatever the relationship brought. In each of these examples, the net strength of the relationship is about the same, even though the relationships are qualitatively different.

Second, dimensions that are important at the early stages of relationship formation may be relatively unimportant as the relationship matures. This is most obvious when looking at the history of elderly married couples. When they began dating, romantic interest was foremost in their minds. They worked hard to be as attractive as possible to each other. As the relationship deepened, they became loyal allies, and this bond got so strong that it eclipsed their other family relationships. They developed more in common as they raised a family. Trust, respect, liking, and mutual disclosure all grew as the years went by, and kept the relationship strong long after the physical features that created the initial attraction had changed.

So we've seen that it's important to be able to diagnose what's going on in our relationships. This allows us to shape them in ways that benefit the organization, and us, too. We'll next see that an effective diagnosis also helps us to heal relationships when they get damaged.

Healing Relationship Damage

Interpersonal relationships are crucial to managerial effectiveness. But we know from our own life experiences that managing relationships doesn't always go smoothly: we end up strengthening some relationships and damaging others.

Damaged relationships can be abandoned, left damaged, or healed. In most situations, abandonment isn't a real option. As a teenager, you may have been able to abandon the relationship when you broke up with a sweetheart who lived in another town. But as a manager, you're probably stuck with whatever relationships you create.

If you can't abandon a relationship, you're better off doing something to make things better. That usually makes more sense than trying to live with a damaged relationship. Fortunately, there are several tactics that will speed the healing process. It usually helps to use several of these in combination. It also helps to remember that *when strong relationships are damaged, they can take time to heal;* so don't expect instant repair, followed by a resumption of the relationship as if nothing had happened.

Here are some options. In explaining how they work in practice, we'll assume the person you're at odds with is a man named John.

1. Apologize. This is the simplest of all techniques. It's also the single most important thing you can do to begin healing a damaged relationship. An apology acknowledges that something has happened that could threaten the relationship. The alternative is denial—acting as if nothing has happened. Denial makes the situation more difficult to deal with.

An apology is also an acknowledgment that you had some role in what happened. The statement "I screwed up. Obviously I wasn't thinking" takes all the blame. An alternative statement, "I should have seen this coming. I wasn't paying enough attention until too late," doesn't take all the blame, but rather shows a willingness to share blame. Taking none of the blame, but saying, "I wish I could have done something to prevent this from happening," expresses a desire to preserve the relationship and invites a reciprocal statement that can get you and John talking about the problem.

An important component of apology is the *expression of regret.* This signals that you're sad about the strain in the relationship. Expressions of regret also have a wide range of possibilities, from personal to situational. A personally focused regret describes feelings about your own behavior: "I screwed up, and I feel awful about it." Situationally focused regret takes the form, "I feel awful about what has happened." By signaling that you care about the relationship and you want to restore it, it will make you more appealing as a relationship partner. That should increase John's motivation to make an effort at healing.

Apologies also can differ in their degree of personalization. At one extreme, you can single out John and deliver a private apology. At the other extreme, you can issue an impersonal "official apology" by posting a memo for whoever might happen to read it. In general, *the more personal the apology, the greater its impact, and, consequently, the greater its healing power.*

At this point, you may be asking, why spend all this time dissecting an apology? Why the heavy focus on what *you* might do when it may well have been John who screwed up? There are at least two reasons. First, although you might feel certain the other person is responsible for what happened, you may be wrong. Your own view could be flawed—by psychological defenses or biases, for example—blinding you to your own responsibility. Second, even if you're right about John being responsible, it's very hard to heal a relationship if John is a defensive person, and *you* may have to be the one who initiates the apology process if you want to restore the relationship to its former strength. Let me elaborate.

A defensive person is one who's uncomfortable admitting that she or he did something wrong, and devotes energy instead to defending his or her actions. Defensiveness arises from the need for approval. Everyone makes mistakes from time to time, and a healthy reaction is to recognize and acknowledge the mistake, and then resolve not to repeat it. But defensive people such as John don't like to admit they screwed up. Somewhere in their childhood, they learned—perhaps wrongly—that they have to be perfect to be accepted and loved: admitting they made a mistake gets associated with being unlovable.

We've all encountered defensive people. They'll argue incessantly that what they did was justified, even though it's very obvious to everyone that they've made an error in judgment. There's no point arguing back, hoping they'll admit they were wrong and then take steps to correct the problem. If you argue, the focus will shift from healing the relationship to winning the argument. That'll make you more frustrated, and the strain in the relationship may end up worse rather than better.

Here's where your skill at apologizing comes in handy. If you apologize to the degree that would be credible in the situation, this has an effect on John. First, it *models* conciliatory behavior: you set an example. Your implicit message is "Here's what real professionals do in a situation like this: they admit the extent to which they had a role in what happened." Second, your apology sets up pressure for reciprocal behavior. If you've made an effort to repair the situation, it's only fair that John make an effort too. Third, your apology takes some of the sting out of John's taking on blame. You're letting him off the hook to some extent, implying that perhaps he wasn't 100 percent responsible. But here's where you may have to choose between being right and being effective. Remember that *it's difficult for defensive people to shoulder all the blame, even when they deserve it*. They're much more comfortable owning up to a share of the blame. There's less fear of rejection if it doesn't look like one party is all good and the other all bad. At the subconscious level, it's comforting to think that nobody is perfect: this means John can still be lovable even though he makes mistakes.

I'm not implying that it's easy to take the initiative in apologizing when other people screw up. Your emotions are likely to generate revenge fantasies, not contrite behavior. You want them to suffer as much as you have, and a good way to ensure their suffering is to see them go through some self-abasement. In colloquial terms, you want to "rub their nose in it." But if the people you're dealing with are defensive, it'll be very difficult to get them to engage in any act of contrition: their fear of rejection will get in the way. So you have a choice: either you take the initiative to heal the relationship, or you may have to accept permanent relationship damage. It's not fair, I realize. But it's realistic.

The reason I'm devoting space to catering to defensive people is that they tend to gravitate toward business careers, and many of the most valuable employees are defensive by nature. Defensiveness has the same source as need for achievement. Both are rooted in a childhood need for approval. The same shortcoming in early family life that drives people to "succeed"— even at the expense of not having a life outside of business—makes them hesitant to accept responsibilities for their mistakes. So if you're going to be good at dealing with high achievers, you'd better be good at dealing with defensiveness.

Finally, apology plays an important role in signaling the termination of hostilities. Conflicts have a natural tendency to escalate. Apology transforms the nature of the interaction from hurting the other party to rebuilding the relationship. At the symbolic level, the apology says, "Look, I don't want to fight any more. Let's fix this problem." From this perspective, the *act* of apologizing is more important than the form it takes.

2. Don't Avoid. We've all had the experience of wanting to avoid someone after an unpleasant encounter. Interacting with the person is stressful because it rekindles negative emotions. Therefore, it's easier, in the short run, to find ways to avoid contact. But avoidance can have very high relationship costs: it can make the situation much worse, for two reasons.

First, psychologists have documented a phenomenon they call the *recency effect.* The encounter people most vividly recall is the most recent one. Suppose you've had lots of good encounters with John, but you did something during the last one that strained the relationship. Now you're avoiding each other. In that case, the last encounter will tend to dominate John's memory of you. But if you keep on interacting, even if it's a little stressful at first, the most recent encounter won't be the unpleasant one.

Second, when you do things that strain your relationship with others, they'll have a tendency to demonize you—to stereotype you as all bad. This happens because our emotions shape the meanings we give to events. The stereotyping remains plausible so long as there's no interaction. But in reality, nobody is all bad—or even all good. So if you don't avoid them, you'll continue to expose your multiple "sides." Their day-to-day observations won't match the all-bad stereotype, so dissonance will set in to erode the extreme negative view.

Deliberately continuing to interact also works if the other person has been the one primarily responsible for straining the relationship. The unwritten rules of social equity say that if one person extends himself or herself to make amends, the other should reciprocate. The pressure to return the gesture is much more powerful when the person who has been mistreated is the one taking the initiative. Westerners praise such behavior, making admiring comments like "He was *big enough* to be conciliatory." It's a little macho, I grant you. But it expresses cultural admiration for taking the initiative in healing relationship damage.

3. Bond with Their Friends. Another way to get dissonance working in your favor is to cultivate relationships with John's friends. This can't be done as an obvious ploy. Otherwise John will see you as manipulative, and the people you're suddenly paying more attention to will feel "used" and resent it.

The stronger your bonds with John's friendship network, the more difficult it will be for John to see you as all bad. Dissonance arises when people John likes and respects don't share his viewpoint. He needs to either revise his opinion of you, or decide that his friends aren't worth listening to. It's usually easier to soften his negative opinion.

4. Induce Empathy. Suppose you're the one who screwed up. Chances are, the other person is pretty narrowly focused on what you did, and how it hurt, inconvenienced, or disappointed her or him. He or she probably isn't thinking about how *you* might have construed the situation—the context, your mood, what you were thinking at the time. If the other person understood all the circumstances surrounding your actions, you'd seem less of an ogre.

Take, for example, the case of two firms that have been operating as a strategic alliance supplying complementary financial services to businesses. Vivian is a fast-track manager reporting to Bill, the managing partner. But Vivian wants to leave Bill's firm and makes a confidential inquiry to Arthur, the managing partner of the other firm. Arthur urgently needs a replacement for a key VP who has just resigned, and Vivian is perfect for the job.

Vivian wants to switch firms because she's going through a difficult divorce and wants to leave the city in which Bill's firm is located. She likes her job and enjoys working for Bill, but the stress of living in this city with an "ex" who has begun stalking her is too stressful. She tells this to Arthur in confidence. Arthur gives her the job.

Bill is furious. His awareness of Vivian's past loyalty to him and his firm convinces him that Arthur must have *stolen* his star employee. He speculates that Arthur must have offered her a 50 percent pay increase—or stock options. He sees Arthur's access to his own firm's employees as a cost of the close working relationship between the two firms. He resolves to put more distance between the two firms so that Arthur doesn't pirate any more of his employees.

Arthur needs to do some relationship healing, at two levels—between the two firms, and between the respective managing partners. Inducing empathy is very helpful in accomplishing this. Arthur should ask Bill to understand his dilemma. He needed to respect Vivian's request for confidentiality regarding her divorce situation, but he also needed to preserve the relationship with Bill. That put him in a bind. He might ask what Bill would have done in the same circumstances.

Arthur could then point out that if he hadn't offered Vivian the job, she would have resigned from Bill's firm anyway, because she needed to relocate. That would mean her talents and experience would be lost to the strategic alliance[8]—and furthermore, upon leaving, she might have taken away some of their customers who had developed a personal attachment to her. In realizing that he might have done the same thing under the same circumstances, Bill is prevented from demonizing Arthur. Thus, inducing empathy makes it harder for Bill to treat Arthur as an outgroup member[9]—and the relationship, though shaken, remains intact.

5. Find a Scapegoat. When the strained relationship arises at the corporate level, pinpointing a scapegoat can be an effective way to heal the relationship. (Notice that we're treating the *fairness* and *effectiveness* of this tactic as separate issues.) A scapegoat is a person designated as deserving all the blame in a problem situation. If I can get you to attack the scapegoat, you won't attack me. You'll have exacted revenge for whatever went wrong, and the relationship will remain intact.

Suppose an organization has done a poor job of serving its customers, its employees, and its strategic alliance partners. A lot of healing is needed. One effective way to give the strained relationships a fresh start is to fire the CEO. Certainly the CEO didn't cause all the problems that had arisen, but the CEO is ultimately responsible for them. The CEO has operated a system that holds subordinates accountable for results, so it's only fair that the Board hold the CEO accountable for results, too. Firing the CEO is a "cleansing ritual." It signals that the offending element has been removed and they can look forward to a different relationship with the organization from that point forth.

Scapegoating sometimes causes greater problems than benefits, however. For example, many managers use the union as a scapegoat. This deepens the rift between union and management, and makes the ingroup-outgroup dynamics more harmful to the organization. Sometimes it's the workers who are the scapegoats. When managers say, "You can't get good help any more," they're often passing on blame for poor management practices. This tactic increases divisiveness within the organization, and reduces the likelihood that empowerment programs will be successful. Worse still, the people most likely to be scapegoated are those who are different, such as women and minorities. This increases hate and discrimination in organizations, at a time when they need to be inclusive in order to be effective.

Despite its disadvantages, scapegoating is very appealing to certain types of managers, particularly defensive people. They prefer to avoid blame themselves, so they're likely to rely on this method of healing a relationship. But if the technique is overused, it actually damages the relationship. People have less respect for someone who won't accept blame appropriately, particularly when scapegoating has the effect of victimizing low-power people, or people who have a history of being discriminated against.

6. Hold Out an Olive Branch. Recall the earlier warning that strained relationships are seldom repaired instantly. People ruminate about relationship problems. They assign meanings to words, gestures, and behaviors, and mull them over until a new understanding emerges that makes sense. Healing therefore takes time.

It's very helpful, during this period, to have made a positive gesture.

The gesture signals that you haven't abandoned the relationship; instead, you wish to restore it. This increases the other person's motivation to participate in the healing process. Healing is very difficult if one person is doing all the work: it feels like an uphill battle. The positive gesture communicates that whenever the other person is ready, he or she will be making the effort at healing in partnership with you.

The challenge is not to get too frustrated or resentful while waiting for the other person to do her or his share of the healing work. The other person may still be angry, ashamed, or intimidated. She or he may find it easier to avoid you rather than to make the investment in fixing the problem. But if you've offered an olive branch, you've dramatically increased the probability that healing will take place if healing is possible.

COMPARTMENTALIZED RELATIONSHIPS

Just as we have multifaceted needs, we also have multifaceted relationships. A person is more than one thing to us, and this is true for groups and organizations, too. Let's consider two examples.

Our boss is in one sense a contractor—as an agent of the organization—for our labor. The boss hired us, and probably can dismiss us. Beyond this organizational role relationship, the boss can be a social acquaintance, and perhaps even a close friend. We can be glad to see the boss each morning, and we may share confidences, hang out after work, and have entwined family lives. The boss can also be an evaluator, and may serve as a teacher, coach, or mentor. Finally, the boss is likely to be a source of rewards and discipline.

These multiple facets of relationships sometimes coexist easily, as in the case of mentor and friend. But some roles clash, as in the case of friend and disciplinarian. When this happens, people experience role strain—the discomfort of being torn by incompatible demands on the relationship. Here's where compartmentalization helps you cope. Compartmentalization is successful when a person acts according to the relationship dimensions that are relevant *in that particular situation.* The boss might say, "Look, I care about our relationship outside the office, but I also have a job to do and a responsibility to the organization. This is a performance appraisal review and there are some problems we have to address."

Inability to compartmentalize relationships is a familiar phenomenon. We describe someone who is having difficulties as "unable to set boundaries." The evidence would be that the person is responding to a relation-ship in a way that's unsuited to the context. Many problems with sexual harassment result from managers or co-workers who are unable to set boundaries. The amorous-suitor role seeps into the domain of the boss or co-worker role.

Compartmentalization also underlies the phrase "This is not per-sonal." It signals that whatever comes next in the conversation has nothing to do with the social relationship—good or bad—with the person being addressed. It has to do with responsibilities in other relationships. The abil-ity to depersonalize when necessary is an important component of profes-sionalism, and, in some instances, ethical conduct. Let's look closer.

"Favoritism" indicates that a social relationship has superseded an organizational relationship. An important aspect of the social contract—between organizations and the individuals who work in them—is meritoc-racy. A meritocracy is a system in which organizational benefits (such as promotions, desirable work assignments, growth opportunities, choice office locations, etc.) go to the most deserving person. People are hypersen-sitive to fairness. They want to believe that everyone has the same opportu-nity to succeed, and if they do excel, they'll be rewarded. If they believe that social ties are influencing these decisions, they'll become angry, disap-pointed, and alienated from the organization. Favoritism is, in essence, a breach of trust. Workers hold managers responsible for their failure to compartmentalize relationships, and rightly so.

Discrimination is the flip side of favoritism. It, too, implies that some consideration other than merit is influencing organizational decisions. The most obvious form of discrimination involves decisions that are distorted by a manager's negative relationship with people who are different—perhaps a different race, gender, or ethnic background. But discrimination also occurs when a strained interpersonal relationship is allowed to affect organizational decisions. Whether or not you like someone should have no bearing on how you treat him or her at work. You have a responsibility to do what's best for the organization and you're abusing your power—and the organization's trust in you—if you allow a grudge to impact your decisions. As an old boss of mine used to tell people, "If you don't like co-workers, don't invite them to your cocktail party. But do the right thing when you're on the job." He was talking about compartmentalization of relationships.

We should note that people's attributions of favoritism or discrimina-tion are subject to biases in our thinking. As a result, our perceptions may or may not be accurate. We tend to take credit for our successes and look for external factors to explain our failures. As a result, in some organizational situations, we may suspect greater favoritism or discrimination than is actually occurring. This doesn't mean that we should always discount our perceptions; only that we should recognize the potential for exaggeration or, in some cases, misjudging the situation.

RELATIONSHIPS INVOLVING GROUPS AND ORGANIZATIONS

The next two chapters expand the scope of the discussion we just began. People have interpersonal relationships in group and organizational contexts. But they also have relationships to the group and to the organization. Likewise, groups have relationships with other groups, and to the organization in which they operate. Finally, there are relationships between organizations that are analogs of relationships between individuals and between groups. All of these need to be understood and shaped—and, sometimes, healed—if the manager is to be effective in the new era.

NOTES

1. Psychologists have identified several defense mechanisms that protect the psyche from bad feelings. Most relevant here are suppression (where the intellect consciously overrides bad feelings) and repression (where the psyche pinches off the bad thoughts and feelings before they ever get to conscious awareness). Colloquially, we say that an individual is "in denial" when not experiencing the thoughts and feelings one would normally expect under the circumstances.
2. Clinical psychologists refer to this process as "transference." We'll explore the effects of transference throughout the book.
3. To be more precise, whatever exchange occurs between close friends is symbolic rather than economic. For example, giving gifts and lending personally meaningful items are gestures that reinforce the bonds.
4. See Greenhalgh and Chapman, "Relationships between Disputants: An Analysis of Their Characteristics and Impact," in S. E. Gleason (Ed.), *Workplace Dispute Resolution* (East Lansing: Michigan State University Press, 1997), pp. 203–29. See also Greenhalgh and Chapman, "Negotiator Relationships: Construct Measurement, and Demonstration of Their Impact on the Process and Outcomes of Negotiation," *Group Decision and Negotiation* 7 (1998): 465–89.

5. We will explore this phenomenon, and its implications, in some detail in the last two chapters.
6. Some people might view the continuum as ranging from love to hate, but love is a complex concept, and hate usually blends dislike with anger, hostility, resentment, and other emotions. You can use whichever continuum works for you.
7. This responsibility has broadened from the realm of ethics to the realm of law in the United States. Managers are held responsible for intervening when co-workers have created a "hostile work environment."
8. Note that this is a *commonwealth* appeal.
9. We'll discuss ingroups and outgroups in detail in the next chapter. For now, think of treating someone as an outgroup member as defining her or him as "not one of *us*."

CHAPTER 3

RELATIONSHIPS INVOLVING GROUPS IN ORGANIZATIONS

People have a natural affinity for groups. It's part of being a social animal. Certainly we're capable of doing things alone, but this isn't our preference, at work or at play. In fact, throughout history, people have worked in groups to get things accomplished unless someone has intervened and imposed a different structure.

During the Industrial Revolution, Western capitalists adopted the hierarchical model for organizing their business enterprises. This architectural form prescribed how *individuals* should carry out routines. There wasn't any role for groups. As a result of this history, our understanding of group relationships in organizations is poorly developed. It just hasn't had the emphasis given to such topics as job design, work layout, and productivity improvement. Yet groups are vitally important to organizational effectiveness—from the lowest-level work group to the top management team. So it's important for managers to understand and manage group relationships.

INGROUPS AND OUTGROUPS

A group is a set of people who have a sense of membership: they know who's a member and who isn't—and why. Thus, the group has an *identity* that members recognize and agree on. The common identity is a basic relationship bond.

The power of common identity in galvanizing groups was made very evident by a simulation conducted in the late 1960s and early 1970s. Jane

Eliot was a teacher at a junior high school in the U.S. Midwest. Her eight-year-old students were all Caucasians, and got along very well.

The students had been taught the evils of racism, but to reinforce the learning, Eliot decided to show them how it felt. So one day, she convinced all her students that blue-eyed people were better than brown-eyed people. She said blue-eyed people were more intelligent, cleaner, and more desirable to associate with. To reinforce the superiority, she reserved use of the drinking fountain and playground for blue-eyed students, and gave them other privileges. She also forbade them from playing with brown-eyed students. Meanwhile, the brown-eyed students were required to wear special cloth collars, so they could be identified at a distance.

It took only 15 minutes for the blue-eyed students to form a cohesive group and to ostracize their former friends who had brown eyes. The brown-eyed students lost self-esteem and motivation, and their scores on an intelligence test suddenly dropped way below those of blue-eyed students. They also behaved like an inferior caste, isolating themselves: they didn't even try to associate with the "superior" blue-eyed students. Thus, within the space of a single school day, making eye color the basis of common identity transformed a homogeneous group of friends into two incompatible factions. And these were students who had been trained not to discriminate on the basis of physical characteristics.[1]

The next day, the teacher announced that what she had told the class the previous day was incorrect. There was, indeed, a difference between blue-eyed and brown-eyed people, but it was *brown-eyed people* who were superior. So the blue-eyed students were made to wear the collars, and the brown-eyed students got all the privileges. The effect instantly reversed itself. Now the brown-eyed students were treating the blue-eyed students as inferior and unworthy of their friendship. And the blue-eyed students responded the same way that the brown-eyed students had acted the day before. One would think that having experienced oppression as an underclass the day before, the brown-eyed students would have too much empathy for their classmates to put them through the same experience. But there was no inhibition at all.

Jane Eliot's simulation highlights the power of sharing something in common in galvanizing group identity. Let's be sure to note that the focus is not simply on what we have in common. We all have noses, for example, but the presence of a nose doesn't create group identity. *Group identity arises from something that makes group members the same and nonmembers different.*

Thus, the group is defined as much by those people it *excludes* as by those it includes. Exclusion by another group binds you tighter to the group that includes you. And if you're normal, it also makes you resent the group that excluded you. Thus you're not indifferent to the exclusive group: you're antagonistic toward them. This leads to a basic dynamic: wherever groups operate—there's both solidarity and divisiveness. The solidarity occurs within the group, the divisiveness between groups.

Anthropologists have seen these basic dynamics operating in every society they've studied. In anthropological terms, an *ingroup* is the group you identify with. It can be an informal grouping of people who are similar: a clan, a tribe, a race, an ethnic group, or even a nation. *Outgroups* are groups you don't belong to. They're seen as adversaries—usually either enemies or competitors.

Ingroup members tend to have common perceptions of outgroup members. This is due to stereotyping of outgroups. All outgroup members are seen as sharing certain characteristics that make their members different from ingroup members. The differentiating characteristics are judged according to ingroup standards. That is, outgroup members are different because of the ingroup characteristics that they lack. Anthropologists refer to this as *ethnocentrism*—using one's own group as the ideal standard against which others are judged.[2]

Ethnocentric judgments have a predictable outcome: the outgroup is always stereotyped as inferior. Outgroup members are seen as less moral, less justified in pursuing their own interests, less intelligent, less powerful, and less cohesive as a group. This makes them subhuman, if we use this term literally. And if they're subhuman, you don't have to use human standards of morality in dealing with them.

Thus, most societies have rules that forbid murdering, raping, or stealing from ingroup members, but these are often suspended when the victim is an outgroup member. Even in the most advanced societies, we can't kill our fellow citizens without risk of severe punishment, but we can kill someone our society defines as an enemy. Think about it: it's only ingroup membership that distinguishes serial killers from war heroes.

It's easy to see how the formation of these groups shapes relationships. Ingroup members are never *allies* of outgroup members. Nor do they *accept* them: after all, outgroup members are inferiors. There's a deemphasis on what they have *in common* because their identity is defined by how they're different. They can't be *respected* or *trusted* because the stereotype views them as low in morality. As a result, it's not surprising that such groups view each other as adversaries. In fact, a cold war is often the best that one can hope for.

We'll use the ingroup-outgroup terminology to refer to this basic tension between groups. We'll also see that our natural ethnocentric biases make it difficult to manage relationships across group boundaries, even though doing so is vital to managerial effectiveness in the new era.

RELATIONSHIPS BETWEEN CORPORATE FUNCTIONS

The natural enmity between ingroups and outgroups explains why different functional areas of a conventional hierarchy rarely cooperate. The corporate strategy cascades down from the CEO. The strategy is well understood, and it's pretty obvious what each functional area must do to carry out its role in achieving the organization's strategic objective. It's also obvious that the functional areas need to work together to coordinate their contributions. Yet it's a real challenge for the manager to get this to happen.

The manager's problem is that the functional areas have many of the characteristics of ingroups. There's a common identity within the function, and a stereotyped view of other functional areas as outgroups—which makes them enemies of sorts. Thus, for example, R&D engineers are stereotyped as egghead technicians who have no regard for what customers want, but instead design products that are technically interesting to them. Production managers are stereotyped as caring only about production efficiency. Sales people are stereotyped as flamboyant extraverts who have loyalty to their dealers and customers, but not to the company.

These characterizations show how a corporate ingroup gains solidarity by sharing a common stereotype of the outgroup. The presence of a common enemy makes it more important for group members to stick together. The solidarity within the ingroup comes at a cost, however. The functions are likely to be at odds with each other when the organization needs them to work together collaboratively.

The ingroup-outgroup schism is difficult to sustain if the groups interact closely and really get to know each other. People's direct observation disconfirms the stereotypes: they see that outgroup members aren't less moral, less intelligent, less powerful, or less anything. They're just people doing a conscientious job in a different organizational role.

ORGANIZATIONAL SILOS: A BARRIER TO COMMONWEALTH

Ingroup-outgroup divisiveness adds to the problems created by the architecture and systems that are typical of conventional hierarchies. The chain of command principle specifies that the functional groups aren't supposed to be working things out between themselves: that's the role of higher management. Furthermore, hierarchical incentive structures are usually designed to optimize each functional area, with no rewards for cross-functional collaboration: therefore, there's no encouragement for managers to make decisions that would benefit the organization as a whole, and no sense of commonwealth. For example, imagine that adding a product feature increases production cost by a small amount, but raises the profitability of the product dramatically. It might be rational for Production to *resist* this change if they're rewarded for holding costs down. That's how accountability works when it works badly.

These schisms result in the silo organization shown in Figure 3-1. The architecture detracts from competitive advantage. Apart from the suboptimization that we've already noted, the organization isn't as adaptable as it needs to be because each functional area "does its own thing." Adaptability requires that several areas shift direction in concert. For example, switching to a just-in-time inventory system requires close coordination between the Purchasing, Materials Handling, and Production Planning departments. If one department won't cooperate, the strategic initiative is doomed. To make matters worse, the organization isn't good at time-based competition because it takes forever for proposals and approvals to move up and down the silos. The slowness is inevitable when only upper-level managers are empowered to make decisions. The gaps between functions in Figure 3-1 represent deep rifts—in our terms, very distant working relationships.

Obviously, the chain-of-command principle—which says you can't coordinate laterally—needs to be replaced with rules that insist on cross-functional coordination. And control systems have to be changed so that there are no rewards for optimizing departmental performance *at the*

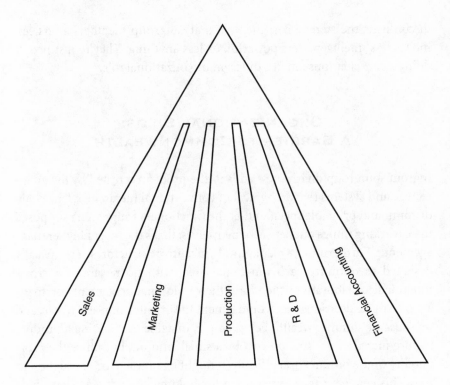

FIGURE 3-1 Organizational Silos

expense of other parts of the organization. If there are disincentives for collaborating, it isn't likely to happen.

But the organization still needs to do something about groups' ethnocentric tendencies to treat their own members as allies and other groups as enemies. One way managers can counter these tendencies is to empower task forces to plan and implement new initiatives. The task forces would have members from different functional areas united around a common mission. Because unity increases when there's a common enemy, it's important to focus the group's animosity on competitors.

Collocation[3] also helps minimize the silo problem. It fosters the formation of *broader-scope* relationships. For example, people who interact with each other informally discover that the stereotypes don't hold up and they have many things in common with outgroup members. They may also find them interesting, likable, trustworthy, accepting, worthy of respect, and empathic. It's difficult to view someone as an enemy in the presence of this many positive relationship dimensions.

ORGANIZATIONAL CASTES:
A BARRIER TO INCLUSION

There's another set of rifts that divides conventional organizations in unhelpful ways. These are horizontal rifts that separate the organization into layers, shown in Figure 3-2. The gaps between layers reflect social-class barriers within the organization. A social-class barrier exists when people sense that a relationship beyond task-related interaction is unwelcome and inappropriate.

The relationship problems arising from caste divisions reduce organizational effectiveness. *An organization can't be inclusive if it has a caste system.* And if it's not inclusive, it's less effective because it doesn't have all people putting in their best efforts and working collaboratively.

Most Western managers are uncomfortable with the notion of workplace castes, because social inequality isn't consistent with democratic principles. If your national creed says that all people are created equal, then

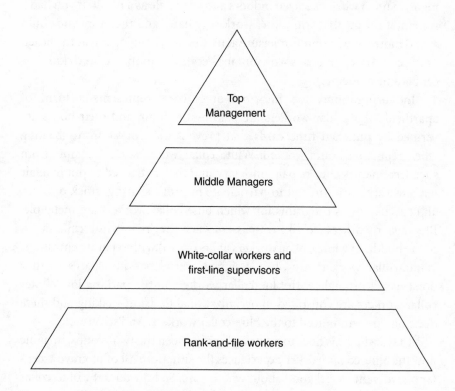

FIGURE 3-2 Organizational Castes

it's a bit awkward to be operating a caste system that says they're not. As a result, managers don't readily own up to its existence or their part in sustaining it. But everyone knows it's there. It's hard to miss.

One obvious display of caste membership is the wearing of uniforms in conventional hierarchies. These don't look like military uniforms, but everyone recognizes them for what they are. A basic caste difference is between blue-collar and white-collar employees, as they're known in the United States. Whether or not you perform manual labor determines the most basic organizational caste distinction.

The association between manual work and lower-caste membership has been fairly stable across time and across cultures. When agriculture was the prominent occupation, upper-caste people avoided exposure to the sun. People got suntans when they worked in the fields, so the paler you were, the "classier" you looked. This led to the wide-brim-hat fashion among Western women and the popularity of whiteners in cosmetics. When factory work replaced agriculture as the dominant form of employment, manual workers stayed indoors and were pale as a result. If you had a suntan, it meant that you didn't work very hard, and therefore you could spend more time in outdoor leisure activities, like hanging out at the beach or the country club. That's why suntans became fashionable (and skin cancer became epidemic).

In corporations, the informal dress code represents a form of apartheid. Blue-collar workers are paid by the hour, and their hours are verified by punched time cards that prevent the worker from cheating when reporting hours worked. White-collar workers are "exempt" from such treatment.[4] They're paid on salary, and they're trusted to put in a fair day's work; they're invited to participate in profit sharing, stock options, and special bonus programs for which blue-collar workers are ineligible. Blue-collar workers feel like trespassers when they're in white-collar areas of the building; white-collar workers are provided with separate entrances. White-collar workers are often assigned special parking spaces so they don't have to mingle with blue-collar workers in the parking lot. White-collar workers are consulted in organizational decision-making and these decisions are announced to the blue-collar workers. And so on . . .

To see what this does to relationships between the two groups, imagine how the blue-collar worker experiences the situation. All of us crave acceptance: we want to feel good about who we are. So how does the blue-collar worker respond to being excluded from salary systems, profit-sharing plans, white-collar areas of the building, good parking spaces, and decision-making?

Again, we have a dissonance problem. Blue-collar workers have trouble reconciling feelings of self-worth with being treated as second-class citizens. Something has to give. The dissonance gets resolved at the expense of the relationship. Their exclusion doesn't hurt so much if they define themselves as being outside the system. Instead of seeing themselves as members of the organization, they see their participation as "just a job" that deserves minimal effort. Their relationship with white-collar workers is that of an ingroup dealing with a hostile outgroup. As this dynamic unfolds over time, each stereotypes the other in unhelpful ways. Add in the resentment that blue-collar workers naturally feel when they're treated as inferiors, and it's easy to see how they would view white-collar workers as more of an enemy than an ally.

The caste system doesn't just operate at the informal level. The upper caste eats in the executive dining room; middle managers eat in the cafeteria; blue-collar workers bring lunch boxes, eat from vending machines, or buy food at the canteen down by the manufacturing area. Company cars—and convenient parking spaces—are assigned according to caste. So are offices and furnishings. There's no functional reason for providing luxury cars or opulent work space to executives: it doesn't make them more effective in doing their jobs. Similarly, the class of air travel paid for by the company reflects the *class* of the flyer: top management flies in a company plane—and upper-middle management in first class—so they won't have to associate with the riffraff.

These arrangements may nourish the egos of the top-level managers who foster them, but they reduce organizational effectiveness. *Castes create divisive relationships between organizational levels.* They ensure that ingroup-outgroup dynamics operate, creating unity within a level and negative stereotyping of other levels. Middle managers, for example, view people lower in the hierarchy as lazy, intellectually slow, and not committed to the job. They have even more derision for higher levels of management. They say things like "Those buffoons at Headquarters have no idea what's going on here. They make decisions without even consulting us, then they blame us when things go wrong." You must have heard people say this. It's classic ethnocentrism, isn't it?

ORGANIZATIONAL FRACTIONATION

If we combine the rifts due to silo formation with the rifts due to castes, we get a badly fractionated organization. This is illustrated in Figure 3-3. As you can see, the relationships are remote and antagonistic between sets of people who ought to be working together. It's impossible to achieve true organizational excellence with this situation.

The key to understanding fractionation is to see the systematic *inclusion* and *exclusion* that happen between groups. A vicious cycle operates that managers need to understand. Membership in one's *in*group is gratifying because it provides us with a sense of being *in*cluded. There's a sense of common identity and "belonging" that's reinforced in symbols, rituals, and common understandings. But nonmembers tend to feel excluded. As members of an *out*group, they're treated as *out*siders and an adversarial relationship develops toward the groups that excluded them.

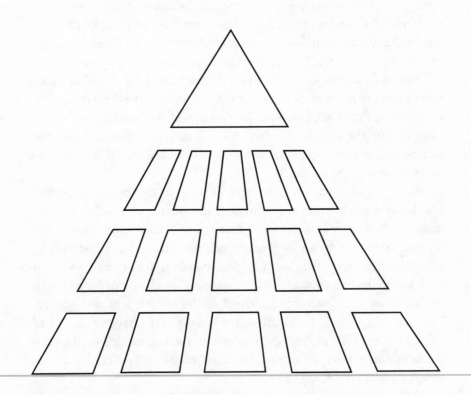

FIGURE 3-3 The Fractionated Organization

Now, this dynamic is a positive force if you have sports teams organized in a league. The adversarial relationships within the league increase the entertainment value of the sports contests. In fact, the more adversarial the relationship, the greater the spectator interest, as is evident in attendance at contests between archrivals. But the same adversarial relationships within an organization are paralyzing.

Managers can counteract these natural tendencies toward divisiveness by creating a *culture of inclusion*. They do this by providing a sense of corporate identity that's stronger than any group identity. At the same time, they must avoid imposing accountability systems that pit groups against each other—so that they compete instead of collaborating. It helps immensely if managers eliminate the caste system[5] that creates superiority-inferiority (another form of exclusion). And they can proactively foster inclusion by conducting events that draw the community together.

Let's look more closely at some of the practices that create a culture of inclusion. Many Japanese organizations have successfully created a strong corporate identity. Employees wear work uniforms that display the company logo, and begin each workday with communal ceremonies. The ceremonies include some calisthenics, but the bonding ritual involves recitation of the company's strategic plan. For instance, workers at the Komatsu plant used to begin every day by chanting "kill Caterpillar" (Komatsu's archcompetitor in the heavy construction equipment business). Here, the presence of an outgroup focuses attention on the organization's common enemy. This reduces the motivation for groups to treat other groups *within* the company as their enemy. Japanese companies also minimize differentiation of different layers of management: salary multiples are low, compared to U.S. companies, and the vacation policies are the same.

Many people believe that Japanese workplace practices can work only in Japan, where the workforce is homogeneous and the national culture emphasizes hard work and company loyalty. But this can't be true. Japanese companies have opened plants in the United States ("transplant factories") that have been very successful. The quality and efficiency levels have been so high that they've manufactured the product in the United States and then shipped it back for sale in Japan. This is strong evidence that it's *the way* you manage—rather than who you manage or where you locate—that makes the difference.

Western managers can easily eliminate most of the relationship barriers that arise from hierarchical caste systems. They can also take positive steps to draw the levels together as a unified community. One such step is to call regular "town meetings," as is done in General Electric's "Work Out!" program.[6] These are gatherings in which there's an open dialog between organizational levels. Everyone's opinion is important and everyone is treated as a peer. The principal benefit of this program is the sense of inclusion that arises. The caste system is at least temporarily abolished as everyone's input is treated as equally important, and management acts on the suggestions of previously disempowered castes.

Management can also eliminate social distance by spending time at the work stations of lower-level employees. The practical benefit is that managers gain first-hand knowledge of how the work is progressing as well as suggestions for improvement. The deeper benefit is that relationships with workers are improved when managers "come down to their level." There are enough success stories involving this approach that it has earned a name: MBWA—Management by Walking Around.

The discussion thus far has highlighted the negative aspects of the way groups operate. This doesn't mean that groups are undesirable in corporations: the opposite is true. Managers need groups in order to be effective. But group relationships have to be managed well.

Union and Management Groups

Union and management are a special case of groups becoming polarized in opposition to each other. Let's start out trying to understand why unions appeal to workers. Recall that people seek a sense of community because of their social nature. It's especially important to find it in the workplace because this is where people spend most of their waking hours. If the company is organized as a conventional hierarchy, management offers employees little sense of community. They aren't viewed—or treated—as full members of the organization: they're simply rented labor, paid by the hour. *Unions offer the sense of community that management denies them.*

The union has many of the characteristics of a group: the members have a sense of identity; they know who's a member and who isn't. Their common bond is the relationship itself, embodied in the word "union." Members are allies, referred to as brothers and sisters, who must stand up to a common enemy—managers, who are stereotyped as remote, unfeeling, and exploitative. Management, in turn, responds by behaving like an embattled ingroup. Each group deals with the *stereotype* of the other, further polarizing the two groups.

The stereotypes are particularly rigid because they serve a positive function for both groups. Management gets someone to blame when anything goes wrong. "I tried, but the union wouldn't let me." This blame tactic not only sidesteps accountability, but also helps them feel good about themselves. Psychologists have identified a fairly universal thought pattern they call "the fundamental attribution error." Basically, we tend to attribute successes to our own actions, and failures to external forces and constraints. So instead of feeling bad about our failures as managers, we attribute poor outcomes to union interference. This is better for our self-esteem.

The union, in turn, gains from stereotyping management as evil people who abuse their power because it increases the perceived need for union protection. Members vote to be represented by a union, and they can vote to decertify the union—or get rid of elected officials—if they're discontent. Seeming needed is also important because members have to pay dues and need to believe they're getting value for their money. The greater their fear of management, the more indispensable the union seems.

The union can be very nasty in dealing with management. Some of this is theatrics—putting on a show to convince members that they're getting their money's worth. But managers' understandable reaction is to meet hostility with hostility, and this further polarizes the workplace and entrenches the union. It's smarter to separate inherently adversarial interactions (such as bargaining over wages) from problem solving (such as figuring out how to gain competitive advantage, reduce time to market, increase profitability, or fix environmental problems). One of the best approaches to working together to solve problems is to create a labor-management committee. The idea is to create a new group that draws its membership from both union and management. The "common enemy" that galvanizes the group is *the problem.*

Labor-management committees are trickier to manage than cross-functional management task forces. Members of an all-management task force are supposed to be cooperating, because this cross-functional group is designed to be a collaborative entity. The labor-management committee doesn't start out with these factors working in its favor. The traditional role of the union delegate is to fight management. The traditional role of managers is to make the decisions.

The key to getting through this bad-attitude minefield is to manage the process and to foster union-management relationships that have a broader scope than the traditional one. It helps to separate the two types of union-management interactions into their domains. Adversarial collective bargaining should always be addressed *outside* the labor-management committee context. This rule needs to be explicitly agreed to and rigidly enforced.[7] Conversely, the problem that the labor-management committee is working on shouldn't be addressed at the bargaining table. Otherwise it will get linked to issues being contested.

Another tactic that can be very helpful is to make the committee's outcome be recommendations rather than a binding decision. This wards off opposition from people outside the committee who are nervous about giving up power. If all the committee can do is recommend, then insecure managers and union officials have nothing serious to worry about. In practice, not having final authority to make a decision is less of a problem than it might seem. If the committee members occupy significant positions in the union and in management, and they've agreed to something, it's difficult to disregard their recommendations.

It's also helpful to keep the labor-management problem-solving process out of the limelight. Audiences rarely help labor-management negotiations. Each side begins posturing for its audience rather than addressing the issues in a thoughtful way. The union representatives feel a need to demonstrate to their constituents that they're tough enough to fight against managerial exploitation. Likewise, management negotiators need to show top management that they're tough enough to stand up to the union and to protect shareholders' interests. The result has too much in common with televised professional wrestling.

Private meetings also help committee members develop strong working relationships. In public, they're constrained by their politicized roles and find it difficult to develop a broader-scope relationship. Constituents get nervous when their representatives get out of role. But labor-management committee members need to operate from a broad-scope relationship if they're to be successful. They need to get beyond the stereotyped images of each other that lock them into divisiveness. This will allow them to recognize that they in fact have much in common. They can learn to respect each other, even though their views on some issues are very different. They can discover that they can trust each other, within limits. And as the scope of the relationship broadens, it's easier to move from the enemy pole toward the ally pole. They find that they can be allies in solving the mutual problem, even if they feel a need to behave more like enemies at the bargaining table.

Acceptance may be the toughest relationship dimension to improve. Some managers are so vehemently antiunion that they have a mental block about this. But acceptance of the union is crucial if the labor-management relationship is to improve. Otherwise, management will squander energy trying to decertify or weaken the union instead of enlisting the union's support in tackling mutual problems.

A neutral facilitator can be extremely helpful to a labor-management committee. The facilitator can accelerate relationship evolution and also ensure that the members abide by the process rules they've agreed to. The facilitator is an asset because neither side starts out with an adversarial relationship with this neutral professional.

The facilitator develops bonds with each party. (If the facilitator can't at least muster trust and respect, the parties ought to call in someone else.) If management sees that the facilitator can get along reasonably well with those union people, maybe they're not as bad as the stereotype has led them to believe. A similar shift in thinking can take place among the union members. They see that managers can "act like real people" in their interactions with the facilitator, so maybe they're reasonable people after all. Relationship evolution should get both parties to the point that they can accept the other side, viewing them, say, as "good people in bad roles." That's enough to allow serious progress.

A Case Example of an Improved Union-Management Relationship: Jaguar Cars

Jaguar is a British automobile manufacturing company founded in the 1920s. Its distinctive competency has always been in design and styling. Over the years, Jaguar earned the reputation for producing the most attractive, best-handling cars in their class, offering what Jaguar described as "grace, space, and pace." However, the 1980s brought a number of problems. The worst was unreliable quality. This was a particular problem because Jaguar was selling expensive cars in an increasingly quality-conscious market.

Low quality was interconnected with other problems. The manufacturing facility was old and dilapidated. The resulting poor plant efficiency denied Jaguar the funds it needed to reinvest to install efficient production lines and precision-manufacturing equipment such as robots. Ford acquired Jaguar in the late 1980s and supplied the funding and quality mechanisms to turn around this ailing icon.

Prior to the turnaround, the relationship between management and the union had been awful, and this compounded whatever problems arose from trying to make do with aging plant and equipment. Labor-management problems are fairly common in Britain. This strife reflects a deeper schism within the culture: there's more class consciousness in Britain than in many other Western countries. Management has traditionally been the vanguard of the ruling class. Labor has therefore been engaged in an ideological as well as economic struggle with management. The deep social division has traditionally played out at the national level, with the Labour Party positioned as the representative of the working classes. As a result, ingroup-outgroup dynamics operate at multiple levels of society.

The deep rift between the working class (embodied in the union) and the owner/manager class contributed to the daunting challenges that faced Jaguar. The company could not correct the quality and efficiency problems without cooperation from the union. Furthermore, without union cooperation, it would not have been worthwhile for the new parent company—Ford—to make the huge investment needed to upgrade the plant and equipment.

A shift in union-management relations was signaled when Jaguar brought in a new Managing Director of Production. David Hudson had considerable experience in automobile manufacturing. He had seen initiatives succeed and fail, and realized that forging a new relationship with the union was going to be vital for the success of any turnaround at Jaguar.

Hudson formed a top-level labor-management committee that met weekly at the Coventry plant. This was a departure from industry practice, which makes the union feel excluded from the change process: Hudson made them feel included. Then he began the slow process of reorienting Jaguar manufacturing employees to become more of a unified community. Prior to his appointment, the workplace seemed more like the site of two warring camps.

Unifying the community was made easier by the specter of three common enemies. The first was the upstart Japanese companies entering the luxury-car-market segment. The message to workers was "we need to join together to repel the invaders" of Jaguar's traditional markets.

The second enemy of sorts was Ford Motor Company. Jaguar workers and managers saw a real risk of losing their autonomy. They had strong identification with Jaguar and did not want to see the proud tradition fade into becoming little more than a high-prestige badge on a Ford car. Everyone was aware of instances of this happening at General Motors; in fact, in the industry, it was called "badge engineering." This expression refers to the practice of putting a prestige brand name on an existing automobile, rather than engineering a new car designed to meet brand expectations. At Jaguar, both workers and managers knew that if there wasn't a significant turnaround, Ford would have to intervene to protect its investment. They suspected that Ford managers would make product line decisions that would be Ford-oriented rather than Jaguar-oriented.

The third enemy of sorts was other countries that would have welcomed the opportunity to manufacture Jaguars. Ford was having great success in its manufacturing plant in Mexico, for example. The quality levels were high and the labor costs low. There was no *technological* reason why Jaguars couldn't be assembled in Mexico. In fact, it probably would have been economically more attractive. So there was a worry that Ford might relocate manufacturing if union and management couldn't work together as a cohesive unit.

These problems helped to convince workers and union officers that the present way of operating the plant was not viable. Prior to Hudson's arrival, the gravity of the problems had not been obvious to workers and the union, hence there had been little impetus to accept change or to participate to ensure its success.

Hudson's problem was that the organization seemed stable to people who knew little about the instability in the industry and the seriousness of Jaguar's financial situation. The factory was still producing 20,000 automobiles a year, and providing employment for 4,300 workers. The Jaguar brand was so strong—and the cars provided such a unique driving experience (when they ran)—that loyal customers were still buying the cars despite the quality problems. So the labor-management committee provided the forum in which to share the strategic and financial problems with the union. The union came to realize that Jaguar was in a desperate struggle for its survival as an independent car company.

Another factor that transformed a previously adversarial relationship was the way managers dealt with performance problems. Previously, if something went wrong, managers would punish the person responsible for the faulty operation. Under Hudson, groups of workers looked for the problem that led to the unsatisfactory outcome. Thus the relationship evolved from "policing" performance to joint problem solving. It gave the workers "ownership" (in the sense of personal commitment and the opportunity to make a real difference) of the production process. Previously, refining production processes had been the domain of middle management, following the command-and-control principles of hierarchical organizing.

This is not to say that Hudson delegated all decision-making to workers, so as to create a workplace democracy. To the contrary. His management style was more decisive than that of his predecessors. Previously, major decisions had been "proposed" and then debated at great length with the union. Under Hudson, major decisions were implemented, and the union was welcome to discuss them after the fact. This shift in style was probably necessary until the relationship with the union had evolved from adversarial to cooperative. The risk was that using a decisive style would undermine his efforts to improve the relationship with workers and the union. But this didn't happen, in large part because of some other changes Hudson made at the same time.

"Ownership" of quality was delegated to workers and the union, departing from industry practice of quality monitoring by middle management and reliance on outside consultants to analyze processes. Under Hudson, Jaguar workers were trained in SPC (statistical process control). Production-line workers were selected if they had the mathematical aptitude to analyze the production data. This was a clever approach because feedback and suggestions regarding quality and productivity were coming from a peer, not from a management watchdog. These workers, in turn, trained their peers in SPC, resulting in a diffusion of the knowledge at the level where it could make the most difference—on the shop floor. This process was so successful that workers soon became more knowledgeable than managers. As a result, managers had to undergo some remedial education to close the knowledge gap.

Although transforming the relationship with the union was the most important thing Hudson did, it wasn't the only change that contributed to the turnaround of Jaguar manufacturing. He overcame some of the horizontal schisms of hierarchy by creating cross-functional teams.

Membership on these teams included suppliers where appropriate, thus gaining him some of the benefits of value-chain integration.

The most important of these teams were the VRTs—Variability Reduction Teams. Their purpose was to assure uniform results—in Hudson's words, "to build it right the first time." The previous variability control system had resulted in a lot of adjustment work during assembly. That is, parts didn't just bolt together, as they were supposed to—instead, they had to be fitted. Ironically, it was Henry Ford who almost a century earlier had introduced the principle of interchangeable parts in the auto industry. Any component should fit on any car without adjustment. In the 1980s, Jaguar was plagued with a lot of parts that would sometimes fit, but often required additional labor.

The team spirit caught on, and early opponents became some of the strongest advocates. The VRT recommendations were implemented more effectively than management could have accomplished, because workers on the teams educated their peers about how to assure uniform quality. Soon, it seemed like everyone wanted to be a member of one of these teams, and indeed by the mid-1990s, 70 percent of workers were on at least one team.

By all indicators the factory was operating more efficiently. Downtime had been reduced dramatically, and workers had taken responsibility for preventive maintenance, a job that had previously been done by outsiders. Workers wanted to do it themselves to be sure it was done correctly.

Ford executives gave Hudson a lot of credit for the turnaround, even though Hudson, modestly, deflected the credit to the workers. Hudson handled all of the employee relations issues personally, rather than delegating this task to a specialist. In this way, he minimized the relational distance from his workforce. The teams reported to him and his own management group, thus giving production-line workers direct access to the highest levels of management. This reduced previous caste divisions within Jaguar.[8]

Furthermore, Hudson made sure that individual and team suggestions got *implemented* wherever possible. His guiding principle was that if it's important to the workers, a suggestion ought to be implemented even if management can't see the immediate benefit. He knew that managers are not omniscient, and that it's worse to discourage employee suggestions than to implement one of their ideas that has no net benefit.

At the same time, the union stewards got new roles in the plant. They were trained and certified as ISO9000 auditors, thus their role was to assure quality and efficiency in the plant. This put them "on the same side of the table" as management. They were doing their part to protect workers' jobs.

The adversarial relationship that had developed over decades slowly dissolved and was replaced by respectful collaboration. As a result, Jaguar cars moved from dismal quality in the mid-1980s to world-class quality in the 1990s. It became the best car in the Ford system, and in the same quality league as the mid-1990s benchmark car, the Lexus. The transformation has justified Ford's considerable investment in new production facilities. Output rose from 20,000 cars per year in 1990 to 40,000 in the mid-'90s, while the number of workers dropped from 4,300 to 1,500. The 157 trade union representatives needed to handle employee-relations problems shrank to 21, all of whom were doing factory work.

THE INDIVIDUAL'S RELATIONSHIP WITH THE GROUP

In the preceding sections, we focused on individuals' relationships with other individuals, and groups' relationships with other groups. Another extremely important phenomenon to understand is the relationship between individuals and groups.

Striving for Inclusion

Individuals have a strong desire to be offered membership in groups they care about. Whether they accept membership is another matter: they want the choice to be theirs. Some of the motivation can be traced to the social nature of our species. Some of it can be traced to our quest for unconditional positive regard. Whatever the motive, inclusion makes us feel good and exclusion hurts.

The obvious reason exclusion hurts is that rejection causes anger and sadness. These emotions are so powerful that shunning—communal refusal to interact with an individual who has violated community norms—is one of the most powerful forms of punishment available. The less obvious reason is that exclusion causes dissonance problems that can hurt our self-esteem. We may feel good about ourselves, but if others are rejecting us, they apparently don't feel the same way. The difference in views causes cognitive dissonance, and must be resolved somehow. We can rationalize the inconsistency by thinking the others are just being mean—in which case we'll hate them. Or we can think less of ourselves, believing that we're unworthy—in which case we'll feel depressed.

Everyone has experienced the pain of rejection, and nobody likes being excluded. Despite this awareness, however, it's surprising how many people are insensitive to excluding others. Take the case of the baby boomer who fervently supports the civil rights movement and would never discriminate on the basis of race, religion, or national origin at work. But this same individual is a member of a club that excludes people who are seen to be of different castes. The general point here is that exclusion results from people's choices, not their values. They choose whether or not to participate in exclusive organizations of all kinds.

This kind of exclusion carries over into corporations in subtle ways. Much relationship-building, information-exchange, and deal-making takes place off-site. This can be done inclusively or exclusively. Suppose, for example, these interactions take place on a golf course. Not everyone is equally likely to be a golf player. In the United States, golf tends to be a game played by men rather than women, and by Caucasians rather than people of color. Thus, golf course interactions have *the effect* of excluding even when this is not a conscious intention of the choice to conduct business discussions there.

It's astounding how many employees feel they're "kept in the dark" about corporate affairs. This practice also tends to exclude because it's hard to maintain a sense of identity with the company if people one level up won't let you know what's going on. In fact, much of the information being kept from subordinates is in the public domain, and subordinates would have access to it if they went to some trouble to look. So why not give it to them? The reason is that information hoarding often reflects managerial caste membership rather than the need for secrecy.

Sometimes the group's *process* has the effect of excluding people. That is, the way the group conducts itself leaves some people on the outside. For example, imagine a group meeting where the dominant members engage in a heated argument over the issues, swearing and yelling at each other throughout the meeting. Many Western men enjoy this kind of meeting, which they would describe as "a spirited debate." But many women and people from other cultural backgrounds experience this same meeting as unpleasant and stressful. The group can't be inclusive if it doesn't adapt to the sensitivities of its members.

Sometimes it's not crude and boisterous behavior that excludes, but rather "in-jokes." An in-joke is humor that's understood only by members of the ingroup. When everyone present can appreciate the humor, in-jokes can help to bond the group. However, these same jokes can make newcomers feel excluded. Remember the last time you walked up and joined some people who were already conversing. If they had carried on talking as if you weren't there, you'd soon have become very uncomfortable; in-jokes can have the same effect.

The Boss's Relationship to the Group

A special case of individual-group relationships is the one between the work group and the person assigned to be the boss. It's better for the boss to be viewed as an ingroup member, but bosses usually hire and fire ingroup members, evaluate their performance, discipline those who violate expectations, and set pay levels. These tasks create relational problems.

It's hard to experience *acceptance* if the boss is evaluating you and deciding whether you're worth keeping around. Neither would you see someone as an *ally* whose primary loyalty is supposed to be to top management. This will also reduce the boss's *trustworthiness*, because your well-being will have lower priority than the organization's interests. The conventional boss will also offer only a *narrow-scope* relationship, sticking closely to the boss role, and *disclosing* very little about herself or himself. The boss may also see you and other group members as potential *competitors* vying for the title of boss. Thus, even though you *like* and *respect* your boss, and see him or her as *empathic* and having much *in common* with you, the other dimensions will likely get in the way of a strong overall relationship.

Managers in new-era organizations don't experience the same relationship barriers because they have different roles and relationships. Consider, for example, the first-line manager of a reengineered organization. This person *supports* (rather than micromanages) the groups that carry out the reengineered process, serving as an ally helping the groups solve problems. There's no loyalty conflict because the group's sense of common mission is shared with the manager: there isn't a sense of "us-versus-them," but rather, a sense of commonwealth. Evaluations don't put the manager in a "policing" role; rather, the group does some form of 360-degree assessment. If there's a problem within the group, members may seek the manager's help (whereas in the conventional hierarchical organization, this same behavior would be seen as "ratting on" a co-worker). And the scope of the relationship between the manager and the group is probably very broad, because the egalitarian culture of the flat organization tends to erode caste differences. The role of supporter, facilitator, and coach allows the boss to be a full ingroup member, thereby meeting his or her own need for inclusion.

Of course, not every manager would thrive in the role just described. While all managers have a need for inclusion, some have a stronger need to dominate, to be treated as a superior, and to tightly control the performance of their unit. These needs are personality traits[9] that shape their approach to managing. Subordinates refer to such personalities as micromanagers, egomaniacs, and control freaks. Individuals with these traits serve a useful role in some organizations, but they're generally better suited to working in conventional hierarchies than in new-era organizations.

A Case Example of Positive Boss-Group Relationships: MBNA

MBNA New England is a credit card company located on the Maine coast. The credit card industry is a mature market, so MBNA has many competitors: many U.S. households are offered a new credit card every few weeks. In this competitive environment, MBNA's objective is to get customers to carry—and use—the MBNA credit card rather than a competitor's.

Service quality is one of the few ways that credit card companies can differentiate their card.[10] So, what is quality, in this context? It involves both technical excellence and positive interactions between customers and MBNA employees. Technical excellence is easier to achieve. The design of data-processing systems can be outsourced to suppliers who have a distinctive competency in doing this. So any credit card company ought to be able to match MBNA's technical excellence.

Competitive advantage must therefore come primarily from excellence in interactions with customers. Most contact between customers and the company is over the telephone. MBNA is not like a local bank branch or a store, where customers walk into a building to receive service. Instead, paperwork is sent through the mail and anything beyond paying the monthly bill is handled over the phone. Thus, the key indicator of quality is how MBNA's "Customer Advocates" deal with customers when the conversation is a difficult one.[11] The difficult calls involve dealing with problems—such as when people get behind in their payments, balk at paying a particular store charge, or decide to terminate their account.

Success in handling the difficult calls depends on the relationships Customer Advocates form with customers. Customer Advocates are vastly more effective in these tense interactions if they generate rapport with customers. But this is not easy. Much of the telephone contact with delinquent customers takes place in the early evening, after these customers get home from work. Customers are tired, and typically don't look forward to dealing with hassles of any kind. Besides, anything related to their debt situation tends to be particularly stressful and embarrassing. So they'd prefer to avoid dealing with the Customer Advocate altogether, never mind form a good relationship.

With such a tough job facing them, you'd expect that Customer Advocates would dread coming to work. Yet these MBNA workers display high morale, and their success in dealing with customers is phenomenal. Let's look at how MBNA does it.

First, the selection process is long, because MBNA wants to be sure to get workers who are relationship-oriented. Then, the first day they report to work, they meet the upper-level managers. This makes them feel *included* in the company from day one. They get the message that they're important enough to be worth top management's time to drop everything and meet with them.

Next, they're carefully educated to deal with difficult interactions with customers. This involves a lot of role-playing, because this method of learning puts the new employee in simulated situations just like they'll encounter in their work. But developing the skills needed to manage relationships with customers doesn't end there. The culture of the company constantly reinforces this dimension of quality. Over *every* doorway is the admonition "Think of yourself as a Customer." At the very least, this reminds employees of the importance of *empathy* in dealing with customers. If they, themselves, were on the other end of the telephone line with a credit card problem, what would they be experiencing? How would they want the credit card company to be dealing with them? What would represent high quality from their perspective if they were the customer?

The Customer Advocate's goal is to transform the relationship with the delinquent customer. The relationship is likely to start out adversarial. After all, one person is a bill collector and the other isn't keen on paying up right away! The Customer Advocate has to change the customer's perspective. The Customer Advocate treats the situation as one in which both parties are trying to solve a mutual problem. Metaphorically, the customer starts out viewing the Customer Advocate as sitting on the opposite side of the table, arguing over how scarce funds will be spent. The Customer Advocate has done a good job of relationship management if the customer comes to feel like both parties are sitting on the same side of the table facing the problem. In terms of the alliance dimension of relationships, the Customer Advocate moves *from enemy toward ally*.

If progress can be made in moving away from the enemy pole, other relationship dimensions can improve—such as *trust, respect,* and other *scope-broadening* dimensions. In fact, if the interaction goes well, the customer may actually grow to *like* the MBNA Customer Advocate. After all, this person helped the customer solve a problem and alleviated some of the stress of financial difficulties. The Customer Advocate seems more like the doctor who relieves pain than the traffic cop issuing fines in a speed trap.

The work of Customer Advocates is done in groups that specialize in certain functions—for example, dealing with people who are unable to keep up with payments, or people who are thinking of closing their MBNA accounts. The integrated group is necessary for quality because customers need to have the same high-quality interaction no matter which Customer Advocate contacts them. Group members also pass on tips about persuasion techniques that have worked well, and give each other support after stressful interactions with hostile customers.

Now let's look at the management system that supports these front-line groups. One might expect groups to have an adversarial relationship with their supervisors, who unobtrusively monitor their telephone calls. Having a supervisor spying on them seems like something that would add to the stress of an already difficult task. Yet this key aspect of supervisory behavior is neither onerous nor resented. Let's look at how MBNA New England is organized.

The MBNA customer is at the top of the organization chart. This is understandable in a service business operating in a highly competitive market. Brand-switching costs are insignificant for most customers. They typically have several credit cards in their purses or wallets. They switch brands by simply not using their MBNA credit cards. A dormant credit card is not much different from a canceled credit card.

The integrated groups of telephone callers at MBNA are the company's direct link to these customers. That's why it's so important that each call be a relationship-strengthening experience. And each call is unique in some way—the Customer Advocate has to adapt to a new combination of customer personality, emotional state, and communication style, as well as the specifics of the situation. So the Customer Advocate has to exercise considerable judgment during each call. Thus, the quality of MBNA's service often boils down to the decisions employees make in real time while on the phone.

Because the calls are so important to MBNA's success in this market, supervisors must know how the calls are being handled. So they listen in. But the monitoring isn't experienced as "spying on" the Customer Advocate because it's done for the purpose of coaching and supporting. If it resulted in punishing and weeding out poor performers, there'd be more of a "big brother is watching you" feeling to it. The positive tone is established by the way that the supervisor conducts the feedback sessions following the monitoring. Supervisors praise employees for what they do well and jointly explore what might have worked better in the particular situation. This puts supervisors and employees on the same side of the table trying to figure out the best way to approach a difficult problem, rather than on opposite sides of the table wrangling over a performance evaluation.

At MBNA, the supervisor seems to be accepted as an ingroup member. This is helped by MBNA's policy of promoting from within, which ensures that supervisors have a lot in common with subordinates. There's also plenty of empathy because managers at all levels are required to make a certain number of telephone contacts themselves every month. This reduces the tendency for caste differences to arise: telephone reps aren't doing work that supervisors won't do.

Other MBNA policies and practices help to avoid the vertical fractionation portrayed in Figure 3-2. Supervisors dress like the telephone reps, have office cubicles that look the same, and don't have special parking places, dining facilities, or other special privileges. Everyone's on salary, everyone's on a first-name basis, and everyone participates in an incentive program. As a result, there's little social distance between supervisors and Customer Advocates.

As a result, supervisors are able to serve in a support role rather than the micromanagement role that occurs in conventional hierarchical organizations. They provide their teams with resources. They solve problems so that workers can go about their work unimpeded. They pass on information from higher levels of management, and hold discussions of trends in the business and the industry. They coach. And they add to the social support provided by the Customer Advocates' peers, thus helping to ease the stress of difficult telephone interactions.

Another major function of supervisors is to administer the various incentive systems. MBNA has one of the most sophisticated employee involvement systems being used today. Certificates and plaques recognize employee contributions of many types, and these are proudly displayed at employee workstations. The recognition programs range from quality of everyday work—which can be determined by experienced supervisors monitoring calls—to the usefulness of suggestions. This is backed up by an incentive system, so that employees genuinely share in the company's prosperity and improvement. As a result of the way they're implemented, the incentive systems actually reinforce employee identity with the company. They also strengthen the relationship with the supervisor, who's highly involved in the program.

Groups do compete with each other to some degree as each strives for excellence. But MBNA has found a way to avoid the divisive side effects of intergroup competition. The design of incentives is guided by the corporate principle that individuals or groups can't be doing well if what they're doing comes at the expense of someone else. So people are discouraged from withholding cooperation as a means of coming out ahead.

In sum, MBNA has found a way to achieve operational excellence by *managing relationships*. As we noted earlier, any MBNA competitor could achieve the same technical excellence, by installing the best systems. But MBNA's competitive advantage comes from its relationships with customers, the creation of constructive competition between groups, the sense of inclusion that binds the employee to the organization, and the relationship between supervisors and workers.

CONCLUDING THOUGHTS ABOUT GROUP RELATIONSHIPS

People *need* to feel included in groups. This is a facet of human nature. Conversely, people dislike being excluded. They'd rather be invited to join the group, even if they don't particularly want to be a member. Someone who turns down an offer to be included is at worst indifferent to the group, but more likely positively disposed to it. Someone who's rejected becomes an enemy.

It's vitally important to manage the relationship between individuals and groups. *The organizations that will survive and prosper in the new era will be integrated networks of high-performing groups.* This requires that workers possessing essential skills form strong bonds with the groups. It also requires the participation of a wide variety of people, because diversity enables groups to adapt to novel challenges. If groups exclude people who are different—even if they don't mean to—they'll fall short of becoming high-performing groups.

The manager's job, therefore, is to manage group relationships within and between groups, as well as interpersonal relationships. In the next chapter, we'll see that it's also important to manage relationships within and between organizations. The discussion will build on what we've just learned about groups, and what we learned about interpersonal relationships in Chapter 2.

NOTES

1. This simulation was later used with adults, with many of the same reactions.
2. See, for example, the classic book *Ethnocentrism* by Levine and Campbell (New York: Wiley, 1972).
3. Collocation involves putting people in the same physical location, rather than keeping them separated in different areas, on different floors, in different buildings, or at different sites.
4. In the United States, they're actually referred to as "exempt employees." Note that exempt implies being excused from something onerous. For example, it would sound weird to say "I'm exempt from having fun." You get exemptions from taxes, exams, prosecution . . . and punching a time card.
5. This is usually the easiest step to take, and much of the initiative can be accomplished instantly. For example, travel policy can be amended so that all employees are allowed to book upgradable coach-class fares. People who then wish to fly business class or first class can use frequent-flyer credits or pay the difference. Employees can likewise be given a flat allowance to lease or buy company cars. Those who want a more opulent vehicle can pay the difference. Parking places can be allocated on a first come, first served basis. And the company can save a lot of money by eliminating apartheid dining facilities. Note that some managers and executives stuck in the old paradigm will object to this policy evolution, complaining that it will be harder to recruit upper-level

management without these caste perquisites. (We would expect this reaction, based on what we saw in the Jane Eliot blue eye/brown eye experiment.) The rejoinder is that new-era companies probably shouldn't be hiring managers who will only join the organization if there's an exclusive caste system creating fractionation and alienation.

6. We examine the GE "Work Out!" program in greater detail in Chapter 5. For additional information, see the book by Robert Slater, *Jack Welch and the GE Way* (New York: McGraw-Hill, 1999).

7. See, for example, McKersie, Greenhalgh, and Jick, "The CEC: Labor-Management Cooperation in New York," *Industrial Relations* 20 (1981):212–20.

8. It helped immensely that Jaguar's charismatic CEO at the time, Nick Scheele, was seen as very approachable.

9. We'll be discussing personality traits and their impact on managerial thinking in the final two chapters.

10. Another way is to offer an affinity card—such as when a small donation is made to The Nature Conservancy or some other charity every time the credit card is used. But even people who have a motive to use an affinity card will not put up with bad service.

11. Seventy percent of MBNA's 100 million telephone calls a year involve customers seeking MBNA products. These calls require less skill to handle.

CHAPTER 4

RELATIONSHIPS INVOLVING ORGANIZATIONS

Old-paradigm managers are puzzled when they learn that a major contract between two large Japanese companies is often only one or two paragraphs long. An equivalent contract between two U.S. companies would probably be at least a hundred pages, because it attempts to provide for all contingencies. The contingencies may arise from shifts in consumer tastes, evolving technology that makes possible new product or service features, regulatory changes that create new options or constraints, or responses to new competitors entering the market.

Just as enigmatic was the behavior of individual IBM employees dealing with an upheaval in the computer chip industry in the early 1980s.[1] Many workers at the computer-chip plant in Vermont volunteered to do work that was far outside their job descriptions in order to help their company through a business crisis. For example, office workers transferred to the production line, and engineers painted unsightly sections of the plant. These were not workers so desperate to keep their jobs that they would do any job to avoid unemployment. They were highly skilled workers with great labor market opportunities. They had *volunteered* to work outside their job descriptions because they wanted to help the company. Higher management had explained the business problem to them and asked for their assistance.

U.S. consumers who buy Saturn automobiles are another source of puzzlement. The Saturn is a good car, but doesn't have unique mechanical properties or exotic styling that would explain buyers' attachment to the brand. In fact the brand is positioned in the "commodity" segment of the market. Potential car buyers can visit—in person or electronically—a series of local dealerships offering different brands of comparable economy cars and get each of them to undercut the others' price. This will get them maximum economic value: they will be buying from the dealer willing to take the lowest profit margin. Yet hundreds of thousands of Saturn buyers have been willing to pay more than they need to for an economy car.

These examples display apparent irrationality when viewed in the context of classical theory, which assumes individualistic motivation. That is, individuals—and businesses, which are viewed as corporate "individuals"—are supposed to make choices in pursuit of their self-interest. Others need to do the same thing, to protect themselves from exploitation. If all behave individualistically, we're told, then the system will be in equilibrium. Good attorneys will catch opposing attorneys trying to slip an exploitative clause into a contract. Workers will move to jobs with the best combination of wages, job security, and attractive job features. And smart consumers will shop to find the best deals, driving inefficient producers and high-margin distributors out of the market.

Yet the examples above show us that people don't always do what classical theory predicts. What's missing from classical theory is an adequate account of the role of *relationships* in decision-making.

The reason Japanese business leaders don't have to provide for every contingency is that they *trust* each other. They know that circumstances will change, but can rely on the other to live up to the *commonwealth* spirit of the agreement. As new circumstances arise, they renegotiate so that the terms of business remain fair to both organizations, as well as responsive to the new challenge. The IBM example illustrates a particular relationship between the company and its employees. They were *loyal* to IBM because IBM had been loyal to them. The Saturn example portrays a relationship in which customers feel *included* in an extended family of sorts.

So the apparently irrational behavior isn't so puzzling when we factor in the full spectrum of *relationship dynamics*. What's puzzling is why classical theory has given so little attention to relationships, in the face of so much commonsense evidence of their importance.

Instead of launching a comprehensive study of how relationships drive and shape business, scholars have relied on the simplistic relationships used in economic models. When I use the term "simplistic," this is not a criticism of economics. Economists create and manipulate ideal models. These models are extremely valuable when used to understand system dynamics, but can be misleading when applied inappropriately to specific organizational situations. This is exactly what many organizational scholars have done: they have overemphasized and misapplied theory that was never intended for application beyond economic models.

We'll see that due to intellectual laziness or lack of real-world organizational experience, many old-paradigm scholars focused on three particular types of relationships in business: hierarchical relationships, exchange relationships, and competition. We'll look at these in some detail before proceeding further. It's important to understand what the old paradigm has to offer, and what makes it inadequate for managing new-era organizations.

RELATIONSHIPS EMPHASIZED IN CLASSICAL THEORY

1. Hierarchical Relationships

During the Industrial Revolution, hierarchy became adopted by Western businesses as the means of coordination and control. Hierarchy gives rise to three relationship dynamics that have some serious drawbacks in addition to the benefits they provide.

First, hierarchy creates *superiority-inferiority* relationships. Managers report to their superiors. Superior implies better, in terms of caste. They work with peers, who are the same social class. And they, in turn, are the superiors of their workers, which makes them inferiors, even though we don't say it to their faces. With superiority-inferiority comes *social distance.* This isn't bad if you're ordering paratroopers to jump out of a perfectly serviceable aircraft and land in a minefield. You don't need to be their pal. But there's no reason to suppose that this same social distance increases *managerial effectiveness.*

Second, hierarchy creates *dominance-subordination* relationships. These involve power differences. Bosses tell their workers what to do. Their workers are even called "subordinates," just to be sure they get the message about being obedient. But there's a real question whether dominance helps managers more than it hinders. If people are only doing what managers *force* them to do, then managers need a pretty good surveillance system. And if they spend all their time monitoring, there's little time to devote to such forward-thinking activities as strategic planning, refining processes, managing strategic alliances, ensuring future resources, upgrading systems of all kinds, and preparing work groups for greater empowerment and continuous improvement.

Third, hierarchy creates and emphasizes *role relationships*. The hierarchical structure is, in essence, a system of intermeshed roles.[2] Middle managers create job descriptions that prescribe not only what an individual is supposed to do, but also how that individual relates to others in the organization. The accounts payable clerk is a processor of invoices from the mailroom, a seeker of verification from the purchasing agent, and a supplier of data to the cost accounting clerk. These roles are analogous to cogs in a machine: the machine runs smoothly if the gears run at compatible speeds and mesh well. Any other relationship dimensions that develop are irrelevant or distracting.

The problem with this way of thinking is that people aren't gear cogs, even on a bad day. They naturally form complex relationships with other people and do the organization's work *in the context of such relationships*. People are not indifferent, for example, to role occupants they don't get along with: they don't easily cooperate with such people. This can produce coordination problems if a peer is disliked, discrimination and suboptimization if a subordinate is disliked, and subtle insubordination if a boss is disliked.

Furthermore, classical theory assumes *individualistic* behavior by role occupants, yet people naturally gravitate to *groups*. They eat lunch together, congregate at breaks, help each other out, and treat other group members' enemies as their own enemies. *Groups can be committed to improving organizational effectiveness, or to undermining it.* They can accept a person assigned to a role, or reject that person and not collaborate with him or her. Groups can cooperate with other groups, compete with them, or undermine them. So relationships within and between groups are also extraordinarily important to organizational efficacy. Yet these relationships are overlooked in the hierarchical model. Groups don't fit into the machine imagery, so organizational theory developed assuming that group relationships were as irrelevant as interpersonal relationships.

2. Economic Exchange

Exchange involves a balance between contributing something and getting something in return. According to classical economists (and sociologists), exchange is the basic relationship linking people, groups, and organizations.

The elevation of the exchange dimension of relationships to such prominence comes as no surprise if we take into account economists' fascination with *transactions.* They see transactions as the fundamental unit of business. A transaction is a one-time deal. When you rent a building, retain an attorney, take a job, or form a joint venture, economists view it as a transaction, even though most of us would experience these events as the beginning of an ongoing relationship. Economists recognize that the benefits and costs of the arrangement can stretch out over an indefinite period. But their mathematical models allow them to reduce the stream of future benefits—and future costs—to an equivalent lump sum that has a "net present value." This allows them to *conceptualize* all business deals as if they were transactions. Managers misapply economists' models when they act as if all business deals are transactions.

In practice, *one-time deals are rare in our business and private lives.* The context of most of our actions is a complex ongoing relationship. We usually have some sort of past history with the person we're dealing with, and we expect to deal with him or her in the future. We often share mutual friends and acquaintances, and we care about our reputation among this broader network. So when we think about real-world deals, we take into account real-world relationships. The exchange perspective distorts this reality by overemphasizing costs and benefits in the current transaction. And when it looks at ongoing interaction at all, the exchange perspective treats it as *a series of transactions.*

Treating an ongoing relationship as a serial exchange process is misguided. Marriage, for example, is not a series of dates in which each party reviews service level, costs, and various proposals from alternative providers. If it were, spouses would constantly be comparing the available cohabitation offers rather than living up to their commitments.

Another way in which the exchange perspective distorts our thinking about relationships is the view that transactions need to be *balanced:* we should get fair value in return for what we give up. This means that if you came out better in the last transaction, you now owe me. Over time, it needs to come out approximately even. This thinking has become so ingrained in Western thought that few people bother to ask whether it's valid. It often isn't.

In real-world relationships, there's a persistent imbalance. Anyone who's raised children knows that parenting is all giving, with no hope of ever getting your economic investment back. Some economists have theorized that parents make sacrifices so that their offspring will be obligated to take care of them after they retire. But that's not *really* why you were born. The truth is, any potential parent who's looking for a balanced exchange should either remain childless or expect to be disappointed. It's the same in couples. People stay together because of attachment bonds, not exchange. If you focus on achieving exchange balance in your long-term relationships, you probably won't have many of them.

We can look at other examples of long-term relationships to find imbalance as the norm. Senior managers who are serving as mentors to junior managers characteristically give more than they get back. The person being mentored will probably never be in a position to return the favor. But mentors don't expect them to. They're acting on nurturing instincts rather than creating indebtedness. Similarly, companies never equally benefit in joint ventures or supply relationships. It's one of those apples-and-oranges situations. One gets some needs met, the other gets a different types of needs met. The issue is not whether exchange is perfectly balanced, but rather whether needs are met in a way that preserves the relationship. So the whole notion of balanced exchange is largely a myth. Life is not that simple.

Classical theory also assumes that the parties to the exchange are motivated to maximize their self-interest. This is the Economic Man thesis: individuals make self-serving choices that maximize their utility and minimize their disutility. With both parties trying to maximize their self-interest in transactions, exchange is inherently adversarial. The parties don't expect the transaction to be balanced, and struggle to make it unbalanced *in their favor.*

From the perspective of economic ideology, this adversarial relationship is good. It fosters an economic merit system that favors those who are good at exchange, and penalizes the less able. The system is revered as "economic Darwinism." The winners are those who can bring more power to bear on the other party, or exercise greater guile so that the other party *believes* that an outcome is fair even when it isn't.

This brings up another point, that the exchange relationship accepts distrust as "a given." Trust, as we learned in Chapter 2, involves the knowledge that the other party has your well-being at heart. But in the classical notion of exchange, the parties are supposed to be looking out for themselves—not each other. Each party *expects* to be exploited in the transaction. It's part of the game.

The institutionalized distrust leads to principles of business such as *caveat emptor* (Latin for "let the buyer beware"). The buyer needs to beware because the seller runs off with the cash, while the buyer is stuck with whatever was bought in the transaction. Obviously, this principle is incompatible with the notion of being customer-oriented, a foundation of modern marketing strategy. The systemic distrust also leads to principles of Western law such as "due diligence." This implies that people should not take the other party's word for what they're getting in a transaction; rather, they should check for themselves. This is incompatible with the notion of strategic alliance in business deals. You shouldn't *have to* exercise due diligence with an ally. If an ally proves to have misled you, there has been some sort of mistake. Allies correct mistakes, which is why Japanese contracts can be so short.

In sum, *exchange relationships are a basic building block of economic theory.* But in real-world situations, exchange is a dangerously oversimplified characterization of relationships. Indeed, field research that asked people what's important about their relationships with others showed that exchange was not the major dimension economists have led us to expect. It turns out to be of only minor importance to most people.[3]

3. Competition

The third system dynamic emphasized in classical theory is competition. Competitors are parties (i.e., individuals, groups, or organizations) vying for whatever is scarce. They may be competing over who gets to sell to a customer, who obtains raw materials, who buys a patent, who acquires a takeover target, and so on. The relationship is considered zero-sum in the sense that one's gain is the other's loss.

For example, GE's Aircraft Engine Division competes directly with Pratt & Whitney, a division of United Technologies. They both have engines available for the Boeing 737, and each company tries to "capture" airline customers. Either one company gets that business or the other does: there's no way to split the order so that GE gets half an airline's order and Pratt & Whitney gets the other half.

This is a textbook case of competition. An economic textbook, that is. In reality, competition is only one aspect of the relationship between the two companies. Both are huge conglomerates, so at times they're value-chain partners. In terms of number of airliners owned, GE Capital has the world's biggest fleet. It doesn't operate as an airline, but leases planes to airlines throughout the world. So GE Capital is a customer of Pratt & Whitney's whenever an airline specifies Pratt & Whitney engines on the planes it leases. United Technologies (Pratt & Whitney's parent organization) owns the Otis Elevator Company. It uses electric motors. GE has a division that supplies electric motors. Thus United Technologies is a potential customer of GE's. So we have to be very careful when we use the term "competitor" to characterize a relationship.

Even within the jet engine business, GE and Pratt & Whitney are not always competitors. When Boeing began work on its enlarged 747 jumbo jet, Pratt & Whitney joined GE in a collaborative effort to develop an engine for the new plane. Each has distinctive competencies, and the companies together could produce a better engine than either could alone. This is an important source of competitive advantage, because foreign manufacturers are vying for this same business, and could form their own consortium that might outcompete either GE or Pratt & Whitney working alone. There are also the daunting development costs—and associated risks—of a new engine program. GE and Pratt & Whitney were probably better off sharing the costs and risks. So the relationship between the companies is in fact poorly described by the term "competitor." Yet classical theory doesn't offer us alternative words that describe the more-complex relationship.

Worse than the inaccuracy of the terminology is where it takes you. A pure competitor is a pure enemy. Their gain is always your loss. Suppose your competitor is gearing up to offer a product line that's outside of your strategic domain. You may want to offer a competing product even though it's off-strategy for your company. The reason for this is that if a competitor generates revenue in an uncontested business area, this money can be used for R&D or advertising expenditures in the contested product line, or as a cash cow to sustain a predatory pricing campaign. So, from this perspective, there are no domains that you can comfortably cede to a competitor.

The notion of competitor-as-enemy is not simply an abstract notion. Airbus Industrie has behaved this way toward Boeing. During the early 1990s each company developed preliminary designs for a Very Large Transport (a VLT). Initial conceptualizations visualized a VLT twice the size of a Boeing 747. The market for such an aircraft is not big enough for two manufacturers. Airbus announced, however, that if Boeing entered the VLT market at all, Airbus would develop its own VLT, thereby ensuring that *both* companies would *lose money*.[4] Development costs of a plane this size are around $10 *billion,* so Airbus's threat was the economic equivalent of a suicide bombing. This approach to competition precludes a relationship that can be mutually beneficial. For example, Airbus and Boeing might both be better off forming a strategic alliance to build VLTs, even while competing in other domains.

These examples illustrate that it's shortsighted—and often misleading—to define another person, group, or organization as a competitor. It's better to specify the domain in which the parties are competing, the nature of the competition, and who, precisely, is the competitor (it may be a single entity within a larger grouping, for instance). Then it's necessary to identify other dimensions of the relationship. This is the step most people skip, to their disadvantage.

Finally, it's wise to assess the other possibilities: what *could* the relationship be? In general, *the more simplistic a manager's assessment of a relationship, the worse off the manager and the company are.*

RELATIONSHIPS BETWEEN ORGANIZATIONS— A NEW PERSPECTIVE

The chapter has thus far shown that three relationships tend to dominate the theoretical models—hierarchy, exchange, and competition—and these work well in pure economic applications (particularly in computer simulations). However, these limited choices are inadequate for the manager assessing relationships among people, groups, and businesses in new-era organizations. They're too simplistic, and lead to simplistic decisions that don't serve the organization well.

So next we'll look at the forms that organizational relationships can take. This will make it obvious that we need to expand the old perspective to fit the realities of the new era.

Competition between New-Era Organizations

As we noted earlier, competition between organizations has traditionally been viewed as an impersonal response to scarcity: whenever something important is in short supply, there's potential for this form of competition.

The relationship between the organizations involved depends on the *nature* of the competition between them. The traditional view of competition was of the benign, impersonal variety found in economists' ideal models. It overlooked all the really vicious stuff that goes on when competitors really go after each other. So let's consider the full range—from implicit, situational competition to targeted competition.

Implicit competition is very impersonal in the sense that competitors may never see or deal directly with each other. For example, if a potential customer has a couple of leisure hours available, these can be spent taking in a movie, going to a shopping mall, or working out at a health club. The movie theater, the shopping mall, and the health club are therefore competing with each other. If one of the three is chosen, the other two are not. This is benign competition because you don't even know who you're losing to—or winning against.

At the other extreme are archrivals, such as Coca-Cola and Pepsi-Cola competing directly for soft-drink customers. If you buy a six-pack of Coke, it's likely to be *instead of* Pepsi. Likewise, if you buy a Ford pickup truck, you're unlikely to also buy a Chevrolet pickup truck. In these either-or situations, the nature of competition is qualitatively different. This is because you can gain competitive advantage either by making your offerings seem more appealing or by undermining your competitor. If you choose to undermine your competitor, you transform the relationship.

The most familiar means of undermining a competitor is through comparative advertising. For years, Visa advertised an aspect of their credit cards that made them a better value than American Express cards. Many more retailers accepted Visa cards, so if you carried an American Express card, you'd have to have a Visa card too, because you couldn't be certain that a particular store would accept American Express. If you had to carry a Visa card anyway, it didn't make sense to pay the high annual fees for the American Express card. This is *targeted* competition.

The most ruthless means of undermining a competitor is to attack its source of competitive advantage. The company begins a campaign of moves and countermoves designed to undermine the competitor's strategy. The company with the better organizational architecture generally gains the advantage in such contests, because it's more adaptable to rapidly changing business situations and is nimbler in time-based competition. Hypercompetition[5] involves repeatedly seizing the first-mover advantage in a series of strategic initiatives. This allows a company to switch to a new strategy as competitors catch up and begin to nullify the advantages of the previous strategy.

Undermining tactics may work effectively when there are only two competitors (in economic terms, a true duopoly). But such economic warfare also takes its toll on the company that "wins." Seeing the market leader bruised and weakened may tempt a healthy new competitor to enter the market, perhaps from overseas.

It's generally unwise to use the most severe tactics unless you can put your competitor out of business. If the competitor lives through the assault, the company launching the offensive will be a bitter enemy. Creating enmity may deny you future opportunities to form a hybrid relationship to tackle common problems, such as a threat to the industry. Targeted tactics are designed and used in such a way that it's hard *not* to take it personally. For example, if you have thousands of Komatsu workers beginning each day by chanting "kill Caterpillar," how are Caterpillar executives supposed to feel? Caution is advisable because in a rapidly changing world, it's hard to predict who you'll need on your side in the future.

Buyers and Sellers

Economic theory is concerned with what happens in markets. Keep in mind that a market is a concept, rather than an actual place where people transact business. It's an impersonal mechanism in which relationships are purely instrumental: that is, sellers have something buyers want (goods or services) and buyers have something that sellers want (money). According to economic theory, sellers don't care who buys the product, so long as they come up with the money; likewise, buyers are indifferent as to whom they buy from, so long as they get what they need. Also, the relationship is assumed to be inherently adversarial in that the seller wants to get the highest price and the buyer wants to pay as little as possible.

Some buying-selling relationships actually resemble this theoretical model: stock markets and commodities markets are two examples. But additional examples are hard to find in real-world business situations. Therefore, we must use caution in relying on the economist's model as a way of understanding buyer-seller relationships. Furthermore, as we look at the multiorganizational architecture of new-era organizations, the market concept seems even less applicable. The emphasis is shifting toward integrated value chains.

The value chain is an important concept for three reasons. First, if you know which processes add value to the product or service, then you know which ones *do not.* Getting rid of the ones that don't add value gives you a lean manufacturing or service-delivery process—and also a lean organization (lean means efficient, profitable, and hard to compete with). Second, knowing where the most value is created tells you where you devote most of your attention if you want to preserve competitive advantage. Third, the value-chain concept gives us a different perspective on strategic business relationships. The old-paradigm notion of competition envisions two organizations competing against each other. The new-era notion envisions two *value chains* competing against each other.

When value chains compete, businesses may gain competitive advantage from beyond their own boundaries. For example, success in the auto industry depends on quality and efficiency. Suppliers that can provide integrated one-piece subassemblies enhance both. The use of such subassemblies has become such a competitive advantage that by the mid-1990s, more than 70 percent of the content of Chrysler Corporation automobiles came from suppliers with these sorts of distinctive competencies. The other large U.S. automakers wanted to do the same, but two sets of *relationship problems* got in the way. The General Motors experience is illustrative.

The first obstacle was GM's relationship with its union. That relationship had been mutually adversarial for decades. The deep enmity surfaced with the issue of outsourced subassemblies, which was viewed in zero-sum terms. Outsourcing meant less work for GM assembly-line workers. The union fought subassembly outsourcing, and GM's competitive position suffered as a result. Due to their antagonistic relationship, both parties lost an opportunity for mutual gain. If GM made a better luxury car, it gained market share over rivals such as Ford, Mercedes-Benz, Lexus, and Audi. This would mean more work for union members and higher stock prices for shareholders. In highly demanding markets, *if a supplier can do a better job, but the union-management relationship precludes outsourcing, then neither union nor management reaps the benefits.*

The second obstacle was, according to the industry press, GM's relationship with suppliers. GM was one of the largest purchasers in the world. This purchase volume gave the company immense power to dictate terms to suppliers. According to suppliers, the GM approach was to bludgeon suppliers into selling components to GM at the lowest possible profit margin. Wielding that power gave GM some short-term savings, but produced a relationship that hurt GM in other ways. Some suppliers reported having so much resentment toward GM that they made innovations available to competitors before they would offer them to GM. And if parts were in short supply or there was a batch with marginal quality, GM's competitors got preferential treatment. At best, these angry suppliers would do nothing "extra" to help GM be successful beyond what was written in the purchase contract. Its *use* of power put GM at a competitive disadvantage.

The lesson from this is that new-era buying and selling require new-era relationships between businesses.

Value-Chain Partnerships

Companies need to be *partners* if the value chain is going to be stable and highly integrated. They won't be able to achieve the same competitive advantage if they're simply engaged in temporary market transactions because they won't be able to sustain system-level continuous improvement. Being partners is very different from being conventional buyers and sellers. Partners feel like they're members of a common ingroup. This gives them a sense of identity and a common purpose, as well as *commonwealth interests*. The rival value chain is viewed as an outgroup, which cements the alliance of the partners.

Partnered companies need to deal with each other in ways that preserve the sense of partnership. You want your suppliers to have a primary loyalty to you. But you can't expect such loyalty if supply contracts are put out for competitive bidding as soon as they expire. If that's your way of doing business, then you need to be aware of the message you're communicating—intended or not. You're signaling that you have no loyalty to your current supplier.

More specifically, your solicitation of bids announces that you're indifferent as to which company is your supplier: all you care about is the lowest price. Even if you *say* you value long-term relationships with suppliers, the *process* you choose says something different: it says there's no loyalty. It also says the relationship is adversarial. If your objective is to get the lowest price for yourself, you intend to minimize the profits of your supplier. That's an adversarial I-win-you-lose situation. An alternative approach is for partners to achieve cost reductions through systemwide continuous improvement.

You want customer loyalty as well as supplier loyalty. So you need to be aware that the process you use in selling may harm relationships downstream in the value chain. Suppose you have something scarce to sell, such as the first production batches of a new-generation computer chip. The computer manufacturers all want to get these chips first, because the new technology will give them a temporary competitive advantage. They get a lot of free publicity when computer magazines review the new technology in use, and the early adopters tend to be opinion leaders who influence others' purchase decisions.

If you auction off that first batch of new-generation chips, you might gain the most short-term revenue. But you might also destroy the *brand loyalty* of a key long-term customer, who views your selling process as inappropriate in a value-chain partnership. Auctions create an adversarial relationship. They put you in the role of getting every possible dollar from a buyer in a transaction. Your gain is the customer's loss. As a result, *the better you fare in the auction, the more relationship damage.* Even the customer that wins the auction will be angry that you put its supply at risk. And if your auction brings you the highest price the market will bear, this won't be treated with indifference. A market price may not be seen as a *fair* price to charge partners.

The customers who lose the auction are likely to be even more estranged. It's only in the ideal models used by economists that people accept "market outcomes" philosophically. Real people in real situations are not so unemotional. They hold grudges, band together to harm you, and become passive-aggressive when you need them to be cooperative. Value-chain partnering calls for a different way of doing business.

Contracts and Value-Chain Partnerships

Written contracts can harm relationships within value chains more than help them. The role of contracts in Western business has grown over the last fifty years, especially in the United States, so this has become a serious issue for managers to consider.

An agreement exists when the organizations' representatives have made commitments. Sometimes, the agreement is confirmed in writing. But it's never a good thing to confuse the agreement with what ends up written in a contract. Written, legal-style contracts simply add specificity to an agreement.

There are three problems with Western contracts. First, the person who writes the contract is rarely the same person who negotiates the agreement. This can lead to different understandings of what's expected of each party. People who write contracts—attorneys—are trained to be good adversaries and tend to stress rights and penalties. Their approach can undermine the relationship.

A highly specific, written contract may send the wrong signals. Many lawyers assert that you should not trust other people. Instead, you should build "trust" into the contract clauses. Lawyers' advice is based on the assumption that people behave like Economic Man: they'll act "opportunistically"[6] and abandon an agreement if they see a better opportunity. Lawyers write penalty clauses that make breaking the contracts seem less attractive, in terms of self-interest, as though a manager's word means nothing.

Second, the contract tries to anticipate anything that could happen, and specify responses in advance. The problem here is that contingencies are becoming less foreseeable. Technology has been changing at an increasing rate, new competitors can suddenly upset the market, globalization puts business at the mercy of whatever is going on in various countries (and currency markets), and deregulation destabilizes industries in ways that reverberate throughout their value chains. Thus, as business becomes less predictable, it's hard to know in advance what could happen and what would be the best response. The actions required by the contract may not make sense at the time managers have to respond.

For example, imagine that some time ago, your organization had drawn up a long-term office-supply contract that covered typewriters, adding machines, carbon paper, and telegram forms. This commitment to a long-term, high-volume purchase got your company a very low price. But despite the dollar savings, the contract could actually impede the organization from keeping up to date with business technology. The agreement would make more sense if it were a general understanding that this supplier of office products would be the company's first choice in obtaining business-support equipment and materials. A condition of enjoying a privileged value-chain partner role would be that this supplier keep up with advances in office technology, and be proactive in continuously improving your organization's efficiency. This is actually how Japanese businesses would word the same agreement. That's why their contracts are so short.

Third, a preoccupation with the legal contract shapes the way managers think about the relationship between the businesses. It highlights the instrumental value of each business to the other. This leads managers to pay more attention to the *terms of exchange* than to their loyalty bonds as value-chain partners.

This shift in the relationship is hard for most managers to recognize, even though it's easy to appreciate in other contexts. For example, prenuptial marriage contracts simplify the process of subsequently getting divorced. But they also change the relationship between the couple that's about to marry. First, it sends the message that at least one of the parties isn't taking the vow "until death do us part" very seriously. This reduces the strength of *the other's* commitment. Also, by emphasizing their rights as individuals, the prenuptial contract deemphasizes their identity as a couple. Finally, specifying all the things that can go wrong, and what will happen in each case, keeps the parties at a wary distance from each other. Why would you let yourself become too close if there's a significant probability that your spouse will abandon you? And so it is with highly specific business contracts.

Because of these problems, a comprehensive written contract is necessary *only* if the relationship is bad. It serves as a substitute for trust and goodwill—but it's not a *good* substitute. Managers would be better off fixing the relationship.

Coordination within Value-Chain Partnerships

Ultimately, competitive advantage comes from creating superior value for customers. Value is a combination of product (or service) features, quality, and price. Marketing specialists do their research on customer needs and expectations, then establish a "price point" for a particular target market. Let's say the product is an automobile and the price point is $20,000. From this starting point, suppliers have to come up with component specifications and prices that will allow the total product to be sold for no more than $20,000. But new-era assemblers don't go out and shop for the low-price supplier, as they did in previous decades: they draw suppliers into joint problem solving.

The component suppliers need to work with the assembler—and with one another—to wring costs out of manufacturing. Suppliers may recommend design changes, or even major changes in product specifications. Suppliers can also be very helpful with benchmarking.[7] They've seen the innovations other manufacturers have used to improve quality and efficiency, and often can make useful suggestions. Assemblers working alone may not know where to look for improvements: outsiders can offer a fresh perspective. For example, when Motorola was redesigning its production lines, it investigated the "industry best practices" of Pink Floyd, the rock band. Pink Floyd was noted for the speed at which it could set up and break down elaborate stage sets as the band traveled from one engagement to the next.[8] There were potential lessons to be learned about making production lines more flexible while minimizing efficiency losses. But Motorola managers had to "think outside the box" to realize they had something to learn from an industry they were unfamiliar with.

Outsiders can help a lot—but they'll do so only if the relationship induces them to make a broad contribution. To be competitive at the value-chain level, suppliers have to collaborate to achieve cost and quality targets. The collaboration may extend as far as stationing workers in the assembler's factories, and possibly the factories of second-tier suppliers. Intermingling employees from different stages in the value chain is one of the best ways to improve design-for-manufacturability-and-assembly (DFMA). If you can see how your components are handled at the next step in the value chain, you can see where improvements would be helpful. Intermingling of employees also gets a new set of eyes looking at problems. But perhaps most importantly, intermingling breaks down the barriers that are normally present at each organization's boundary. In anthropological terms, mingling of employees can give everyone a sense of ingroup membership. In strategic terms, mingling helps create an *integrated* value chain.

Locating a supplier's plant close to the assembly plant produces economic advantages even when there's an arm's-length buyer-seller relationship. Geographical closeness reduces transportation costs. It also eases the coordination problems inherent in just-in-time delivery systems because it's easy to take care of a rush order if you only have to deliver next door. But collocation offers greater benefits in terms of value-chain integration: it makes it natural for workers and managers from the different companies to get together and work on system-level improvements. Now, no supplier would uproot itself and relocate next to an assembly plant unless it had a special relationship with the assembler. The relationship isn't special if the assembler solicits a new round of competitive bids each time the contract expires.

The deep ties we're describing suggest that integration of value-chain partnerships is driven more by *agreements* than by the highly specific, written contracts that are prevalent in arm's-length buyer-seller relationships. The agreement isn't simply a purchase order. It's a broad understanding of the contributions expected from each partner.

Transforming Conventional Buyer-Seller Relationships

Imagine that you're a corporate strategist. You want to create an integrated value chain that will take a dominant position in a new market. Ideally, you'd create partner relationships with your suppliers and customers from the outset. But few of us get the opportunity to "start with a clean sheet of paper." Instead, we have to transform something that already exists. So how do you transform arms-length buyer-seller relationships into value-chain partnerships? Here are some of the issues you should consider.

Picking the Right Contact People. If the people doing the buying and selling have adversarial tendencies, they'll approach partners in ways that make it more difficult to develop close ties. The relationship probably won't evolve much beyond the zero-sum struggle that's emphasized in economic models.

Aggressive people are most likely to turn potential value-chain partners into adversaries. This personality type may have been selected for a purchasing position as someone who "takes no nonsense" from suppliers—or, for a sales role, as someone who "knows where to draw the line" in dealing with customers. These appointments reflect an old-paradigm belief that the buying-selling relationship is inherently adversarial and that people need to be aggressive to take care of the organization's interests.

Competitive people are also likely to create adversarial relationships. These people strive to "win" any encounter. They're selected for their competitive spirit, which can be an asset in some situations, but is more likely to be a liability when dealing with value-chain partners. If a competitive negotiator "wins" an encounter with a supplier or client, there may be a short-term profit advantage. But the long-term cost could be much higher if the resulting strain on the relationship threatens the strategic alliance.

The debater is a third personality type whose approach is likely to get in the way. There's a popular misconception that good debaters are good negotiators. But debaters spend their time arguing, rather than strengthening the relationship—to ensure ongoing loyalty, establish trust, and develop the sense of alliance that fosters discovery of new opportunities for mutual gain. The best that an arguer can achieve is to have the other person give in. But you don't want your value chain partners to *give in,* you want them to *join in.*[9] That is, you want them to share your sense of commonwealth and strongly commit to a course of action that benefits the whole value chain—and makes it more effective in competing against rival value chains.

Is Accountability Helping or Hurting? It has become fashionable to "hold people accountable" for the effectiveness of their work. A preoccupation with measuring what individuals do leads us to focus on what's easily measurable, which may be different from what's important.

Let's look at sales or purchasing, the contact points between value-chain partners. What's easily measurable is price—how much money the purchasing agent saved, or the sales representative was able to wring out of a customer. What can't be measured as easily—but is of greater strategic importance—is the robustness of the ongoing relationship. Thus, we have to check whether the monitoring and reward systems are inducing our sales representatives and purchasing agents to optimize transactions at the expense of the relationship.

The tendency for accountability systems to induce adversarial tactics is greatest when performance is below expectations. Here's the scenario. A U.S. company has a tough quarter, due to factors beyond its control—let's say it's due to bad weather, a depressed market, and the rollout of a new product line by its major competitor. The company's stock price takes a dip as a result of the bad news. Because they're held accountable for short-term results, high-level managers take immediate steps to reduce costs. The easiest target for cost reduction is outside purchases. So the purchasing department is told to slash costs. If the company is very large and has a lot of power over its suppliers, purchasing agents can force them to accept lower margins.

But they can't do so without harming the relationship. Holding a gun to the heads of suppliers creates resentment and erodes loyalty. This is a bad outcome. You want the supplier to be highly motivated to *work jointly* with the company to improve long-term profitability and market share. But gun-to-the-head tactics make the supplier highly motivated to *reduce its dependency* on the company. So it starts courting other customers, offering them the same benefits that had previously been conferred only on its value-chain partner. In this way, the shortsighted cost cutting of the dominant organization erodes the cohesion of the integrated value-chain, which loses competitive advantage as a result.

Dealing with a Bad History. Past events can haunt a current relationship. Suppose, for example, that two businesses had got into a serious disagreement in previous years, and instead of resolving the problem themselves, the managers turned the dispute over to their attorneys. Litigation usually leaves deep scars. The damage is done when attorneys treat lawsuits as single transactions in which each party says and does whatever it takes to win. The attorneys move on to other disputes, but the managers are stuck with a badly strained relationship.

Two approaches to dealing with a bad history will minimize its effect on the current relationship. The first is to try to *repair the strained relationship*. Sometimes managers accomplish this by identifying an external cause. Blaming the lawyers is a common tactic—and is often justified. The manager can say, "The process got away from me and our lawyer did some things I never would have done." This tactic is effective when it draws both parties together with lawyers as the common enemy. The managers come to feel like an ingroup with the law profession as the outgroup.

The blame-the-lawyer tactic also alleviates the dissonance problem. It's hard to remember that the other manager is a value chain *partner* if he or she is putting you through an ordeal in court. But if it's the other manager's *lawyer* who's causing the hassle, there's much less dissonance. Now, in reality, the lawyer is simply the manager's agent, so that the manager is responsible for everything the lawyer says or does. But psychologically, if you experience the lawyer rather than the other manager as the oppressor, then it's easier to restore the relationship with that manager. It's a form of scapegoating.

The second approach is to *appoint a new contact person*. Let's say that a particular sales representative or purchasing agent has developed a bad relationship with a value-chain partner. It may be wise to appoint someone else to deal with that buyer or supplier. People's responsibilities get shifted around routinely, so there's little loss of face if a manager's job responsibilities change.

Of course, not all relationships can be changed, even if all the healing tactics we discussed in Chapter 2 are applied. If past interactions have been *really* bad, lingering anger and resentment will make it difficult to transform an adversarial relationship into a partnership. Once a company becomes seen as a hostile outgroup, it may take years to alter perceptions. When there's a strong revenge motive, each point of contact may be treated as a chance to "even the score" rather than an opportunity to fix a strained relationship for mutual benefit. Thus, it's better to avoid damaging relationships in the first place.

Cementing the Alliance. The approaches we've discussed thus far bring us to a turning point in the relationship, as it moves from adversarial buyer-seller dynamics toward a true value-chain partnership. The first step was fixing whatever made the relationship seem adversarial. The second step was making it easier to manage the boundaries between companies by appointing a new contact person. Now it's time to change interaction patterns so that the extended enterprise increasingly functions as a unified entity.

The most obvious thing you can do is to involve value-chain partners as though they were members of your own organization. Imagine that your company were vertically integrated so as to encompass the whole value chain. (In other words, suppose your company owned all its suppliers as well as the companies further downstream in the value chain.) If all these people were employees of your company, shouldn't they all be participating in meetings where they could make a useful contribution? This way of thinking gets you past the artificial barriers created by ownership boundaries. For example, if decisions about product specifications are dependent on what a second-tier supplier[10] can accomplish, then you ought to have that second-tier supplier at your planning meetings.

Value chain partners should be involved in training programs as well as meetings. It makes sense to have value-chain partners participate in the learning experience along with your own people. This gets everyone "on the same page"—that is, there's a common understanding among the people who must implement new ways of doing things. We should also note that as a side benefit, participation in joint management development facilitates broad-scope relationship building. Managers from partnered organizations interact with each other outside of their organizational roles. This fosters the formation of the deeper bonds.

Another useful approach to overcoming the impediments created by organizational boundaries is to make sure that the interaction takes place at multiple levels. Western businesses tend to delegate company-to-company interactions to specialists. Organizational theorists call them "boundary spanners." Thus, sales representatives and purchasing agents handle most of the interactions between companies. Company executives perform some ceremonial liaison roles, and official statements are made by company spokespersons. But value-chain partners need to coordinate at other organizational levels: engineer to engineer, production manager to production manager, and worker to worker.

Dealing with Multiple Loyalties. Before moving on, we should talk about how to deal with conflicting loyalty demands. The problem arises, for example, when a company is a supplier to several value chains. The relationship strain arises because integrated value chains operate on the basis of loyalty ties. Each is a kind of ingroup, squared off against a rival. This competitive stance encourages the kind of thinking that classifies people and organizations as either allies or enemies. As in war, others who profess to be neutrals are looked upon with great suspicion, and are monitored carefully to detect any sign that they might be helping the enemy.

The sense of being embattled makes it difficult for customers to be open and forthright with neutral suppliers, because without the loyalty bond, there's a risk that the supplier will pass on information to a competitor. But if the customer withholds information, it's harder to be effective in meeting the customer's needs. The supplier is stuck in the old mode of fulfilling orders to specifications, even if this means they're delivering less value than they could if they knew more.

Despite the lost opportunities, the neutral role—treating rivals equally—is the safest one. It's helpful to have different contact people calling on each rival, and better still if different client-service groups can be assigned to each. That way, loyalty is less questionable. Consultants operate this way. They have nondisclosure agreements with all of their clients, and often won't even discuss who their clients are.

STRATEGIC ALLIANCES

A strategic alliance makes sense when each organization has a distinctive competency that, when combined with the other's, produces a joint competitive advantage. One organization may be great at design and manufacturing, for example, and the other at marketing and distribution. These allies need to closely coordinate their actions, which requires that each give up a little autonomy in order to achieve advantages through commonwealth efforts.

In practice, managers are less aware of the relationship between the organizations than their relationship with one or more *individuals* from the other company. So *the success of the strategic alliance may depend on who's interacting with whom.* The old-paradigm approach prescribed interactions by creating roles and standard operating procedures. New-era managers try to encourage consensual interactions by fostering collaborative relationships.

A strategic alliance is more likely to succeed if it has *champions* in each organization. Appointing the right champion involves finding and empowering a manager who really cares about the joint effort. Usually several managers will be sufficiently interested, but not all of them will be equally good as champions. The best champion will have persuasive abilities and a network of internal relationships that will facilitate getting the program implemented. He or she will foster relationship formation at all levels of the organization.

For the strategic alliance to work, relationships at the top management level must be aligned. The allying companies may formerly have been competitors or they may have been in a traditional, arm's-length buyer-supplier relationship. Top managers need to act in a way that signals that this relationship has changed. Otherwise, people below them will carry on acting as though the other organization is an adversary. At the very least, top managers need to proclaim a business *domain* in which the relationship is primarily between partners, rather than between adversaries. Otherwise, the champions interacting at day-to-day operating levels will be hamstrung when trying to mobilize parts of the organization to collaborate with the strategic ally.

We shouldn't underestimate the importance of ceremonial interactions in accomplishing this transition. From an anthropological point of view, ceremonies create, signal, and reinforce relationship changes. The corporate "marriage ceremony" involves a public commitment to the relationship. We know from social psychological research that if someone makes a public commitment, she or he will be more likely to really believe in it and to act in accordance with it. Ceremonial acts or events change the individuals involved.

But ceremonies also have an impact on the broader audience. The marriage ceremony lets the community know that these individuals are no longer available as potential mates—or entertainment partners—for others, and they'll henceforth operate (that is, make decisions, incur debts, and have a social identity) as a couple rather than as individuals. The corporate marriage ceremony sends a similar message.

It's very important to identify who the various audiences are, and what you want them to learn. There will always be an important internal audience. Employees will need to hear clearly that they'd better start collaborating. But the external audiences pose a dilemma. Top management will want to signal to customers that the strategic alliance will do a better job of creating value for them, and to investors that the strategic alliance will decimate the competition. The problem is that these same messages mobilize adversaries. Threatened competitors will try to block the alliance through antitrust litigation and lobbying. Or, they'll learn what strategic advantages the new alliance hopes to generate, then take steps to nullify the advantage. The airline industry today, for example, has everyone offering frequent flyer programs and code-sharing arrangements, with no airline coming out ahead as a result of all this effort and expense.

RELATIONSHIPS BETWEEN INDIVIDUALS AND ORGANIZATIONS

Individuals can experience a range of relationships with organizations. Some of these enhance organizational effectiveness; others undermine it. So these relationships need to be managed well, too. Let's explore three important sets of relationships with organizations: the employee's, the customer's, and the representative's.

Employee-Organization Relationships

We noted earlier that *Homo sapiens* is a social animal, which makes it natural for people to seek out ingroup membership. This means that people will either find a sense of ingroup membership within the organization that employs them, or they'll find it somewhere else. It also means that managers can either reap the benefits of worker identity and commitment, or squander the opportunity and deal with the resulting problems.

It's not surprising that organizations have the power to shape the identities of the individuals who work there. Work is where most people spend the largest proportion of their waking hours. The key to developing a favorable sense of identity is *inclusion*. Managers have to allow employees to feel like they're full members of the organization. But despite the potential benefits of inclusion, Western managers often operate in ways that exclude workers. In the last chapter, we lamented the tendency to segregate employees into castes. This produces a system in which the lower-level workers—those in direct contact with customers and who operate the organization's basic processes—are treated as an outgroup; and who often respond by creating their own ingroup, by forming a union.

We'll see that managers are not being mean when they exclude workers. They're making choices based on old-paradigm thinking. More specifically, they're misapplying economic theories. Let's look at how U.S. organizations construe workers to understand the problem and its consequences.

Rented Labor. Some economic analyses are easier to conduct if you pretend you're paying rent. Suppose, for example, that you own a factory and you've fully paid for the building and land. This doesn't mean that the factory costs you nothing. You're forsaking an income stream by not selling the property and investing the money in treasury bonds, for example. So, for analytical purposes, it's often helpful to pretend you're paying rent. This way of thinking naturally led to the concept of rented labor.

Managers make a mistake when they go from *thinking* of workers' contributions as rented labor to *treating* workers as hired hands being rented by the hour. If you're paying workers an hourly wage and managers a salary, this discrepancy sends an unintended message about inclusion. Workers "hear" that they're not really part of the organization. They're outsiders. Creating distance in the worker-organizational relationship is unhelpful. You need a broad contribution from *all* employees. You want their commitment to show up and work hard, their wisdom and ingenuity in achieving continuous improvement, and their loyalty in helping to fend off competitors.

Now let's be honest. *All* employees—managers and workers alike—have workloads that vary over time. Some days they're really busy, other days they've got some extra time on their hands. So you could make a logical argument for paying everyone a salary, or paying everyone by the hour. What's hard to justify is paying *some* of them a salary and others an hourly wage. People who love to argue can come up with a way of rationalizing this practice, but I've never heard anyone make the case that this form of discrimination makes the organization more effective.

Because Western managers have been paying lower-level workers an hourly wage for decades, they accept it as "the way it is" without thinking about how it affects workers' relationship with the organization. The ingroup is paid a retainer; the outgroup is paid by the hour. The ingroup is trusted to put in a fair day's work for a fair day's pay; the outgroup has to punch a time card so that hours spent in the plant are machine-verified. The ingroup is valued for its overall contributions to the business; the outgroup is valued simply as hired hands (not even whole people!). This compensation practice makes hourly workers feel excluded. They're highly conscious of being treated differently—as a fringe caste. This leads to a strong sense of us-versus-them—in an organization that would be more effective if it functioned as a unified whole.

Not all organizations do this, of course. It's noteworthy that many of today's most highly motivated workers are on salary, even though they're doing the same work that most workers are paid by the hour to do.

Layoffs. The layoff policies in many U.S. organizations also harm the worker-organization relationship because they, too, communicate exclusion rather than inclusion. Thoughtless layoff policies are the result of another misapplication of economic theory.

In some economic analyses, it makes sense to think of a workforce the same way that you think about inventory. But, again, there's a problem if managers *treat* workers as an inventory item—if more are needed, they're acquired; if there are too many, you get rid of the surplus. This impersonal way of dealing with workers can be very costly, yet it's understandable how managers can become so insensitive about disrupting people's lives. We routinely use the term "labor market," as if workers are like any other commodity. In large firms, we even refer to an internal labor market of available workers. Commodity markets are managed by adjusting supply to meet demand.

But *workers are not like any other commodity: they're highly reactive.* Their attitude toward the company makes a huge difference to the organization's efficiency and its ability to adapt to changing circumstances. Job security, in particular, is an extremely important attitude. When managerial policies create low job security, the organization loses competitive advantage.

At the beginning of this chapter, we noted that IBM was able to avoid such workforce trauma throughout its high-performing years. In fact, IBM's relationship with its employees was a major source of competitive advantage. To IBM, workers were about as far from being hired hands as workers can get.

IBM believed it had a commonwealth responsibility to treat its employees as if they were members of the IBM family. That meant that during business downturns, the company needed to do its utmost to preserve their well-being. In practical terms, this meant a no-layoff policy. Without the option of laying off employees, IBM managers got very creative in adjusting the workforce. They developed excellent workforce planning, which enabled them to predict attrition rates with considerable precision. IBM also developed sophisticated job-transfer mechanisms, so workers could easily move from a declining operation to a growing operation.

IBM was able to get through decades of major corporate upheavals without breaking its commitment to provide continuous employment to its workers. Granted, IBM had deep pockets at the time, and therefore could afford to be humane. But to focus on the financial ability to cushion changes misses the point. IBM was able to transform itself during immense technological shifts while preserving the morale and commitment of its workforce. IBM closed down the world's biggest adding machine business, then the world's biggest electric typewriter business, and then completely transformed its computer business, all without a single layoff. What it got back from its workers made it a world-class organization.

This doesn't mean that organizations should *never* lay off workers. This is not realistic in business environments that are becoming more turbulent. Even IBM had to resort to layoffs during the last decade. What it means is that downsizing has to be undertaken in a way that minimizes damage to the relationship between workers and the organization. IBM employees, for example, accepted layoffs as an inevitable business outcome because they were sure IBM had exhausted all the alternatives.

Psychological Contracts. Some scholars believe that employees think about the relationship as if there were a psychological contract in effect. The psychological contract is an informal understanding of mutual expectations. The employee is expected to be on the job when needed, to obey instructions from bosses, and to generally behave in a way that furthers the company's interests. In return, the employee expects to be paid regularly, to be evaluated fairly, and to be offered opportunities for advancement.

Construing the relationship in terms of a psychological contract is of limited usefulness to managers of new-era organizations. Its focus is on fair exchange, ignoring other aspects of relationships. As we noted in Chapter 2, people don't think about fair exchange in their most important relationships. Family members live with unbalanced exchanges of all sorts, especially in raising children, but don't want or need to balance them; this dimension is irrelevant to their relationships as a family. College graduates work 80- to 100-hour weeks for investment banks, consulting companies, and start-ups even though their salaries are fixed. People patronize food co-ops even when they can get equivalent goods for less money at supermarket chains. So the psychological contract doesn't do a good job of explaining the role of commitment and identity, both of which are pivotal factors in relationships between individuals and organizations.

The issue of balanced exchange within a psychological contract is most prominent when there's a problem in the relationship. That is, workers are most concerned with balancing their outcomes with their contributions when managers have denied them a strong identity with the organization. Workers in high-performing organizations don't think about their employer in exchange terms. They think about the organization in terms of their *identity*—where they work is part of who they are. They go to work in the high-performing organization because they're members of an ingroup. And they work hard because ingroup members strive to prevail over out-groups and achieve commonwealth success. There are enough examples of high-performing organizations that this phenomenon can't be written off as a fluke, a cultural anomaly, or something that happens only when the task is intrinsically interesting.

Unless they have a bad case of burnout, most workers crave a job that will elicit their effort and ingenuity. People like to believe in what they're doing, on and off the job, and take pride in doing their best. Don't you?

Customer Loyalty

The organization's relationship with employees isn't the only individual-organization relationship that's important. Organizations also benefit when *customers* have strong identity with the organization.

It's very important to distinguish product or brand loyalty from organizational loyalty. Customers display a loyalty of sorts to a product (or service) when they find something that works for them and establish a buying habit. For example, if you find a hair stylist who can make your hair come out the way you want it to, you're likely to go back to the same salon and ask for the same stylist. In the product sector, if you find a shampoo that seems to work well with your hair texture and body chemistry, you're likely to stick with that product until you have a motive to switch—such as a pattern of "bad hair days." The bond that develops between you and the product is largely utilitarian: the product meets your needs.

Customers display brand loyalty when the product's trademark affects their identity. A Rolex watch, for example, may not keep better time than an inexpensive, high-tech quartz watch, but purchasers may think of themselves as "the type of people who wear a Rolex." They probably care about how other people think of them, and pay a premium for prestige brands in the hope of being envied.

Company loyalty is different still. The individuals feel some sort of bond to the company. This created the competitive advantage of Harley-Davidson motorcycles and Saturn cars in the 1990s. The Harley-Davidson example is the extreme case, given the number of customers who go so far as to *tattoo* the company logo on their bodies (sometimes in really painful places!). Furthermore, many owners are in low-income brackets and must make sacrifices to buy their Harley, which is often the most expensive piece of property they own. Their investment is qualitatively different from that of a Mercedes-Benz buyer who has little appreciation for cars but spends more than he or she really can afford, in order to impress others.

It's also useful to differentiate the company-loyalty motive from responses to economic incentives or convenience advantages. Saturn buyers are repeat purchasers because of inclusion bonds that have formed with the company and the dealer. Buyers are part of the Saturn family. Family bonds tend to be very strong: for example, most people would buy from their own family business before they bought the same product or service from an outsider. Saturn is tapping into this motive structure. In contrast, Ford competed with Saturn using a "customer loyalty program" in the early 1990s by means of a special Visa card. As customers used the card, their accounts earned contributions toward the down payment on a new Ford vehicle. Ford's approach to loyalty focused on economic motivation to stimulate repeat purchases. Ford had to use a different approach because the company didn't have the same relationship with customers that Saturn had achieved, even though Ford products were probably technically superior.

Auto-leasing programs provide a different inducement for repeat purchases. The motive is convenience. If you lease a car, you have to return it to the dealership when the lease is up. That's the time when you're in the market for a new car, and the dealer has you on site, in need of a replacement. It's most convenient for you to lease a new car from that same dealer. Thus, the dealer has a great opportunity to move you into a newer car, or even upscale to a more profitable model.

The leasing and credit card examples show that repeat purchases don't signify that customers are experiencing loyalty toward the organization. The customer may actually be indifferent—or even hostile—to the company, but these feelings may not be strong enough to override the economic or convenience advantages. But companies need true customer loyalty rather than repeat purchases.[11] Loyal customers don't have to be "bought" through incentives, so it's more profitable to serve them. And they're the ones likely to promote the company to other potential customers: the best "sales reps" Saturn has are loyal Saturn customers—because they praise the brand among all their friends and acquaintances.

Individuals Who Represent Organizations

When we think of the relationship with another organization, we picture our relationship with particular individuals. The person with whom we have direct contact *personifies* the organization. Whatever bond develops with that person is experienced as the bond with the organization he or she represents.

As a result, it's very important to choose the right people for customer service roles, and train them well. Thus, if a telecommunications company or other service company wants to improve its relationship with customers, the key thing to improve is how customers are treated when they call in. The person who answers the customer call *is* the company, as far as the customer's concerned. The company can spend all it wants on TV ads promoting a favorable image of the company, but the customer remembers how that representative treated him or her.

This explains the problem the auto companies have in the United States. They spend millions in advertising, lauding quality and product features, but the only interaction the customer has is with the local dealer, an independent business. If the dealer treats the customer miserably, the relationship with the auto company suffers. So the company has to fall back on economic incentives.

Sometimes, companies present a particular individual to their customer audience who personifies the company. Wendy's, a U.S. fast-food chain, features its founder, Dave Thomas, in its TV ads. Thomas comes across as a kind, generous, mellow person. Customers' relationship with Wendy's is being shaped to feel like visiting your favorite uncle's place to get a meal. Ronald McDonald, by contrast, personifies the McDonald's fast-food chain. Ronald is a clown. One way McDonald's generates business is by enticing children to pressure their parents to take them to McDonald's for meals. Thus, the key relationship is between Ronald and children. Other organizational personifiers have been more or less successful. Think about the TV ads you've seen, and how well the person being featured enhances your image of the company. Do you remember Joe Isuzu, the car salesman who told awful lies?

Similarly, employees' relationship with the organization is often deeply overshadowed by their relationship with their boss. This is a problem when bosses are selected for the wrong reasons, as is often the case. Typically, a boss is selected because he or she was a good subordinate. Promoting that person has two shortcomings. First, you take that person away from a task that was being done very well, and it may be hard to find a replacement. Second, *managing* work calls for different skills than *doing* the work: a good subordinate may be a lousy boss.

The personification issue is also an important determinant of the organization's relationship with its union. Typically, the U.S. organization delegates all interactions to an industrial-relations director, who is too often selected for an ability to be tough in adversarial interactions. When no one else from higher management interacts with the union, the relationship with the IR director *is* the union's relationship with the organization. Meanwhile, the union selects a tough negotiator to deal with management, with the result that the union leader personifies the union. When adversarial people are selected for these roles, the union-management relationship will be adversarial, at the expense of both parties.

Relationship Managers

Some companies have created a special liaison role to ensure full coordination with their corporate partners. The relationship manager can serve a very useful role. Suppose a divisional manager in a multidivisional firm decides to sue a customer to resolve a disputed debt. This may put other divisions' business at risk. The divisional manager may be making a good decision as far as his division is concerned, but the costs to other divisions may be enormous. The relationship manager is supposed to have greater breadth of vision. She or he sees the entire business relationship, and may recommend conceding the dispute rather than risking the overall business.

The relationship manager can also be an advocate who represents the interests of the partnered organization. The advocate may be an employee of your own organization or an employee of the partner organization who is collocated on your premises. For example, in manufacturing industries, it's not unusual for key suppliers to locate their personnel on-site, with designated workspace and administrative support supplied by the manufacturer. The person is treated much like any employee—as an ingroup member.

The account manager has a more specialized role—to learn, in depth, the other organization's needs, and to ensure that his or her own organization meets those needs. An appropriate metaphor would be that of the general practitioner (GP) in medicine. The GP knows your medical history, your lifestyle, your idiosyncrasies, and your preferences. The GP does a diagnosis and then arranges to have services performed by appropriate specialists.

In the financial-services industry, this works well for both the service provider and the client. The client may not know what services are actually needed. For example, a growing company may engage a financial-services company to help with an initial public offering (IPO) of stock. This will provide the equity financing needed for expansion. A year or so later, the company may be ready for further financing, but may not know what all the alternatives are and which one is best suited for the business at that stage. Later, the company may be ready to grow by acquisition, and needs the services of mergers and acquisitions (M&A) specialists. The account manager can arrange all of these services, functioning as a consultant as well as a sales representative.

Not everyone is equally appropriate for this role. Certainly expertise is important. In the financal-services industry, we would expect account managers to have deep knowledge of the client's business situation. The account manager also needs a deep knowledge of his or her own company, and power to make things happen. But more important than either of these considerations is the individual's ability to form personal relationships with managers in the client organization. Trust and respect are crucial: if clients are comfortable with the account manager, they'll more easily disclose their true needs.

The relationships formed with the account manager may be more powerful determinants of customer retention than the objective value of the services provided by the organization. Companies realize this when account managers leave one organization to begin working at another, and take all their clients with them. This is enough of a problem that many employment contracts have explicit clauses that preclude this. The customers' motive is to stick with the person they trust and respect. They're loyal to the relationship, not to the supplier organization.

Case Example of the Importance of Organizational Relationships: Japanese Suppliers

Japanese companies' relationships with suppliers are very different from what one finds in Western countries. Premier Japanese companies don't issue requests for bids and buy from the cheapest supplier. Instead, they pick *two* best suppliers for an essential component. A condition of getting the business is that the two help each other. This means sharing trade secrets, opening up your operations for each other's perusal, and coaching each other on the ways you have gained competitive advantage.

Helping your competitor to get better seems bizarre when viewed from an old-paradigm, Western perspective. But it makes strategic sense. Competitive advantage can come from many points within the value chain, so Japanese companies want to ensure that each supplier makes the greatest possible contribution. Just because one supplier is better overall, this doesn't mean that the supplier is better at everything it does. Thus, each supplier has much expertise to offer the other. If both suppliers help each other to do the best possible job, the extended enterprise will prosper and the suppliers will too.

The advantage to the two suppliers goes beyond getting more business due to the commonwealth success of the value chain they're participating in. If they started out as the two best, it won't be long before the two of them widen the gap between them and their next-best competitor. So even though they lose competitive advantage over each other, the two suppliers gain competitive advantage over everyone else in the business.

Concluding Thoughts on Relationships

The effective manager in the new era is a manager of relationships. The old-paradigm approach gives primary attention to planning, organizing, directing, and controlling. The alternative approach involves tying into relationship networks, learning who has a particular distinctive competency, earning trust, building commitment to long-term joint prosperity, forging bonds between people in different organizations, managing the conflicts that strain relationships, learning from others' strengths, building human capital *and* loyalty, and dealing with the relationship challenges that come with diverse workforces and global business.

Managing relationships means influencing how they evolve. Relationships are not static. They change over time as people face challenges together, work though conflicts and other relationship strains, and mature as individuals.

In the next chapter, we'll conclude this discussion of relationships by showing how inattention to relationships has distorted Western knowledge about managing, at the expense of competitive advantage.

NOTES

1. For further details, see Greenhalgh, McKersie, and Gilkey, "Rebalancing the Work Force at IBM: A Case Study of Redeployment and Revitalization," *Organizational Dynamics* 14 (1986): 30–47.
2. See Chapter 5 for further details.
3. See Greenhalgh and Chapman, "Negotiator Relationships: Construct Measurement, and Demonstration of Their Impact on the Process and Outcomes of Business Transactions," *Group Decision and Negotiation* 7 (1998): 465–89.
4. See Mecham, "Airbus Tells Boeing: We'll Build Superjumbo If You Do," *Aviation Week & Space Technology* 141, 19 (Nov. 7, 1994): 37.
5. See Richard A. D'Aveni, *Hypercompetition* (New York: Free Press, 1994).
6. Economists introduced this term to their models so as to make screwing other people sound respectable.
7. The process of benchmarking involves comparing the way your organization does things with industry best practice.
8. Cited in A. L. Velocci, Jr., "Pursuit of Six Sigma Emerges as Industry Trend," *Aviation Week & Space Technology* 149, 20 (Nov. 16, 1998): pp. 52–57.
9. These points are elaborated in Chapters 6 and 7.
10. A second-tier supplier is your supplier's own supplier.
11. According to some studies, it costs several times as much to recruit a new customer as it costs to retain an existing one.

CHAPTER 5

MANAGING OLD ORGANIZATIONS IN THE NEW ERA

Chapter 1 showed the degree of organizational integration a manager needs to achieve to be effective. Relationships are at the very center of the "SPARSE" model (see Figure 1-1) and need to be managed well in order to align all the components of management (strategy, processes, architecture, resources, systems, and empowerment). Chapters 2, 3, and 4 deepened our understanding of relationships involving individuals, groups, and organizations. As a result, we now have the tools to understand relationships and design extended organizations (value chains with multiorganization architecture) that will work well.

The problem is, few managers get to design organizations from scratch. Most work in an organization that's been around for quite some time. So they inherit problems that arose from old ways of thinking.

We'll learn that previous generations of Western managers abandoned the naturally occurring communal organizations that had prospered for centuries, and that had been effective as a result of their inclusion and sense of commonwealth. These were replaced with hierarchical organizations hamstrung by adversarial relationships.

This unfortunate legacy makes modern managers' jobs more difficult. However, by understanding exactly what happened, we can gain insight about how and where to make improvements in these hierarchies. We'll begin with a brief look at the evolution of Western organizations, noting especially the relationships we once had and the relationships that developed as a result of twentieth-century thinking. Then we'll explore the adaptations managers can make to increase the effectiveness of their organizations.

TRADITIONAL ORGANIZATIONS

People have been involved in commercial enterprises for thousands of years. From a sociobiological perspective, *Homo sapiens* is a social animal that relies on relationships for survival and prosperity. This makes us different, say, from leopards, which live their lives alone except during mating. We do things in groups. So it's not surprising that our early ancestors formed communal organizations to increase their success as hunter-gatherers and producers of food, tools, and other goods. Let's look at the form early organizations took.

The Cottage Industry

Most early enterprises were cottage industries, so called because members of the extended family worked out of the family cottage. The organizational form was a network of close relationships rather than a mechanistic system of roles, rules, controls, and workflows. The relationships arose from loyalty bonds and a strong sense of commonwealth. Coordination was easy because communication was instant and their interests were joint and largely indistinguishable. Each person made contributions because these were needed and he or she was in a position to make them.

Now, this doesn't mean that these relationships were conflict-free. To the contrary, every family encounters sibling rivalries, adolescent resistance, marital conflict, mother-in-law problems, disagreements over how money is spent, and all of the other strains of everyday life. But contributors to the cottage industry had a very strong sense of direction, purpose, and common fate that helped them put disagreements into perspective— that is, into the context of an ongoing relationship that was of central importance to them.

There was a division of labor based on each contributor's areas of competency. But they all knew each other's job and would pitch in and help as needed. The adults in the family took a strong role in managing internal relationships, but also maintained relationships with the village community—with customers and suppliers.

When the family was the only supplier to their community, as was often the case in small villages, they had dependent customers and no competition. Yet the family members worked harder than they needed to, turning out the highest-quality product they could achieve, and they left money on the table by not charging the maximum price that the market would bear.

Viewed superficially, their behavior seems economically irrational. They could have made their lives easier, charging more for products that were "good enough." But their performance wasn't irrational because it wasn't motivated by the singular focus on self-interest that's assumed of Economic Man. Rather, it was the result of their role in the community being at the center of their *identity*. For example, if the family business involved weaving, they would see themselves not just as ordinary citizens, but as the community's textile supplier. They would even take on a role-related surname, such as Weaver (or perhaps Webster, or Woolworth).

Identity is a core existential belief. It tells you who you are, how you fit into the world around you, and—most importantly—what your relationship is to people and institutions. Because it's so central to the psyche, identity shapes beliefs, attitudes, and values, which in turn shape behavior. As a result, workers had as strong a relationship to the organization as is possible. A song like "Take This Job and Shove It" would have seemed absurd to anyone working in a cottage industry.

Cottage industries were very effective as business enterprises. Even when judged against modern criteria, they'd be evaluated very positively. The operation was efficient, given the technology available. The workers were highly motivated, with their social identity being inseparable from their work and their organization. In effect, they had a perfect "employee stock ownership plan": each worker prospered if the business prospered, and payroll costs were minimized during lean times. The workers were cross-trained, and more than willing to work beyond their job descriptions as the need arose. They knew what created value for the customer and strove to deliver it. They had a perfect communication and coordination mechanism that facilitated cross-functional collaboration, just-in-time inventory, design-for-manufacturability-and-assembly, continuous improvement, flexible manufacturing, minimization of scrap, and recycling. They also had job security, a system of job sharing, and a responsive flextime system.

Modern executives in large conventional organizations would pay dearly for their businesses to have all these self-sustaining characteristics. Indeed, they pay consulting companies a fortune just to get them a little closer to these ideal states. Ironically, even today, start-up businesses have many of the characteristics of the cottage industries of old. Naive entrepreneurs set them up in the way that has made sense for countless years. These organizations attract good people and bring out their best efforts. They fail much more often than they succeed, but rarely because of problems with the organizational structure. Cash-flow problems and inability to sustain competitive advantage are much more likely to be the cause of their demise.

The Extended Enterprise: A Communal Industry

As the villages grew, cottage industries became less self-sufficient. For centuries, the Weaver family (whom we just used as an example) had been herding and shearing its own sheep on their farm in the north of England, carding and spinning the wool into yarn, weaving it into cloth or blankets, dyeing it to produce the colors customers wanted, and selling it in the village. But the Weaver family wasn't equally good at all these things. They had a distinctive competency in weaving, in the sense that nobody else in the village was as good at this particular skilled trade.

Other families developed distinctive competency in the complementary value-chain functions; therefore it made sense to have a *community-wide* division of labor. So the Weavers outsourced sheepherding to the Shepherd family, who in turn outsourced the shearing to groups of young men who moved from farm to farm. Spinsters were "first-tier suppliers" of yarn to the Weavers. The term spinster—used today to refer to a woman who remains unmarried—originated with women who spent their adult years at the spinning wheel rather than raising a family. Colored yarn came from the Dyer family business. The Dyers obtained yarn from the spinsters, but their craft involved the very messy business of soaking the yarn in tubs of dye. They stomped color into the yarn filaments with their bare feet, sometimes gaining the surname Walker to reflect how they spent their days.

Downstream in the value chain were the Taylors, whose specialty was sewing woven cloth into garments. This called for a set of skills the Weaver family didn't possess, so it made more sense to let the Taylors do the sewing and for the Weavers to concentrate on production of bulk cloth.

The Weavers and Taylors had two channels of distribution available. The direct channel involved goods made to order, and the agreement was made in conversation with the customer. The indirect channel involved the merchants who bought up the surplus fabric and apparel, and sold it in other villages and towns, or to merchants who would export it.

The Weaver family also outsourced many of the functions required to maintain plant and equipment. Smiths worked in metal, Wrights in wood.

So if anything broke on the loom, one of these specialists would be brought in to fix the problem. Thatchers repaired the roof, an important maintenance activity in a cool, rainy climate since a leaking roof could mean water damage to the woven goods. Colliers supplied the coal necessary for heating the cottage so that weavers' fingers weren't too cold and numb to operate the loom. Coal was the only available source of fuel because all the trees had been clear-cut when the land was transformed from forest to fields.

We therefore have, in 1700, a well-organized value chain operating as an extended enterprise. The network of family businesses was held together by communal relationships. People's identity arose not only from what they did for a living, but also how they fit into the value chain. The Weaver family was the principal buyer of yarn from the spinsters and Dyers, but also sold cloth to them. The Weavers supplied fabric to the Taylors, but also bought clothing from them. When special customer requirements arose, the Taylors would set up a meeting with the Weavers, spinsters, and Dyers, with the customer fully participating. Smiths and Wrights would also be in attendance if equipment needed to be altered to accomplish a specialized task. Everyone would collaborate to come up with a product that met the customer's needs.

It's worth emphasizing that *relational bonds, rather than market forces, were the basis on which business was conducted in this extended enterprise.* Customers didn't "shop around" to get the best deal on tailored clothing; they discussed terms at length and came up with a price that was reasonable compensation for the Taylors and fair value to the customer. The Taylors, in turn, didn't invite weavers in nearby villages to bid on the fabric order. They had a long-standing single-source supply arrangement with the local Weaver family and it would have been unthinkable to buy fabric from someone else. The Weavers, in turn, had several spinsters from whom they could buy yarn. The choice of a supplier would usually be based on a particular spinster's need. The spinsters, in turn, would coexist in parallel rather than in competition. They would hand off work during overloads, share information and innovations, and coach one another on technique. The Shepherds were suppliers of meat as well as wool, and were purchasers of clothing, fabric, and support services. Their sheep grazed on the Weavers' five acres of fields in exchange for wool and meat.

The extended organizations of 1700 were very effective business enterprises. Judged against modern criteria, they would be evaluated very positively. The value chain is optimized, given the technology available. A highly motivated family group runs each business, just as we saw during previous centuries. But the system is more effective because tasks are allocated on the basis of distinctive competency—each business is doing only what it does best. The businesses are interconnected through strategic alliances, in complex reciprocal relationships. The alliances operate through negotiated agreements that specify how the businesses should collaborate to create customer value. The businesses remain responsive to the customer because the customer is included as an integral element of the system. This arrangement ensures that the value proposition remains closely aligned with the customer's needs, and that customer loyalty is enduring.

Interestingly, Japanese businesses did not abandon the communal organizational architecture during their Industrial Revolution. They updated it to take advantage of technology and scale. The result is an extended organization—an integrated value chain—known as a *keiretsu*. A *keiretsu* is, in essence, a network of strong relationships. It's a natural communal form. But Western organizations chose a different evolutionary path.

WESTERN ORGANIZATIONS OF THE INDUSTRIAL REVOLUTION

The Industrial Revolution transformed the textile business, as mass production became possible. Steam engines and waterwheels generated power, which was distributed throughout the factory by steel driveshafts that spun all day at a constant speed. In the earlier production process, skilled craft workers had turned out one item at a time. The new process allowed unskilled workers to tend several machines. The machine-tenders' work was supported by a variety of specialized roles—such as materials handling, machine maintenance, and various finishing operations.

The technology of factory production was so efficient that cottage industries couldn't compete. The Weavers closed down the business that had supported the family for generations. They, along with most of their neighbors, went to work in the factories.

Managing the Factory

The factory owners had a problem. They had no experience in coordinating the activities of several hundred workers dispersed throughout the plant, each performing specialized but highly interdependent roles.

In the cottage industry, coordination hadn't been a problem. People took on roles as the need arose. Communication was simple and direct, so workers knew what everyone else was doing and what they needed. These spontaneous feedback mechanisms made the work process self-adjusting, so that the Weaver family was constantly engaged in business process reengineering. And the workers had a strong commonwealth bond that made them highly committed, so they took challenges and setbacks in stride. The factory owners had none of these factors working in their favor.

These early capitalists were, in fact, pioneers. There were no books on organization theory, no management gurus or consulting companies to tell them what to do, and no large-scale industrial organizations to emulate. The two large organizations in existence at the time were the army and the church. The church had basically copied its structure from the army, and so, in turn, did Western factory owners.

Several military principles guided how this factory organization functioned. The first principle was that the organization needed to have a clear chain of command. This meant that every subordinate reported to only one superior. The reporting relationships were crystal clear from the lowest-level employee all the way up to the president.

The second principle was that the pathway of communication needed to follow the chain of command. Subordinates received instructions and information only from their immediate superior. If there was any upward communication from subordinates, it was *to* their superior—and no one else. Thus, if an employee needed to coordinate with a worker from a different department—let's say the other worker was screwing up a previous step in the production process—the employee couldn't simply walk across the aisle and tell the other worker what was wrong. Instead, the employee had to tell her or his own superior, who would tell the other employee's superior, who would in turn tell the worker that there was a problem. This sounds inefficient and rigid until one remembers the military origins of this way of communicating. This principle gave rise to the organizational silos that have been getting in the way of internal coordination ever since (see Figure 3-1).

The third principle is that the span of control should be limited to no more than seven people. In the military, the upper limit of seven subordinates made practical sense under battlefield conditions because communication was made difficult by the noise and smoke of gunpowder. The number seven seemed logical in the factory too, because superiors were supposed to be micromanaging. If you have to *plan* every subordinate's activities in detail, *organize* the department so that each person's role and tasks dovetail nicely with everyone else's, *direct* the workers' activities on a minute-to-minute basis, then seven subordinates would present a full workload for a superior. As factory workforces got large, so as to take advantage of economies of scale, this principle made for very tall organizational structures—with high overhead costs.

The fourth principle involves reporting and control. *Control* involves checking up on subordinates. It's not enough for a supervisor to make clear what subordinates are supposed to do; he or she must compare reports of what subordinates did with what was expected of them.

The hierarchical model is mechanistic, as we've noted before. It views workers as cogs in a machine, and managers as designers, controllers, and operators of their part of it. Machines consist of components that are interchangeable—gears can easily be replaced—and their value lies solely in what they accomplish. Accordingly, it's no surprise that scholars and managers considered workers as simply "one of the factors of production" along with equipment, working capital, raw material, and finished-goods inventory. This view shaped workplace relationships in ways that diminished competitive advantage.

As we look back, we can conclude that the early capitalists showed poor judgment in simply copying the organizational structure of the military. Workers were unmotivated in these structures, and the layers of managers created inefficiencies. Capitalists would have been better off developing a structure directly tailored to their exact needs.

MISAPPLICATION OF ECONOMIC THEORY

Adopting a military-style model wasn't Western capitalists' only mistake. They relied on economic theory as the primary lens through which to view business relationships. Economics focuses on divisive dynamics, particularly competition and self-interest. Industrialists certainly needed to be aware of these dynamics, but they had a much stronger need to know how to foster collaboration and commonwealth.

In earlier chapters we noted that economic thinking led managers to view workers as rented labor and relationships with other organizations as inherently adversarial. That same perspective portrayed self-interest as the essence of human nature. Let's look closely at the impact on organizations of the Economic Man assumption.

Economic Man and Incentive Motivation

The Economic Man thesis posits that people's basic motivation is to maximize utility and minimize disutility. People are viewed as self-interested, calculating, rational decision-makers. Utility Theory has some good uses beyond economists' ideal models: it's a satisfactory explanation, for example, of why you order peas rather than spinach with your dinner: you like peas and you hate spinach. But when you move away from uncomplicated choices, Utility Theory has strong limitations that managers need to be aware of.

Actually, the fact that you're reading this page means there's something wrong with Utility Theory: if the thesis were valid, you'd never have been born. Children, from an economic standpoint, are all cost. At conception, a college-bound son or daughter in the United States has a net present value of minus $100,000—or more. Economists sometimes reason that it's worth investing in children because they'll support you financially in your old age. Don't count on it. Whatever validity this thesis might have had a century ago, it's a myth in most Western societies today. So if couples were really economically rational, they'd put their money in a mutual fund and be very careful about birth control. And Economic Man would become extinct in one generation.

Utility Theory is extremely individualistic, despite the ample evidence that *Homo sapiens* is naturally communal. Utility Theory sees self-interest as the primary motivator, and ignores other motives. But we *know* that workers have motives to maintain relationships at work, to feel included rather than excluded from social groupings, to contribute to the success of an institution that forms part of their identity, and to honor commitments. All of these forms of motivation are outwardly focused—on the individual *in connection* with something or someone—whereas Utility Theory presumes an inward focus.

So imagine the capitalist of 1800 who is scratching his head trying to figure out what to do with the workforce. His workers are visibly depressed, angry, and resentful, and are putting in only minimum effort. The most comfortable explanation—that he must have hired lazy workers—strains credulity: this is the same set of people who not too long ago had enthusiastically worked their fingers to the bone in their cottage industries. This is when the capitalist turned to economists for ideas.

We now know that when worker-organizational relationships are bad, workers ponder whether to put in more effort than the minimum necessary to avoid being fired. Under these conditions, incentive compensation can be used to influence workers' contributions. Not knowing that it would be smarter to fix the bad relationships, industrialists sought to manipulate behavior through incentives. The idea was simple: measure workers' output, and if they produced more than normal, pay them a little extra.

Incentive compensation *seemed* to be effective: output increased. But the industrialist was addressing the symptoms rather than the cause of his productivity problem—a bad relationship with workers. The incentive-compensation system was not a success if we compare its results against what workers *were capable* of producing; in fact, these results usually look good only if we compare them against what disgruntled, alienated workers were previously producing.

Workers, we now know, *can respond to an incentive system in two ways: they can produce more than normal or they can "play games" with the incentive system.* When gaming the incentive system, workers devote their efforts to depressing the standard for what's normal, or find clever ways to give the appearance of greater productivity (such as by skimping on quality). In nineteenth-century factories, their relationship with the capitalist was dismal. It was obvious to them that the capitalist and his managers cared nothing for their well-being. So, in the absence of goodwill, the workers strove to keep the standard low and output high. The adversarial relationship has persisted to this day in many workplaces.

Incentive pay is usually a negative motivational intervention, something to be used only in the context of bad workplace relationships. In a well-run organization, incentive pay could actually be a demotivator because of the meanings workers attribute to incentive pay. Let's see why.

To see the possible negative effects of attributions, think about how your mother would feel if you tipped her for good table service at Thanksgiving dinner. Or how your new spouse would feel if you left a $100 bill on the pillow after a delightful wedding night. Or how your boss would feel if you gave her or him an envelope stuffed with unmarked $20 bills after giving you your promotion. Incentives can actually backfire.

Often, incentives aren't needed at all. Some of the most productive and innovative organizations pay all their workers straight salary. The workers are on the job sixty to eighty hours a week with no time card to punch. They don't consider themselves irrational. They actually enjoy their work. If the company does well and they share in the profits by means of a bonus, they're happy because it reinforces their sense of commonwealth. The bonus communicates inclusion. *Thus, incentives have to be assessed in the context of the relationships in which they're being offered.*

If the employees' relationship with the organization is calculative—which means they'll make contributions only in exchange for compensation—workers and managers will be highly attuned to fairness. They'll look at what they contribute to the organization—the hours, obviously, but also their experience, education, and whatever else they consider of value to the organization. Then they'll look at what they get back as rewards—their paychecks, primarily, but also any status that comes from the job, friendships at work, career opportunity, and whatever else is of value to them. Because it's hard to objectively evaluate whether the rewards are appropriate to their contributions, they'll make comparisons with the obvious rewards and apparent contributions of other employees.

This is where incentive pay gets companies in trouble. People have a natural bias toward overvaluing their own contributions. So any time they see another person getting more, they're predisposed to see it as unfair. Unfairness makes them indignant, and motivates them to do things to rebalance the reward-to-contribution ratios. The most common way to restore equity is to put in less effort (or, if output is closely monitored, cut back on quality). Or, workers may quit, complain, or join a union. In practice, it seldom occurs to people to work harder to earn a pay increase, because they've already judged the system to be unfair.

Incentives can also have adverse effects on business-to-business relationships. The most promising architectural form for the new era is the extended enterprise. This is an integrated value chain in which each business entity is making contributions according to its distinctive competency. It's a communal organization—a strategic alliance of value-chain partners bonded together by commonwealth interests. Yet the tendency for Western managers—particularly Americans—is to tie the organizations together by contracts with clauses specifying penalties and rewards. The contracts induce contributors to focus on self-interest when the success of the extended enterprise depends on everyone focusing on commonwealth interest.

As we noted in Chapter 4, business contracts shape relationships between business partners the same way prenuptial contracts shape relationships between marriage partners. If the contracts communicate distrust and estrangement, they are likely to create these divisive dynamics. You don't want your partners to be weighing the costs and benefits of living up to the commitments they have made; incentive clauses invite them to think this way.

So we see that here, too, the Economic Man assumption—and the business policies and practices that have arisen from a preoccupation with self-interest—have held business back. Compensation is an effective motivation tool only when it increases participants' sense of inclusion—that is, when it's consistent with the relationship you want. This means that group-based pay and profit sharing are likely to be more promising managerial interventions than micromanagement through incentives for individual performance alone. In addition, a sense of commonwealth is likely to create greater competitive advantage for an extended enterprise than the most comprehensive contract clauses. The general point here is that *incentives shape behavior, but they also shape relationships, sometimes in unhelpful ways.*

THE DARK AGES

Throughout the nineteenth century, managers struggled to make their organizations operate effectively. As Western economies made their slow but steady transitions from agriculture to manufacturing, more workers ended up in factories. And more problems arose. In fact, productivity, morale, and working conditions in industry deteriorated to the point that, by all accounts, the nineteenth century truly was the dark ages for workers. It's worth noting some of the developments of this era that haunt us to this day: adversarial union-management relations, restrictive business regulation, and antitrust legislation that impedes strategic alliances. Let's look at each of these developments from a relationship perspective.

The Union Movement

Our managerial ancestors created an adversarial relationship with workers that was so awful that it has lasted to this day. A manager who wants a different relationship with her or his workforce had better understand the problem in some detail.

Military hierarchies were effective because the superior had the power to compel subordinates to do what he said. Soldiers who disobeyed could be punished severely. Officers made a point of doing the flogging—or executing—in front of the other soldiers to make sure that no one missed the lesson.

Managerial hierarchies didn't offer the same degree of coercive power. The greatest punishment managers could inflict was dismissal. If the labor market was fluid, this wasn't much of a punishment: fired employees could find work for the same pay in another local factory. So, to increase their control over workers, managers found ways to make workers highly dependent on their current employer.

First, they developed a blacklisting system. The name of a fired employee was put on the "blacklist," a document that was circulated among managers of different factories in the area. The worker blacklisted by one factory would be denied employment at the other factories. This "benefited" all factories because it had a chilling effect on employee opposition.

Second, factories provided credit and housing to impoverished workers. This made it easy to enforce discipline, because a worker who didn't readily obey faced losing more than a revenue stream: his or her family could be evicted and he or she could be made insolvent. Remember that in the old days, insolvency got you sent to debtors' prison.

This induced dependency also allowed managers to pay wages to their existing workers below market rates. There was nothing illegal about this practice. After all, nobody had *forced* workers to accept factory-owned housing or factory credit.

The result of having the power to minimize wages was that businesses became more profitable and workers became poorer. This dynamic ushered in a particularly grim era in industrial society. People worked long and hard—usually as long as there was enough daylight to see what they were doing. Their only day off was the Sabbath. There was no age limit, so children began working at around age five and spent the rest of their lives in the factory. In effect, dependency turned workers into indentured servants.

Two distinct socioeconomic classes emerged from this system: the power elite (consisting of highly affluent business owners and top managers) and the working poor. The difference in social class became stark, and the term "superior" had an ironic double meaning: bosses were members of the superior class both inside and outside of the factory. This was how the organizational caste system became entrenched (see Figure 3-2).

The power elite also included the people who wrote the laws (because it was only the rich who got educated). Not surprisingly, laws were written—and enforced—in a way that enhanced industrialists' wealth and control. Legislators and industrialists socialized together, intermarried, and took care of each other's interests. Thus, while the rich were getting richer, the working poor were becoming increasingly desperate, giving rise to class consciousness and a smoldering discontent that was to result in concerted opposition to management.

This is the historical context in which labor unions began to form in the industrialized countries. Unions made it hard for management to pay below-market wages, and to single out workers and control them by threatening their livelihoods. Unions made a huge difference in the workers' daily lives, primarily because workers no longer felt quite so helpless. And, as we noted earlier, unions supplied the sense of community lacking in hierarchies.

The beginnings of the union movement placed capitalists at a historical crossroads. Had they been wise, they would have taken steps to heal the strained relationship. They could have reached a truce and made wages, hours, and working conditions less exploitative. They then could have enlisted the union's support in making the factory more humane and more productive. Instead, management fought the unions, using the power of the state as well as their own economic power. The resulting feud left deep scars—particularly mutual distrust—which affects Western labor-management relationships even today.

The Robber Barons

The nineteenth-century industrialists created relationships that workers found intolerable. The industrialists made the same mistakes in dealing with customers. Their simplistic notion of economic wisdom led them to do business in a way that other companies, legislators, and the general public found equally shocking. This time, antitrust legislation was the response. Here's what happened.

A very effective way to maximize wealth is to collude in ways that create a monopoly. Industrialists who did this became known as "robber barons." By eliminating interfirm competition, these industrialists could raise prices to a level just short of motivating customers to substitute another product or service—or do without.

In many cases, the customer could neither do without, nor substitute a different product or service. For example, certain companies were absolutely dependent on outside suppliers for rail transportation, coal or oil, and bulk chemicals to use as raw materials. These were large-scale industries with enormous barriers to entry. So when the robber barons got together to fix prices, the companies that depended on those inputs had little choice but to pay the artificially inflated prices. The robber barons amassed enormous profits—at the expense, ultimately, of the general public.

There wasn't much concern for relationships with customers or the general public during the dark ages. Businesses were supposed to be pursuing their economic interests without violating explicit laws. And that's what they did.

The unfair profiteering during this era was so outrageous that anti-monopoly laws were enacted to preserve market mechanisms. Although badly needed in the days of the robber barons, that same set of laws became an impediment to the formation of strategic relationships between businesses, which can be essential for success in the global markets of the new era.

The Quest for Improved Productivity

As the nineteenth century came to a close, factory productivity was low, employee turnover was high, unions had become entrenched in a "cold war" with managers, workers were doing only what was demanded of them, and customers were disappointed with value-for-money.

In hindsight, the obvious starting point in remedying this dismal state of affairs was to do something to improve the adversarial relationships that had evolved. But turn-of-the-century managers showed no such wisdom. Managers' failure to diagnose the source of the relationship problems is understandable. When they looked around them, they saw that all the other major Western organizations had copied the military hierarchy. And in some cases, there were no better alternatives to hierarchy, such as in manufacturing situations where products are simple and don't evolve, no worker judgment is required, and all controllable factors are easily measured. Even today, plants that fill cans with "classic" Coca-Cola may be best run hierarchically. The classic product recipe hasn't changed much since 1934, and a can of Coke is required to be identical throughout the world. The same is true of McDonald's hamburgers, ammunition for M-16 rifles, and prescription pharmaceuticals.

There weren't many different models in the West to benchmark against. So they kept the existing architecture, accepting the fractionation and relationship strains as unavoidable. To make the best of the situation, they turned to science as a pathway to greater effectiveness.

The idea behind Scientific Management was that there was one best way to do any job, and this could be discovered through scientific analysis, conducted by specialists at the middle-management level. These "efficiency experts" would perform time-and-motion studies and then redesign workers' jobs and develop the optimum standard operating procedures (SOPs). Nobody bothered to ask *the workers* how their jobs could be done better.

Scientific Management produced tangible improvements in the efficiency of hierarchical organizations. But it also caused further estrangement in the relationship with workers. The people who conducted time-and-motion studies were hated. The union denounced production-line changes as "speedups"—changes that brought more profits to management at workers' expense. So workers did everything they could to undermine Scientific Management, from minimal cooperation to sabotage. The cold war continued.

THE CHALLENGES OF THE NEW ERA

The end of the twentieth century brought changes in the environment of business that were difficult for even the most conservative hierarchical managers to ignore. These changes have supplied the impetus to consider new-generation organizational forms. In this section, we'll examine the challenges of the new century and see how the most innovative managers have organized to meet these challenges.

1. The Information Explosion

In conventional hierarchical organizations, the president came up with the strategy and tactics. The president told the vice presidents what they must do to implement the plan. The vice presidents, in turn, established procedures, deadlines, and controls to ensure that their functional divisions did what was expected of them. This process continued cascading down until the first-line supervisors gave specific task instructions to the lowest-level workers, who were supposed to just shut up and do their jobs.

The success of this top-down management process depended on the president knowing what was going on throughout the business and its market. This level of awareness might have been feasible in the nineteenth century, but the information explosion of the late twentieth century swamped company presidents. Decision-making, due to its new complexity, needed to be shared. This alone made top-down hierarchical architecture obsolete.

The president of a modern corporation of any size is basically clueless about what's going on in his or her organization. Anyone with a hat size much larger than size 8 gets into the *Guinness Book of World Records,* so we know that human brain size is finite. As a result, nobody has enough cognitive capacity to take into account all the factors that should be considered in making decisions.

2. Globalization

At the beginning of the twentieth century, the typical U.S. corporation was a domestic business. By 1990, a truly domestic organization of any size had become hard to find. Businesses had flowed across national boundaries and many U.S.-based companies were obtaining components from one country, producing a product in a second country, and selling it on a different continent—perhaps through a three-way strategic alliance involving the host country's government and a local company.

The evolution into these kinds of global, extended organizations made the president's information-overload problem a whole lot worse. Now it was necessary to take into account exchange rates, political risk, transfer pricing, tariff barriers, different legal systems, and different labor and product markets. This further reduced the ability of top managers to make knowledgeable decisions that would cascade down through the company.

Perhaps more important, though, it became less desirable and less politically feasible for organizations to have central control. Expatriate Americans couldn't understand the culture, markets, business systems, and infrastructure in the way a native of the host country could. Nor could they form the kind of working relationships necessary for effective functioning in the host country's business system. Furthermore, host governments, with a growing resentment of "economic colonization," insisted on significant local control of business decisions. Together, these factors have increased the pressure on global businesses to adopt an architecture that comprises multiple structures, each tailored to the local business situation.

The challenge is to manage relationships with the various subsidiary businesses so they'll all contribute to the overall strategy.

3. Technological Changes

Even if hierarchy was suited to an industry at one point in history, times change—or, more precisely, technology changes over time. *In general, as technology has evolved, the relationships inherent in classical hierarchies have become less appropriate.*

Modern technology provides superior mechanisms for communication and control. This eliminates much of the day-to-day work that used to be carried out by hierarchical managers. One reason span of control used to be limited was that a manager could only give instructions to a limited number of subordinates. Now the manager can communicate with thousands of employees dispersed all over the globe through such devices as e-mail, voice mail, and video links. Electronic communication also improves control systems. This eliminates a major responsibility of hierarchical managers—surveillance, assessment, feedback, and corrective action. Instead, sophisticated sensors, bar-code readers, and automatic monitoring systems alert managers when something isn't going according to plan. Technology thereby allows one person to manage a very large number of subordinates.

The management structures that seemed appropriate for one technology (such as hordes of telephone operators who would mechanically connect telephone lines) may not be appropriate for its replacement (electronic switches, which can make thousands of connections per second, serviced by software and hardware specialists). And new technology creates the need for "knowledge workers" who are valued for what they know, not for the specific tasks they perform. They consider themselves associates rather than subordinates, and want support rather than supervision. This calls for a very different manager-worker relationship.

4. Shrinking Product Life Cycles

"Time to market" has become a source of competitive advantage. Time-based competition wasn't seen as important until recent decades. All organizations used to be slow developing new products, because they didn't fully realize the advantages of being fast—for example, establishing early market share, and reaping profits from the price premiums paid by eager early-adopters. The emphasis was on production efficiency, not seizing a first-mover advantage.

Organizational processes slow down to a snail's pace in a siloed organization (see Figure 3-1). They're constrained by hierarchical reporting and delegation relationships. The chain of command ensures that information and decisions only travel up and down *within* each functional area. New products, for example, were designed by middle managers in the Product Development silo. Paperwork was routed from that silo to the next, with approvals being given at every level. Then it went to the next silo. If someone discovered a problem along the way—perhaps a design problem was only discovered when the manufacturing people saw the blueprint—it would have to be sent back to a silo that had already approved it. This approval process took forever, sapping competitive advantage.

5. The Quality Revolution

Quality expectations rose dramatically in the 1980s. This was largely due to the increasing global prominence of Japanese manufacturers, who were guided by a different way of thinking.

Prior to the 1980s, Western managers visualized a price/quality trade-off: if consumers wanted good quality, they had to pay a higher price. Higher quality meant fewer defects, which meant higher costs—because of two assumptions. The first was that a fairly stable proportion of manufactured items would be imperfect. If the standards were set very high, fewer imperfect units could be passed on to customers, and a smaller proportion of the output would earn revenue. Therefore, the net cost was higher when quality standards were higher. The second assumption was that fewer defects required more labor per unit, or more-expensive raw materials and components.

Relationships with customers and workers, rather than production economics, shaped Japanese thinking about quality. If empowered workers did the job right in the first place, they could achieve both high quality *and* lower costs. With high quality, the scrap rate would be negligible, and the yield very high. Thus, by committing themselves to high quality, they might turn out fewer total units—but more sellable units—per hour. Additional efficiencies came from not having to pay inspectors to do the monitoring, or to pay other employees to rework defective products.

Japanese managers sought and fostered loyalty in their relationships with customers. They viewed customers inclusively—as an integral element of their business—and treated them accordingly. It was logical to strive for the highest quality level attainable. Why would you do less for someone you cared about? This relational rationality—commonwealth logic—gave Japanese manufacturers a competitive edge.

Not only did the quality revolution raise the bar on minimum quality, the *concept* of quality evolved. From the beginnings of the Industrial Revolution until the mid-1980s, the ultimate quality standard within hierarchical organizations had been zero defects. This was achieved when every product produced met the minimum acceptable standard. Responsibility for results was assigned to the Quality Control Department, not the production worker. There were four shortcomings to this way of thinking. First, the people who generated quality weren't the ones who controlled it. Second, quality was viewed simply as meeting the minimum standards. Third, products weren't expected to improve as workers learned how to build them better. And fourth, it didn't take into account how consumers assess value. The Japanese didn't encounter these shortcomings because they approached the quality issue from the perspective of *kaizen* (continuous improvement).

The flexible, group-oriented Japanese management structures facilitated continuous improvement, while the classical hierarchies of Western competitors tended to discourage it. Recall that designers of Western organizations had envisioned businesses as "well-oiled machines." Machines are built for specific purposes and need to be reconfigured for different purposes. But continuous improvement means doing things differently every time you find a better way. From this perspective, the decentralized Japanese system for achieving continuous improvement is "out of control." New ways of doing things or new product features violate established standards. In Western businesses, improvements were prohibited until they'd been proposed through the proper channels, decided upon by specialists at the middle-management level (who had less contact with the customer or the production process), and implemented by means of new controls.

Now, obviously, workers can't be given carte blanche to change anything they want, any time they want. Some changes will have an effect beyond the worker making the decision: these need to be coordinated. *But the rate of continuous improvement is immensely higher if every employee views it as part of her or his job,* and management is oriented toward fostering rather than restricting improvements. As we noted in Chapter 1, empowerment needs to be aligned with strategy and systems.

6. Unsustainable Competitive Advantage

Facing only a few domestic competitors, a classical hierarchy could prosper three ways. It could increase its efficiency. It could differentiate its product. Or it could grow large and thereby achieve economies of scale as well as dominate market segments. But changes in the environment of business have made these approaches somewhat obsolete. As a result, competitive advantage may no longer be sustainable.

The biggest problem is that domestic markets have become global markets. So having a conventional hierarchy that has held its ground against domestic competitors is no longer grounds for complacency. It's an open invitation for competitors with superior organizational architecture and better value-chain relationships to enter the market.

Not even large organizational size assures sustainable competitive advantage the way it once did. Large size gives an organization "deep pockets"—the financial resources that are sometimes necessary to enter new markets, to weather recessions in an industry, or to survive a sustained price war. But size can also be a liability, because huge organizations tend to be unmanageable and top-heavy.

ORGANIZATIONS OF THE NEW ERA

There's hope, however. New architectural forms can improve competitive advantage. *The best organizations are those that are flexible, lean, inclusive, and empowering. Their success depends on relationships, not structures, and the key means of coordination is negotiation.* Let's start by looking at what makes a virtual corporation successful.

The Virtual Corporation

Business opportunities arise when markets are poorly served, new technologies become ready for commercial application, or existing businesses are slow to respond. The "virtual corporation," illustrated in Figure 5-1, was designed to take advantage of these opportunities. Let's look at how this organization operates, then we'll see how conventional hierarchies can apply some of the same organizing principles for their own benefit.

The integrator organization—the core of the virtual corporation— *identifies the target opportunities, then negotiates a network of strategic alliances to swiftly capture market share and early profits.* Overhead costs are kept low because the virtual corporation is purposefully lean. Time-to-market is fast because it's unhampered by bureaucratic processes. Its business is dynamic, because the core managers continually improve the resources being assembled.

At the center of the strategic alliance network is the integrator organization itself. This consists of a core group of managers with strategic and day-to-day coordination responsibilities. The core group may be comprised of as few as 12 employees, and even a "large" organization (in terms of sales volume) is likely to have less than 100. They establish the strategy, create optimum architecture by forming the necessary strategic alliances, then coordinate strategy implementation.

The first step in assembling a strategic alliance network is to determine what creates value for customers. This knowledge drives the other deci-

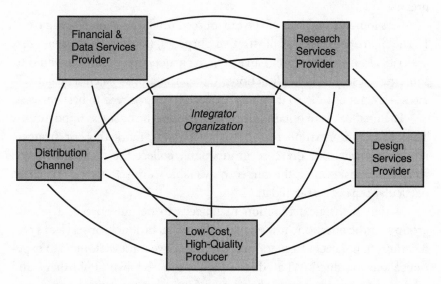

Note: Lines connecting nodes indicate coordination of functions

FIGURE 5-1 Integration of the Virtual Corporation

sions. Then the strategists identify the best combination of suppliers that will create an unbeatable value proposition. Each of the key suppliers must have distinctive competency in its area of contribution. The core managers coordinate the various functions to make sure the outsourced activities are tightly integrated. Their primary task is to ensure alignment of all the elements of the SPARSE organization, as shown in Figure 1-1.

Because there's no hierarchical power to force value-chain partners to comply, core-group managers must *negotiate* all arrangements, and mediate disputes between partners. In other words, their job is to *manage strategic business relationships.* That's how they achieve competitive advantage.

The virtual corporation can adapt very fast. It selects agile suppliers, and can quickly reshuffle suppliers in response to market shifts. Prices can be kept competitively low due to the "sparseness" of this extended enterprise: it's a low-overhead operation that selects lean suppliers and holds inventory carrying costs to the minimum by means of just-in-time deliveries. Its quality is hard to beat because its selection criterion—distinctive competency—presupposes world-class quality. In short, the integrator organization selects the best-in-class to perform every vital organizational function. This is pretty scary to anyone employed by a conventional hierarchical organization. But it's a reality of the new era that all managers must prepare for.

Let's look next at each of the outsourced functions shown in Figure 5-1. The figure assumes, for illustrative purposes, that five functional areas are critical to success. Core managers are particularly attentive when outsourcing these particular functions. Other functions—such as legal services—are not critical, so they don't have to be outsourced to best-in-class.

The first task is to obtain information about the business opportunity. The needed information may be of a technical, marketing, or strategic nature. Managers in the core group don't collect the data themselves; instead, they ask, who is the currently available world-class supplier of this particular type of research data?

Design is the next function that needs to be outsourced. The core group asks the question, how do we create actual product (or service) specifications that meet customers' needs? How do we want customers to experience our product? What does it look and feel like? Publishers and advertising agencies use graphic-design firms to meet their design needs. Similarly, architects supply design services for commercial real-estate developers, software designers supply computer firms, and costume designers supply the latest fashions for the clothing industry. Outsourcing provides the flexibility to constantly shop for the world's best designs as tastes change.

The next functional area, as we move clockwise around Figure 5-1, is manufacturing. Managers make strategic decisions about who will make the products, and where. The integrator organization is seeking value, rather than simply getting lowest price. Value includes high quality, current availability, the flexibility to adjust production volume, time to market, continuous improvement, just-in-time deliveries, contributions to innovation, environmental responsibility, and a willingness to integrate with other participants in the value chain.

Core managers' jobs aren't over, however, when they've selected the best manufacturer. They may have to manage further "upstream" in the value chain. Subassemblies should be produced at the most efficient point in the supply chain. This means that the manufacturer may be better off buying assembled components. Core managers may therefore have to help select and manage second- and third-tier suppliers, and to mediate negotiations between these entities.

The next functional area to be covered is distribution. The idea of using another company's channel of distribution isn't new. This arrangement has been feasible because some organizations like Wal-Mart have nothing *but* a channel of distribution, while manufacturers like Procter & Gamble don't have one of their own. What's different about integrator organizations is how they *manage* their distribution channels. Conventional organizations tend to act as though their job's done when the product has been shipped from the factory. If there's a problem in distribution, it's the distributor's problem, not theirs. But integrator organizations are concerned with the extended enterprise as a whole and focus on creating value for customers. Thus the distributor's problem is also *their* problem.

The finance and data-management functions may also be best performed outside the organization's boundaries. At one time, managers would not have even considered outsourcing financial functions, viewing them as the heart of running a business. But it's just as legitimate to ask why finance—or any other function—*should* be done in-house as it is to ask why a function *shouldn't*. Data management can likewise be outsourced. Technological advances have greatly facilitated this. As one example, the widespread use of bar-code data for work-in-process inventory, finished-goods inventory, shipments in transit, and sales has generated a wealth of data. Given the ease of data transmission, these data can be processed any-where. By anyone. So management information systems can be fully out-sourced, with managers receiving only the summary information needed for forecasting, control, and decision-making.

Coordination of the Virtual Organization. The relationship between the integrator organization and the businesses supplying goods and ser-vices goes beyond simple subcontracting. The core management group functions like an orchestra leader, helping the component businesses to coordinate their activities with *each other.*

For example, research and design need to be closely coordinated. It's obviously important that the research is closely attuned to the applications; it's equally important that the design take full advantage of the available knowledge and technology. Likewise, collaboration between the producers and designers—and often the research group too—must be fostered in order to achieve design-for-manufacturability-and-assembly, which is often a vital source of competitive advantage. This coordination may need to extend out to include second- and third-tier suppliers, who can be a valuable source of innovation. The integrator organization needs to treat them as an essential partner in the extended enterprise. A related coordina-tion task is to integrate the producer with the distributor. The producer, for example, ought to ship manufactured products directly to the point-of-sale, because any product that ends up being held in inventory creates an inefficiency in the system. Finally, the financial and management informa-tion systems need to be tied in to *all* the other system elements so as to ensure progress, coordination, and efficiency.

If the integrator organization has done a good job, each partner in the system will learn to spontaneously coordinate its efforts, innovations, and continuous improvement with other partners. This will create a structure that looks more like a fully integrated network.

The architecture of a virtual corporation consists of a *network of rela-tionships* rather than a structure. The network operates on the basis of col-laborative interdependence, rich communication linkages, and fuzzy boundaries between the roles of the various participants. The architecture is dynamic and adaptive: it constantly adjusts to new constraints and opportu-nities, and gets better with experience. Coordination is accomplished not by hierarchical command-and-control structures, but by constant *negotiation.* The network of relationships is *inclusive,* so it fosters ingroup allegiance.

And, perhaps most important, participants support and improve each other's operations: they're motivated by a sense of *commonwealth.*

WAYS CONVENTIONAL ORGANIZATIONS CAN RESPOND TO THE THREAT

The virtual corporation is the most formidable competitor to face because it assembles the best of every key function in delivering products or services. There are no organizational silos, or entrenched standard operating procedures, or union-management deadlocks to impede its adaptability. It's free to respond quickly to opportunities.

As we lamented earlier, few Western managers get to create a totally new organization. Most managers have to deal with a preexisting organization that has already spent much of its life as some sort of hierarchy. But they can try to incorporate some of the best features of the virtual corporation into the organization they inherited. Let's look at four such adaptations.

The Joint Venture

From time to time, business publications publish lists such as "the world's ten best corporations" or "the country's most admired companies." The corporations that make these lists are usually world-class in *only one* of their functional areas—and in rare cases two. This means that even the best organizations are *less* than world-class in most of what they do.

To compete in the new era, the organization may need to collaborate with one or more complementary organizations. The resulting strategic alliance may take the form of a joint venture. A *joint venture* (a "JV") *makes strategic sense if it can accomplish things that the sponsoring organizations can't do as well if they're acting alone.*

A freestanding joint venture is the ideal type (see Figure 5-2). The sponsoring companies are little more than shareholders. The JV functions "entrepreneurially" as an integrator organization. It may obtain components and services from the sponsoring organizations, but only when doing so increases the JV's competitive advantage.

The figure shows the JV drawing on each sponsoring organization in only one functional area. A is particularly good at distribution, whereas B is

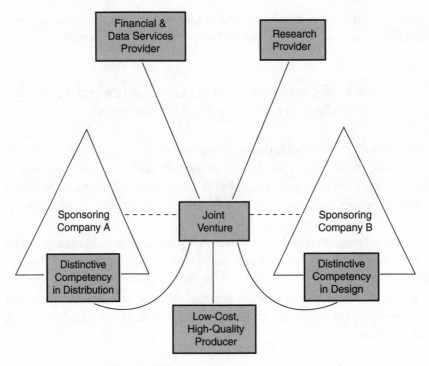

Note: Dotted lines indicate ownership; solid lines indicate source of supply

FIGURE 5-2 The Pure Joint Venture

particularly good at design. Neither sponsoring organization has distinctive competency in the other key areas. So the JV finds best-in-class partners to do the research, manufacture the product, and provide management information and financial services.

This ideal type is a rarity in the West because the sponsoring organizations are usually reluctant to give up control and let the JV operate like a start-up company. Worse, the sponsoring companies often squander their energy arguing over who's going to own 51 percent. The resulting relationship strains may well doom the JV to failure. This is why we avoid the term "parent organizations": custody battles never turn out well for the offspring.

Even if the joint venture isn't torn apart by a custody battle, it can be crippled by accountability pressures within the hierarchical organizations that sponsor it. Suppose, for example, that the JV managers have settled on a strategy of seizing early market share, and have therefore decided to outsource manufacturing so as to achieve rapid time-to-market, low costs, and high quality. Meanwhile, managers within the sponsoring companies are being held accountable for the efficiency of their functional area, so it's rational for them to resist outsourcing. They'll want to spread fixed costs over as large a volume of production as possible, and charge the JV high transfer prices. This wrangling will keep the JV from doing what it needs to do to be successful.

The general point is that a joint venture needs to be viewed as a venture—an independent "start-up" business that needs freedom to pursue its strategic objectives in a way that makes the most business sense. The sponsoring organizations are certainly *potential* suppliers, but they shouldn't be excused from the discipline of the market. If they can present a better value proposition to the JV than outside suppliers, then they ought to get the business. If they can't, they need to improve.

The challenge, obviously, is to be able to manage the difficult relationship issues. The sponsoring organization is both an equity holder and a potential supplier. One role shouldn't be allowed to contaminate the other. If the relationship issues remain unresolved, managing a JV can be a stressful and frustrating task—perhaps a hopeless one. The high rate of failure of Western JVs isn't surprising.

The Empowered Task Force

An empowered task force (shown in Figure 5-3) usually consists of a group of managers from different functional areas. Their task is to pursue a specific strategic objective, and they're empowered to operate "outside the hierarchy" to respond quickly and effectively to whatever opportunity or threat has arisen.

The task force works best when it's given the freedom to act like an integrator organization. It needs to have the flexibility and independence of a "start-up" company. The figure illustrates a situation in which the task force has chosen to use its own organization as a source of research and of financial/data services, and to outsource everything else.

Task force members are usually managerial peers. This arrangement neutralizes hierarchical power. Managers therefore have to negotiate strong agreements with each other. We'll see later in this book that a strong agreement within a task force is one that generates high commitment to the course of action, and is usually the result of an *inclusive* decision process.

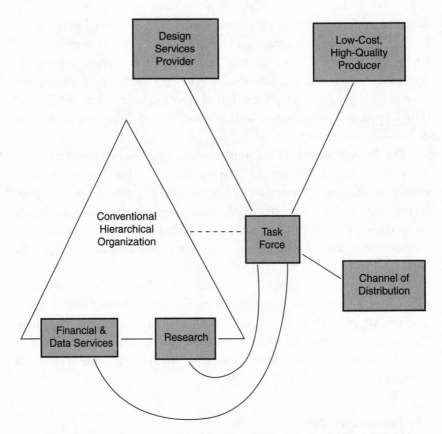

Note: The dotted line indicates a reporting relationship; solid lines indicate outsourcing relationships

FIGURE 5-3 The Empowered Task Force

A striking example of the empowered task force approach was IBM's introduction of the PC. IBM had been the world's premier manufacturer of mainframe computers, which customers leased from IBM. But the market was shifting to miniaturized, "personal computers" that customers would own. This was a new business, in every way, and other manufacturers—notably Apple—had a significant head start. To enter this new competitive arena very quickly, IBM created a task force and freed it from most of the constraints of IBM's traditional way of developing, building, marketing, and distributing computers. As a result, IBM was able to bring a product to market soon enough to establish its market position and become the alternative "standard" to Apple's Macintosh.

The Process-Oriented Organization

Many companies have gained competitive advantage by optimizing processes rather than functional areas (e.g., maximizing production efficiency or minimizing cost of sales). Let's consider an example.

Sometimes, when you get off a plane, you have to rent a car. In the old days, it took you half an hour to get your car because four different people had to carry out independent processes (paperwork, busing, providing a vehicle, and security checks). After extensive process reengineering, the company gave me a number on a plastic card that looks like a credit card. Now all I do is call ahead and give them that number. My number alerts them that I'll be using a particular Visa card, and their computer automatically checks to see whether I'm still solvent on a faculty salary. It also tells them that my own car insurance covers all the supplemental insurance, so they needn't bother to ask, and that I want the most fuel-efficient car available, preferably a nonsmoker's car. I go straight to the courtesy bus. The driver asks me my name, tries bravely to pronounce it, radios ahead that I'm here, and takes me straight to the car. The keys and paperwork are already in it. At the exit gate, the security guard checks my identification and uses a bar-code reader to make sure I have the right car. The whole thing takes five minutes, even on a bad day.

To attribute all of these service-level improvements to technological changes misses an important point. The focus of the rental company's reengineering was on the *process* of renting and how it affects value for customers, and this led them to ask different questions about how technology should be applied.

A focus on processes almost invariably requires a realignment of organizational architecture (recall the sequence in Figure 1-1). Processes usually cut across functions, so the groups that carry out the processes must transcend functional lines. Processes may even cut across organizational lines, such as when suppliers' employees are working alongside employees of an assembler corporation. This means that the role of managers has to change considerably. (See Figure 5-4.)

The first-line supervisors are no longer supervising. Instead, they're supporting the work groups that are carrying out and continuously improving the processes. The primary role of this *support* level of management is to align resources with processes—to provide workers with whatever they need.

The people who used to be middle managers also have a different role. They are now *coordination-level* managers. Their role is to help support-level managers by ensuring that different processes are integrated. They align processes with strategy. For example, in the car rental example we considered earlier, the process of returning a car may be optimized in a way that interferes with the efficiency of the next work group waiting to rent it out. It may be better for the vehicle-preparation work group to have customers drop off the car at a remote location where it's easiest to wash and vacuum the car, refuel it, check it for problems, and leave it in the back parking lot. But it's better, *overall,* if both processes take place in the same location, so that the car is quickly available to be rented again. The coordination level of management also makes decisions about the allocation of scarce resources between processes, something support-level managers couldn't be expected to do.

The next level of management is the *strategic* level. Here, decisions are

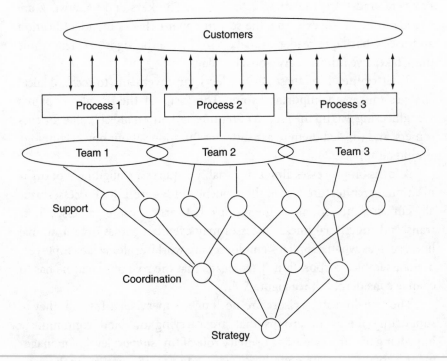

FIGURE 5-4 The Process-Oriented Organization

made that bear on the product line or service delivery system, the markets to be served, the ownership interests, and so on. For example, managers at the coordination level of the auto rental company might think it would be a great idea to rent out sailboats as well as cars, but this is a strategy-level issue. Managers at the strategy level spend most of their time negotiating for strategic consensus and effective strategy implementation.

This organization chart isn't simply a hierarchy drawn upside down. It's qualitatively different.

It's also very flat, with only four levels. From the standpoint of organizational efficiency, flatter is better. You always want a greater proportion of employees doing work that directly produces revenue and a smaller proportion managing them. Of course, management has gone *too far* in flattening an organization when there isn't enough coordination and support.

The Empowered Workforce

Empowerment means that lower-level employees have a voice in decision-making. Voice makes them feel more *included* in a caste system that tends to make them feel excluded. Empowerment runs the gamut from having some input in decision-making—or at least being sure that their suggestions are considered—to operating autonomously as a self-managed work group. *Any* empowerment is an improvement, from a worker's perspective, over conventional hierarchical management practices in which workers are told, not asked.

The value of employee input was demonstrated most dramatically at General Electric—during GE's massive corporate revitalization effort of the 1980s and 1990s. Under CEO Jack Welch, employees were encouraged to participate in open forums, in which anyone was free to question any business practice. The people who were closest to the job, the customer, and the supplier had the most to say. They demonstrated firsthand knowledge of what works, what's wasteful, how to do things better, which practices have outlived their usefulness, and what paperwork and reporting is no longer useful. The "Work Out" program was immensely successful in streamlining GE processes.

Within GE, these gatherings are referred to as "town meetings." This terminology evokes the image of a collaborative *community* trying to overcome the wasteful and obsolete practices that had accumulated over decades. A town meeting changes the relationship between the organization and its employees in positive ways. It's *inclusive,* eliminating some of the caste barriers, and, in so doing, creates a sense of commonwealth.

The gains resulting from corporate town meetings can be striking. The U.S. business press has lauded the success stories of worker suggestions at these meetings. The successes include saving thousands or even millions of dollars; identifying new customers, products, processes, or materials; and eliminating nonessential procedures and departments that had been draining the organization's resources and vitality.

It's striking that these stories are newsworthy. Employee suggestions are a rarity in the United States. It's not that U.S. employees don't have anything to say. The evidence from GE's town meetings shows that employees have a lot of good ideas, and that they're eager to express them. Yet it doesn't normally happen, and the near-absence of employee suggestions is part of the legacy of hierarchical thinking.

Asking for suggestions is the absolute minimum management can do to empower a workforce. Yet when I ask U.S. managers and executives to estimate the frequency of suggestions made by the average employee in their company, most tell me it's at the rate of less than one per year. For comparison, the average employee in some Japanese organizations makes more than a hundred suggestions per year.

This comparison really gets the American managers thinking. None of them believes that Japanese workers are smarter or more resourceful, so they figure something else must be going on. Many attribute the difference to some peculiarity in Japanese culture. The more they think about this, though, the less credible it sounds. Especially when they realize that the same thing happens in some Japanese plants located in the United States, with an all-U.S. workforce. Others assume the Japanese have developed incentive systems that compensate people properly for suggestions. But Japanese workers typically think making suggestions for continuous improvement, greater value for customers, and increased competitive advantage is *part of their job.*

Empowerment programs require considerable training in new middle-management skills, as well as constant top-management involvement, to ensure that the old guard is loosening the reins appropriately. The locus of power shifts from bosses controlling subordinates to peers negotiating working arrangements with each other. The role of upper management is to keep work groups focused on the overall goals, and to mediate conflicts the groups can't resolve through negotiation.

THE LESSONS OF HISTORY

The journey we've taken—from the distant past to the new era—has much to teach us. Organizations have evolved immensely since the days of the traditional industries that flourished before the Industrial Revolution. We can read about today's success stories, or even see them for ourselves, but we have to be very careful what we conclude from our observations.

Some of the evolution of organizations has been positive in terms of increased organizational effectiveness. But organizations are complex, and their effectiveness is determined by multiple factors. As a result, when we see an organization prospering overall, we can't conclude that everything the organization is doing is helpful. Some things may actually be getting in the way, while other factors are compensating for them, resulting in a net positive assessment. We can't learn much if we don't pinpoint what's working and what isn't.

There's no doubt that organizations became more effective in the aftermath of the Industrial Revolution. The biggest gain came from technological advances. Automation makes a big difference. Technology has continued to advance, and is doing so at an increasing pace. It continues to offer productivity gains and other competitive advantages.

Increases in the scale of operations have likewise produced benefits. This is especially true when high fixed costs can be spread, savings can be gained from high-volume purchases, or efficiency can be increased by means of specialization (division of labor), routinization of steps, investment in automation, and so on. At some point, however, the effects of scale are fully exploited, and increasing the scale even further brings no additional advantage.

But effectiveness also results from the way the organization is managed. We've made the case that organizations were, in fact, managed very well prior to the Industrial Revolution, even when judged against modern criteria. They were highly flexible, innovative, adaptive, cooperative, and inclusive; the emphasis on commonwealth drew out the best efforts of workers and value-chain partners; they had low overhead; and they were highly attuned to creating customer value.

We saw that many of these managerial advantages were lost as the Industrial Revolution progressed, because the traditional organization form was replaced by an adaptation of the military hierarchy. During this era, organizations were prosperous, but they prospered *in spite of* the way they were being managed: they were simply benefiting from technological developments and advantages of scale. Efforts to improve them, such as Scientific Management interventions, produced small gains by changing how the tasks were designed and organized. Larger improvements were elusive because managers didn't understand that the hierarchical organizational form—*and the relationships it implied*—inhibited effectiveness. As we get smarter about what it means to manage new-era businesses, further gains are possible.

We're also beginning to benefit from increasing workforce diversity. As business has become more complex, more differentiated, and less stable, organizations need to draw on a broader repertoire of skills. As an obvious example, a U.S. company can't deal with an increasingly diverse domestic market, or with global partners, customers, and competitors, if it has an all-American white-male workforce. Furthermore, women and people from different cultural backgrounds are naturally better at certain managerial roles and functions, so that the workforce homogeneity of past decades is a competitive disadvantage today.

Managers can learn a lesson from modern "start-up" companies. As we noted earlier, these small entrepreneurial ventures have many of the best characteristics of the traditional cottage industry. People work long and hard, doing what needs to be done irrespective of their job descriptions. There's a high degree of coordination, with no constraints on communication. The entrepreneurial organization is a flexible, negotiated order rather than a rigid structure: it needs to be flexible, because it must constantly adapt as it molds itself around opportunities in a dynamic marketplace. The lessons to be drawn from the success and appeal of start-ups lie in asking what's good about these organizations? Why are they able to draw the best efforts out of people?

There's also a lesson to be learned about what *not* to do as these organizations grow. Often, the entrepreneurs move on to found other start-ups. Then old-paradigm managers take over and turn them into hierarchies, extinguishing the communal spirit that made them successful. The once-vibrant start-up becomes just another conventional organization, and sinks into mediocrity.

A Look Ahead . . .

The next two chapters deal with specific relationship-management techniques. Chapter 6 explores negotiation as a means of gaining commitment to a course of action. The chapter is very different from classical discussions of what's involved in effective negotiation in that its central focus is on the relationships involved. You'll see that it matters a great deal who you're negotiating with, and success may be affected more by the kind of relationship you create than by the tactics (such as bidding) that you use. Chapter 7 extends relational negotiation to the group context, explaining how to achieve creative consensus.

CHAPTER 6

MANAGERIAL NEGOTIATION

Managing new-era organizations primarily involves managing relationships. The biggest challenge is dealing with the conflicts that arise in them. People's motivations clash, they misunderstand each other, they get jealous, angry, and disappointed. Sometimes they're simply afraid of the pace of change, and balk at acting. They may become selfish, competitive, or resentful that someone else is calling the shots. All of these things happen among good people with good intentions. Conflict is an inescapable part of all relationships and *negotiating is the principal task in managing relationships*.

We'll use the terms "conflict" and "dispute" interchangeably, to refer to any situations of disagreement. Conflict is present when managers have a difference of opinion, when they don't see eye to eye on what the problem is, or when they want to approach a situation differently. There's conflict when they can't both get all of what they want. It occurs when one of them is going to get more credit, recognition, or reward than the other, or when one has to make a greater sacrifice in their joint endeavor. It occurs when managers err in dealing with each other, and cause the other to feel annoyed, slighted, or frustrated. In sum, conflict arises from the friction of everyday human interaction.

Conflict isn't necessarily bad: in fact, business decisions come out better when there's constructive conflict. The term "Groupthink" has been coined to refer to a decision process that's too consensual.[1] If everyone is overly concerned with agreeing, then decisions won't get the scrutiny they deserve. Conflict can also improve communication when it clears up misunderstandings.

Despite the benefits, conflict is usually viewed negatively. But it's usually *poorly managed disputes* that give conflict a bad name. Conflict is poorly managed when it's expressed—and dealt with—in a way that harms the relationship. For example, psychological distance increases when there's residual anger, loss of social face, or guilt about doing things that have created or worsened the conflict. The relationship suffers even more when one of the parties harbors a grudge—a motive to harm the other.

Managers can deal with conflict either coercively or consensually. The old-paradigm view saw managers suppressing conflict, using the *power* that comes with their position to command, reward, and punish.[2] But power use can cause relationship strains at a time when the need for healing is paramount. Therefore, in new-era organizations, managers need to settle conflicts through *negotiation*.

We'll look at two-party negotiations in this chapter. Then, in Chapter 7, we'll see what other factors need to be added in when the manager is dealing with a group rather than one other person.

What Is Negotiation?

Negotiation is the process of resolving a dispute by achieving mutual agreement. True agreement involves becoming committed to a course of action that meets both parties' needs, to some degree. *Negotiation always takes place in the context of a relationship.*

Negotiation is often confused with arguing. An argument is a contest to determine who's right. It's inherently adversarial because if one person's right, the other's wrong. Argument is very different from persuasion, which results in the other person changing his or her mind. It's instructive that the formal form of argument is debate. In a debate, the objective is to convince *the judge* that you're right and the other person is wrong. There's no pretense that you're trying to convince the other debater.

Many people who end up in business careers love to argue, and believe it's a means of persuasion. It isn't. When you lose an argument, you don't abandon all your prior opinions and adopt the winner's point of view. More often, you give up trying to make yourself understood. You realize that the other person isn't listening to you and that it's pointless to continue trying to get him or her to fully understand and take into account your point of view. You haven't become convinced of anything—other than that you're wasting your time.

In order to simplify the illustrations in this chapter, we'll focus on the two-person case and we'll follow conventional vocabulary by calling the negotiators "parties" rather than "the managers involved." It's a useful shorthand.

OBJECTIVES OF NEGOTIATION

You have three objectives in any negotiation. You need to understand the differences in viewpoint, engage in interdependent decision-making, and build commitment to a joint course of action.

1. Understanding Differences

The parties need to accurately identify what the points of difference are. These aren't always obvious at the outset. The parties may begin by negotiating over one set of issues, only to discover that their interests are actually aligned. Or perhaps there are other issues in dispute that weren't initially apparent.

A starting point in understanding differences is for the negotiators to be able to answer the question "What's this conflict about?" Their answers may not be identical because people's definition of a situation is likely to be idiosyncratic. For example, the buyer of a mountain bike may see an opportunity to have some fun riding with friends; the seller may see an opportunity to get some cash and free up some storage space. The situation is the same—a mountain bike is for sale—but the parties' definition of the situation is very different.

This is not to imply that each party's definition of the situation remains constant throughout their interaction. Indeed, an important aspect of negotiation is modification of your own definition of the situation as well as the other party's. Often, one party's definition of the situation gets in the way of successful negotiation, such as when one party construes the interaction as a game to be won.

Negotiation requires that the parties be able to articulate—at least to themselves—what the specific, tangible issues are that need to be resolved. This condition is important to note, because many disputes don't involve tangible issues. Sometimes the person will say, "Ed just gets on my nerves." Without tangible issues to address, conflicts can't easily be resolved through negotiation.

2. Making Interdependent Decisions

A person makes an *independent* decision when a unilateral course of action will take care of a situation—when no one else has to agree to it. An *interdependent* decision must be aligned with the other party's decision. That's why offers take the form "If you'll do A, I'll do B."

Note that interdependence may be a choice of the negotiators rather than a property of the situation. For example, the situation may allow me to make a unilateral decision but I may figure it's wiser to involve you in a bilateral decision. That is, *the relationship can call for interdependent decision-making when the situation does not.*

3. Building Joint Commitment

The outcome of a negotiation is a commitment by both parties to a joint course of action. Negotiators aren't *forced* to accept an outcome, as in the case of decisions imposed by coercive power. Nor does the conflict become obscured, moot, or resolved, as in the case of conflict resolution. Rather, negotiators stick to the agreement because of the commitment they made.

We'll see that *the process* of negotiation determines whether there's low or high commitment. If people feel pressured, bullied, or deceived, they won't feel bound to honor the agreement. People need to feel they've been treated fairly, fully heard, dealt with honestly, and had an adequate opportunity to express their point of view before they'll be fully committed to the settlement.

THE PHASES OF NEGOTIATION

Negotiation is a complex process, but the various components are easy to understand when they're considered one at a time. Figure 6-1 shows the seven phases of a negotiation. We'll see that most Western negotiators don't follow the sequence, sometimes skip important phases, and overemphasize some phases while neglecting others. This usually makes them less effective than they could be. I'll summarize the seven phases briefly, to give you a "big picture" view of the model. Then we'll explore each phase in detail.

Preparation needs to be done well, and it obviously needs to come first.

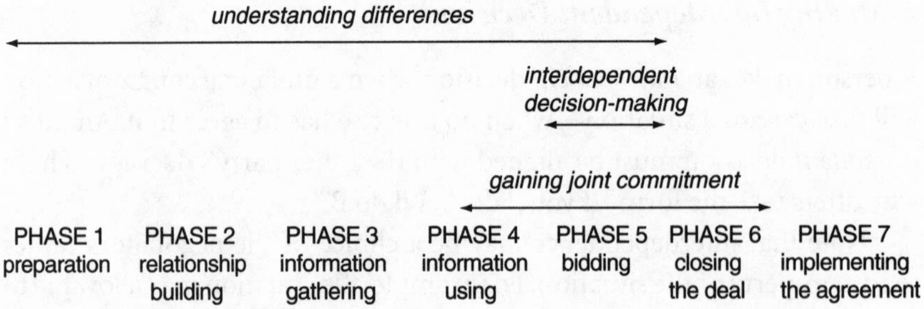

understanding differences

interdependent decision-making

gaining joint commitment

PHASE 1	PHASE 2	PHASE 3	PHASE 4	PHASE 5	PHASE 6	PHASE 7
preparation	relationship building	information gathering	information using	bidding	closing the deal	implementing the agreement

FIGURE 6-1 The Phases of a Negotiation

The manager decides what's important to accomplish and comes up with a tentative plan for how to get there. Some winning-oriented negotiation texts portray preparation as coming up with a strategy for how to get what you want and how to use the threat of walking away as a club to get it. That approach seems inappropriately adversarial for most modern business negotiations, in which managers need to be concerned about the ongoing relationship. Preparation, as envisioned here, involves thinking ahead about the three general objectives we just outlined, studying the situation, and anticipating potential pitfalls.

Relationship building sets the stage for *information gathering*. If a bad relationship has formed, the other party will be hesitant to disclose the information necessary to craft a good settlement. Instead, you'll get no information, or partial information—or worse still, information distorted by "spin" that casts the information in a different light. Your objective, don't forget, is to *understand differences*.

A good relationship is one that puts the other party on the same side of the table as you. We'll see that the sequence of phases is very important to relationship building. If the interaction starts off with adversarial bidding, the relationship will quickly become contentious. It will be difficult to transform the adversarial relationship into something more conducive to solving mutual business problems.

Information gathering is an obvious prerequisite for *information using,* which is the key element in persuading the other party to accept a settlement. You'll be persuasive when you can say, "This is the best way to meet your needs." But you're in no position to do that if you haven't gathered information about the other party's needs.

If you've done a good job with the preceding four phases, the *bidding* phase will be easy. This is the phase in which you discuss alternative out-comes, and mutually decide on one of them. At its best, bidding involves making fine adjustments to a general course of action that'll meet both of your needs. At its worst, bidding is a struggle over who'll make the greater sacrifice to reach a settlement rather than an impasse. Adversarial bidding usually results from screwing up the previous stages. It's unpleasant, stress-ful, and typically leaves the relationship worse off. It's a bad way to approach *interdependent decision-making.*

The close is the phase where you make the other party feel good about the deal. Winning-oriented negotiation texts look upon this phase as lock-ing the other party into a deal that's advantageous to you. You get them to sign a contract, pay you a deposit, or make a public announcement. Then they can't back out when they discover the deal isn't good for them. Good managers don't use that kind of trickery. The ongoing relationship is too important in most business situations. Instead, the closing process is an opportunity to alleviate anxiety about the deal that has just been made. This helps achieve the objective of *building commitment to the agreement.* A good closing process takes surprisingly little effort for the potential benefits it offers.

The final phase is *implementation.* Rarely is a negotiation over and done with when the parties have agreed on terms: the parties now have to actually *do* what they agreed to do. Here, the strength of the agreement—and the impact of the process on the relationship—make a huge difference. If the others feel that the decision was "forced down their throat," for exam-ple, they'll have little enthusiasm for taking the action steps required. Instead, they're likely to drag their feet and be uncooperative when unfore-seen difficulties arise.

I'll explain each of the phases of this seven-step negotiation process in some detail. Then, in Chapter 7, we'll look at how the model needs to be elab-orated when the negotiation involves several parties rather than just two.

Phase 1: Preparation

PHASE 1 preparation	PHASE 2 relationship building	PHASE 3 information gathering	PHASE 4 information using	PHASE 5 bidding	PHASE 6 closing the deal	PHASE 7 implementing the agreement

Typically, people do little preparation for negotiation. Many view it as an interactive process in which they'll figure things out as they proceed. In some negotiations, lack of preparation will hurt them. They'll wish they'd done their research, anticipated the other's viewpoint, tactics, and possible reactions, and developed a tentative strategy. Of course, even in those circumstances, each party needs to be open to learning as the negotiation unfolds.

The degree of preparation that's desirable depends on the negotiation situation. In general, formal negotiations with adversaries require more preparation, whereas negotiations with strong relationship partners require less. But even in the strongest relationships, good preparation can make the process go more smoothly. So let's see how one might prepare for a negotiation, and note how this will change depending on the nature of the negotiation and the strength of the relationship.

There are seven different activities that ought to be components of preparation, which we'll discuss in detail. These are:

- Define the Problem
- Imagine What's Possible
- Develop a Tentative Strategy
- Assess the Emotional Dynamics
- Pick the Setting
- Do your Benchmarking
- Consult your Client

Define the Problem

A key objective in negotiation is to understand the differences that underlie the conflict. Defining the problem involves pinpointing what those differences are. Note that *we only have a problem if our differences are straining the relationship.*

Let's look at different ways negotiators might construe the problem that they're going to negotiate over and how this affects the way in which they prepare.

1. *Disputed facts.* Disputes often involve differences of opinion about what the facts are. An example is a dispute over what has been agreed to. One manager

may believe that a delivery was promised on a particular date; the other may believe that the date was an *estimate* of what was possible, not a guaranteed deadline. Note that the "truth" of the situation cannot easily be ascertained—as it would be, say, if the dispute were over today's spot price of gold.

Reasonable people may disagree on what facts should guide a decision. Preparation, in this sense, involves jointly establishing what's in dispute and gathering factual evidence to deal with the disagreement objectively.

2. *Disagreement about the optimum course of action.* The dispute may not involve contrasting views *of the circumstances,* but rather about what's the best course of action *under the circumstances.* For example, suppose an established airline is beginning to lose market share to a new competitor offering low fares but "no-frills" service on selected routes. Executives of the established airline may agree completely about the facts in the case, but disagree on what ought to be done. One executive might favor starting up its own no-frills subsidiary, another might favor buying out the upstart, and a third might favor increasing its own service level to make the upstart seem even more spartan.

Preparation for this type of negotiation is very different. It involves cataloging the pluses and minuses of your own favored course of action as well as the alternative options. A negotiator will have done a good job of preparing if she or he doesn't encounter any surprises.

3. *Opportunities for gain or sacrifice.* Most negotiations result in getting some of what you want. Typically, you come out better than when you started, but you don't get everything you asked for. Thus, you can focus on what you gain—or what you lose. Your choice will bias your assessment of how well you're doing in the negotiation, and therefore your willingness to make concessions. Therefore, you need to understand this dynamic.

Let's consider an example. Suppose you've received a 10 percent bonus at the end of each of the past three years—during which time your company has been doing very well in the market. Last year, however, the company didn't do very well, and it's now time for you to talk with your boss about the rumor that this year's bonus will be half of last year's. If you frame the negotiation "positively" you'll approach the conversation with the objective of improving on your base salary even in a bad year—and you'll be grateful for a 5 percent bonus. If you frame the negotiation "negatively" you'll approach the negotiation as a struggle to maintain last year's total compensation, and you'll be resentful if you lose 5 percent of your customary bonus. The two negotiations go very differently.

People are subject to many biases like the one we just considered. The biases are patterns in perception (what we notice) and in cognitions (how we think about what we see). If you want to learn more about these, I recommend the various articles and books written by Max Bazerman and his colleagues.[3] For now, you should be aware that these potential biases may distort your thinking. Preparation might therefore involve "thinking out loud" and getting friends and colleagues to critically evaluate your assessment of the negotiation situation.

4. *Dividing a fixed pie.* Negotiators commit the fixed-pie error when they walk into a negotiation assuming that interests are opposite.[3] This creates an adversarial relationship at the outset. In real life, interests are complex. There's rarely a single factor to be considered, such as price. For example, when you're buying a warehouse from a business owner you don't know, price is an issue, but other issues may also be important: when you move in, how the financing will be arranged, and whether you'll keep the forklift trucks that the seller no longer needs.

   Good preparation can be really helpful in counteracting the fixed-pie error. If you assume that interests are opposite, you'll approach the negotiation with an adversarial stance, and it's likely to be a struggle. If, on the other hand, you're open-minded about the possibilities, you might, indeed, discover them. So during the preparation phase it's important to figure out exactly what assumptions you're making.

   Of course, the best way to avoid falling victim to the fixed-pie error is not to think about pies! People trained in economics love this metaphor, but it gets in the way as often as it's helpful in visualizing a negotiation situation. The notion of dividing a pie is powerful because it evokes early memories of fighting with your siblings over who gets the slightly larger piece of a tasty pie. But this metaphor shouldn't dominate your thinking about adults involved in complex relationships.

5. *Solving a mutual problem.* This is a constructive way of framing a negotiation. Remember that the occasion for any negotiation is some sort of relationship strain. The two of you have different interests, different opinions, different ways of going about dealing with an issue, or some other difference. If you construe these differences as a problem that needs to be solved, you're more likely to end up collaborating.

   It's important to remember that two people, viewing the same situation, will have two different definitions of what the problem is. Each person's perspective is somewhat unique, but important to understand. That's why empathy is an important skill for negotiators. You can't be effective unless you have some idea of how the other person sees the situation. Understanding differences is a basic objective in negotiation.

6. *Focusing on the process or the outcome.* Your definition of the problem needs to address whether the negotiation ought to be outcome-focused or process-focused. Let's say the negotiation is over how something that's scarce will be allocated (for example, who'll get the large corner office, who'll get the better deal, or who'll be inconvenienced more): this will be an outcome-focused negotiation. Our stereotype of negotiations assumes that they're *all* outcome-focused. But sometimes they aren't.

   Sometimes people negotiate when the outcome isn't in doubt. Each negotiator has a different perspective, is aware of the constraints and power dynamics in the situation, and knows what will be decided. But they go ahead and negotiate anyway, expressing their diverging points of view. This seems like a waste of time, so why do they do it? They do it because it's important to hear people out. The alternative would be to ignore or silence them, which pretty much assures that they won't buy into the outcome or help implement it.

So, an important preparation task is to define what needs to be accomplished: certain goals will favor a process-focused, rather than an outcome-focused, negotiation.

Imagine What's Possible

It's helpful to visualize a spectrum of possible scenarios for how the negotiation might unfold. Most books assume that the negotiation will center on some sort of bidding process. You're advised to prepare for a negotiation by (1) figuring out what's your best option if you can't reach a negotiated solution, (2) setting limits beyond which you won't agree, and (3) planning an opening bid with supporting arguments about why it's justified. If you do this kind of preparation well, you're likely to have an adversarial negotiation. The two of you will make bids and counterbids, and if you're successful, you'll eventually arrive at a compromise in which you didn't have to give up much. Your preparation will lead you down that adversarial path even if that isn't the best approach.

If you've imagined what's possible, it'll dawn on you that there may be considerable misunderstandings—on both your part and the other party's. Marriage counselors, for example, spend most of their time straightening out misunderstandings before they get to the real differences that need to be resolved. When all the misunderstandings have been cleared up, there often are few real differences. Now think about what this means: if people who live together and know each other intimately can have such a high degree of misunderstanding, imagine the potential for misunderstandings among negotiators who aren't as close!

Thinking narrowly rather than broadly about the possibilities can overlook creative solutions. Consider the case of a purchasing agent haggling over the price of a laptop component. The buyer is under pressure to get a low component price because the company has to hit a particular price point for the new laptop, yet still make a reasonable profit. If the buyer imagines what's possible, rather than being preoccupied with bidding tactics, he or she may discover design revisions that drastically reduce assembly costs. This provides the savings the buyer needs without sacrificing the profit margin the seller would like to maintain. Seeking creative solutions is better than getting into zero-sum (I win/you lose) struggles with suppliers over price.

Another danger of thinking narrowly is that you may be focusing on "shadow issues" (symptoms of the problem) rather than on the real issues. For example, parenthood involves endless negotiations with teenagers. The surface issues are all different, but the real issue for the teenager is autonomy, and the negotiations are about expanding the limits of what they can decide for themselves. The surface issues for the parent are all situational, but the real issue is the anxiety that stems from having strong protective instincts but losing control of the situations teenagers get into. If their negotiations focus on opening bids ("I wanna . . ." and "No way you're gonna . . ."), they may reach livable compromises that provide moderate autonomy for the teenager and a level of anxiety that's within the parents' coping ability. But if, instead, the negotiation focuses on the underlying problem, creative alternatives can emerge, such as "You can go if you keep the cellular phone with you at all times." Just *knowing* the teenager is potentially reachable at any time may allay the anxiety—and the parent may never need to actually call.

Develop a Tentative Strategy

If you've pinpointed the issues in dispute and imagined what's possible, you're ready to develop a strategy for the negotiation. A strategy is a plan that specifies what you're trying to achieve and how you're expecting to achieve it. Let's look at a hypothetical example. Suppose you're a purchasing agent for Microsoft, and your company wants to get a large number of employees to an industry convention in New York City. Let's say that you already have a volume-discount arrangement with Northwest Airlines, but the convention is such an unusual event involving so many employees that it falls outside the structure of the existing discount arrangement. So you're free to shop for a good deal.

You're faced with the same three strategic options that present themselves in any purchasing situation. These are haggling, sweetening, or transforming. Here's what's involved in each strategy:

- *Haggling* is trying to get a lower price while holding specifications constant.

- *Sweetening* is trying to get more value while holding the price constant.

- *Transforming* is coming up with an alternative way to meet your needs.

Maybe you start out haggling. You talk with Northwest, your preferred supplier, and try to get a larger-than-normal discount for such a large number of tickets and plenty of advance notice. If you can't work out a deal with Northwest, maybe you try other airlines that link Seattle with New York. You haggle until you get the lowest price.

Suppose Northwest can't budge on price. For example, they might have a volume-discount deal with the U.S. government that requires Northwest to charge the government the lowest fare that it gives to anyone on a particular route: so there's a problem with a precedent here. So maybe Northwest offers a number of free upgrades to business class, or arranges free bus transportation to and from the airports. The airline will be sweetening the deal by offering greater value at the same price.

Maybe you can get more creative still. Perhaps Northwest will allow you to charter a plane to carry Microsoft employees from Seattle to New York, and back. Chartering is cheaper for the airline because there are no business risks. If some of the savings are passed on to Microsoft, both parties come out ahead.

Assess the Emotional Impact

Disputes can produce strong emotional reactions. This is where good preparation can make a difference. When the other party is likely to be emotionally volatile during the negotiations, your preparation should focus on good ways to introduce the issues. Perhaps the other party tends to be defensive, devoting energy to making excuses for his or her actions rather than solving the problem. If so, some mental rehearsal will make messages "easier to hear." Perhaps the other party risks a loss of face, so your preparation should focus on strategies for minimizing shame and embarrassment. Perhaps there's risk of triggering a broader conflict, in which case preparation may involve a plan for getting agreement from the other person to limit the scope of negotiations at the outset.

Preparation may also focus on your own emotional reactions. If you're aware of your emotional vulnerabilities—particularly things that trigger anger—you can plan to control the *expression* of those emotions. Sometimes, emotions catch us off-guard and we react spontaneously. While such natural behavior is healthy in most circumstances, it can get in the way of some negotiations. With good preparation, you avoid giving in to first reactions.

If you know the negotiation is likely to be emotionally charged and could "get away from you," it's worth planning techniques to suspend the negotiation temporarily. All of us have been involved in negotiations that seem to go from bad to worse, with emotions building in unproductive directions and parties becoming rigid in their stances. So you can make provisions for time-outs before the discussion gets too heated. Perhaps you've warned the other person that you'll have to take a few minutes out to make an important phone call or to consult with your boss. Or simply that you'll need to stop for coffee at some point. Time-outs let emotions cool down so you can start the interaction afresh.

Making the negotiation more public than private is another way to prevent the interaction from becoming emotionally overheated in unproductive ways. People are more restrained when there's an audience. But this runs the risk that the parties will "play to the audience" rather than negotiate in good faith.

All of these emotion-management tactics require forethought. You don't want to frustrate the other person, or suppress emotions that need to be vented. And you certainly don't want to imply that the other person is emotionally unstable and out of control. But with careful planning during the preparation phase, you're better able to orchestrate the appropriate blend of emotional expression and restraint that will allow the negotiation to proceed in a productive direction.

Pick the Setting

How you set up the negotiation can make a huge difference. Suppose your boss has some ideas about where your unit is headed, strategically, but hasn't yet told you that there are issues to be discussed. Consider two alternative scenarios for how the negotiation gets set up.

It's a little after 8 A.M. when you arrive at your office, and the phone is ringing. Your boss's secretary informs you that you're to report to the boss's office, RIGHT NOW. The boss is sitting behind the desk, talking on the phone, and beckons you to sit in the chair in front of the desk. You sit there wondering why you were called in without any notice. You become very nervous, because the company has been undergoing downsizing and many middle managers have lost their jobs. The boss abruptly hangs up the phone and says, "I've been thinking about your unit, and I've come up with a tentative plan. I'd like to hear what you have to say about it." This negotiation would probably start out strained, due to your discomfort and anxiety. You wouldn't be as flexible and open-minded as you normally are.

Alternatively, your boss sees you drive into the parking lot, and waits so that the two of you can walk into the building together. The boss says, "Hey, I've been thinking about where your department is headed, and I have some ideas. I know you've been thinking about it too, so I'd like to hear your ideas. Wanna grab a cup of coffee and chat?"

The two approaches accomplish the same thing—they initiate a negotiation over the business unit's strategy. But they go about it very differently. The first is likely to be an uncomfortable, guarded interaction. Your own ideas and reservations aren't likely to be fully expressed, and you're not likely to become highly committed to whatever course of action is decided upon. It's likely to be a less effective negotiation than the one arising from the second scenario, purely because of the way it was set up—the agreement to meet, the physical setting, and the encouragement to express views openly.

In an office setting, peers are often better off meeting on neutral turf if they wish to avoid territorial undertones. Bosses will want to summon subordinates to their offices if they want to emphasize discipline and power, but they might meet at the subordinate's workstation if they want to minimize the subordinate's anxiety and defensiveness. Subordinates will want to meet in the boss's office when they wish to ingratiate themselves, but over lunch if they want to emphasize rapport.

Sitting behind your desk emphasizes social distance. Sometimes this will be desirable; at other times it'll get in the way. It's good to have alternative furniture available if space permits. Think of settings in which you've been very uncomfortable interacting with others: you'll probably find that the physical arrangements had a significant impact on your comfort level.

Seating arrangements can also have symbolic importance when you're negotiating. If negotiators from one organization are lined up *opposite* their counterparts, this opposition of sides is likely to affect the negotiation process. If you want a problem-solving interaction rather than a contest over who'll come out ahead, being on opposite sides will get in the way. Symbolically, you'll be better off sitting on the same side of the table, squaring off against the problem. When this is awkward, the two negotiating groups can intersperse their members with a similar effect.

Sometimes it's better to conduct a negotiation over a meal. "Breaking bread" together is a ritual of inclusion and tends to affect the relationship in positive ways. It tends to make the other party more cooperative, due to the norm of reciprocity. If I do you a favor, you'll experience some level of impulse to return the favor.

Finally, negotiations between groups are often conducted in physical settings that provide private space in which groups can "caucus." Caucusing occurs when members of a group seclude themselves to review progress and discuss strategy. The practice of caucusing—and providing caucus space—has become so commonplace in Western negotiations that few people question whether it's a good idea. But if a group needs to meet privately, what does this say about the process and the relationship? Doesn't it signal that the negotiation is basically adversarial? If the two groups are committed to collaboration, what do they need to say outside the room that can't be revealed to the other group? One implication of private caucuses is that the group needs to plot against you. That isn't very nice, and it'll strain the relationship between the groups. So during the preparation phase, it makes sense to decide whether providing space—rather than just time—for caucuses will hurt or help.

In sum, there's no one best way to arrange the setting for a negotiation. It really depends on the constraints, what you're trying to accomplish, what the relationship is, and what you want the relationship to become. But details of the setting shouldn't be left to chance.

Do Your Benchmarking

Suppose you're about to graduate from business school and you're negotiating your starting salary at a consulting company. Would you go in without *any* preconceived notions of what you'd like to achieve in the negotiation? Probably not. Instead, you'd study the range of salaries being offered to grads, giving particular attention to how much people made who went to work for consulting companies.

This is called benchmarking, and it's an important aspect of preparation. You're figuring out the terms on which comparable deals were settled. Benchmarking gives you confidence in the goal you're setting for yourself in the negotiation. Otherwise, you may not know when the other party is offering you a bad deal. But it's wise to make sure that other people's outcomes don't blind you to the possibilities of doing something that's out of the ordinary—and much better. Maybe everyone else in the job market is getting salary plus a sign-on bonus, but you can negotiate salary plus stock options—or salary plus tuition reimbursement.

Consult Your Client

We often negotiate as a *principal*—as an individual with only our own interests at stake. But at other times, we negotiate as an *agent*—on behalf of our constituency, whom we'll refer to as the client.

If you're an agent, it's important to understand your client's underlying interests before you proceed very far. Sometimes the client will ask you to take a particular position, or achieve a specific outcome; this may constrain you in a way that makes it more difficult to achieve a good outcome for the client. There usually are several ways of accomplishing a general objective.

You also need to learn your client's goals and limits. What's the client's ideal settlement? Is it a realistic goal? If not, you may need to do some educating. Unrealistic expectations may leave your client disappointed even if you negotiate a fabulous deal. This is a trap for many professional negotiators, such as investment bankers and real estate agents. They're tempted to present a best-case scenario to increase the probability that they'll get the negotiating assignment. But they also need to prepare the client for the very real possibility that the outcome will be short of the best case.

The client's discontent arises from one of the framing effects we discussed earlier. If the client has been focusing on the best-case scenario, the actual outcome will be judged as a *loss* from what could have been achieved. If the client has been focusing on the worst-case scenario, the outcome will be judged as a *gain*—but it's less likely the negotiator will have been given the assignment. So, whatever has been said to "sell" the engagement, it's important to set realistic expectations before negotiations actually begin. Otherwise the client may reject the settlement.

In addition to managing expectations, it's also important to learn the client's limits. On the buy side of a purchase transaction, there'll obviously be some limits on ability to pay. But the limits may involve timing and form of payment rather than the actual amount: with good preparation, you'll learn this. On the sell side, clients may have specific financial needs, but their limits may also involve what they're willing to guarantee. When people are selling a company, for example, they aren't usually willing to guarantee that every "receivable" (invoice billed to a customer) will be collected in full. Nor would they be willing to guarantee that the company would never be sued for something that had happened in the past. They're more likely to be willing to assume liabilities for known, current risks.

At the preparation stage, you may also want to establish and clarify the terms on which you'll serve as an agent. You'll need a clear understanding of what your fee will be. It may be a flat fee, an hourly rate, a percentage of the value of the transaction, or some incentive structure tied to what the client wants you to achieve in the negotiation. But you may also want to make sure there are some limits on your own potential liability. If there's a lawsuit later because the parties can't agree on something after the transaction is completed, you'd want your client to insulate you from the burden of litigation. Obviously, if you've been grossly negligent or guilty of misrepresentation, you'll have to answer for that. But if you simply acted in good faith as an agent, you won't want to get drawn into protracted lawsuits. So it's better to have an "indemnification" clause in your agent agreement that limits your own risk.

In addition, you'll want to provide for delayed decisions. Suppose you're selling a business and, after working long and hard on the deal, the most promising buyer won't meet the price being asked. The seller takes the property off the market and dismisses you as her or his agent. But over time, people's minds change, as do their circumstances. Perhaps, six months later, the buyer antes up more money or the seller cuts the price, and the deal gets done. You want to be sure that you're compensated fairly for your work that set up the sale. So during preparations for negotiations, you'll want to provide for the possibility of belated agreements.

When you're negotiating as an agent, it's likely that the client will want to attend and perhaps participate in the negotiations. A very important preparation activity will be to reach an understanding of *how* the client will be participating. In general, it's better to have people who're affected by a decision process highly involved in it. This makes them more committed to the decision, which helps immensely when it comes time to implement the agreement. But different people have different views, priorities, ways of doing things, skills, and understandings of the situation. So within the client group, there may be serious divisiveness that needs to be managed. Thus, when you're negotiating as an agent, there may be three negotiations that need to take place: the negotiation with the other party, the negotiation within the client group, and the negotiation between you and your client. It's best if the last two take place primarily in the preparation phase.

If these client negotiations are incomplete when the negotiation begins, or if issues arise as the negotiation unfolds, this is a legitimate occasion for caucusing. But it helps immensely to tell the other party, candidly, why you're meeting privately. You'll want to avoid suspicions that adversarial tactics might be discussed.

Phase 2: Relationship Building

PHASE 1	PHASE 2	PHASE 3	PHASE 4	PHASE 5	PHASE 6	PHASE 7
preparation	relationship building	information gathering	information using	bidding	closing the deal	implementing the agreement

Negotiation always takes place within a relationship. Neither you nor the other party can choose *not* to have a relationship, because in approaching the other party, you assume a role. Suppose, for example, you're approaching a complete stranger to negotiate for a job. You'll begin your relationship assessment by seeing this stranger in the role of hiring manager. You'll add more dimensions to the relationship as the interaction proceeds: for example, you might perceive a person who seems well-to-do, shrewd, married, ethnically similar, and much older. These perceptions will shape the relationship, and the process of modifying your perceptions will continue throughout the negotiation. So it makes a difference what kind of relationship you create at the outset: this is what you'll build *on*.

Each party's view of the relationship is idiosyncratic. The accuracy of your—or the other party's—perceptions is moot. People react to the other party on the basis of what they *perceive*. This is a dynamic process: as more information about the other party is assimilated, the relationship evolves.

Your experience of the relationship determines how you act in the negotiation at any point in time. You'll be assessing, for example, can I trust this person? Do I like him or her? Do we have enough in common that we'll be able to see eye to eye when difficulties arise? What is this person's level of integrity? Can I rely on him or her to implement the agreement? Is this person competing with me—treating this negotiation as a contest?

Because the relationship is so crucial throughout the negotiation, it makes sense to *manage* it. You begin by assessing your own initial impressions. What do you expect *before* you actually meet with the other party? People prepare for negotiations by visualizing the interaction and mentally rehearsing what they might do and say when confronted with the actual situation. You've done it yourself, many times: look at all the rehearsing you did before you asked for your first date. That was a negotiation of sorts. This visualization shapes the relationship. We all have stereotypes of bureaucrats, used-car salesmen, accountants, and anyone else we might have to negotiate with. These impressions form cognitive predispositions—they set us up to experience the relationship a particular way. You need to figure out whether your initial impressions are setting you up for an adversarial encounter.

Because initial impressions are so powerful, there's no such thing as "no relationship," even when the two of you are complete strangers. Consider this scenario. You stop your car on the street next to a used-car lot. A red convertible catches your eye, and you have some time on your hands before your appointment in a nearby office building. You're not planning to buy another car, but you're curious about what the interior looks like, how much space there is, and how much dealers charge for second-hand convertibles. You suddenly become aware that a man has walked out of the showroom, dressed in a bright polyester blazer that doesn't match an equally bright tie, and is striding toward you with a big smile. At this exact moment in time, is it true that you have *no* relationship with this complete stranger?

Most people go on the defensive, poised to counter an aggressive sales pitch from a slick used-car salesman. There's already a relationship of distrust, with strong emotions arising from fear of exploitation or preparation for some form of competition. *Nobody* has yet reported being neutral. This shows how powerful initial impressions can be—and why it's important to both manage the impressions you create on others and be aware of the ones you're forming about the other party. Initial impressions are *assumptions*.

How you dress can have an effect on the relationship. If you arrive overdressed for a negotiation, your formality may create an interpersonal barrier: that is, the other party may perceive that the two of you have little in common—or worse, that you consider yourself superior. If the clothing is severe in its style, it can make you seem uptight and unapproachable, and this may diminish rapport. The general point here is that each of us has several sides—what psychologists call multiple *personas*—and we need to be conscious of which one we're presenting during a negotiation. Some of our sides are harder to relate to than others.

As we saw earlier, the setting can shape the relationship, too. If a high-status person invites you to meet in her or his office, you might be flattered, especially if you're treated as an equal when you get there. If a low-status person makes the same gesture, you'll have a very different reaction. You may even become suspicious and see the invitation as some sort of power play.

Concern for relationships ought to be an important consideration when deciding *who* is present at the negotiation table. For example, if the other party brings an attorney, this will probably have an impact on the relationship. You'll be more guarded, more formal, and more distant, even if the other party tries to assure you that the attorney is only there as a resource to answer technical questions. Attorneys take sides. That's what they get paid to do. It's generally unwise to treat their presence with indifference. You'll usually be better off saying that if the attorney's there simply as a resource to answer technical questions, then the attorney can wait outside until technical questions come up.

Sometimes you'll want to include people in your negotiating group who'll likely have a positive impact *on the relationship* between the parties. In business and political negotiations, the parties often invite very-high-status individuals to attend the opening and closing portions of the negotiations. It tells the other party that they're so important that it's worth the time of the organization's most important people to attend. They'll feel as honored as you would.

The relationship is further shaped during our interactions with the other party, as our earlier views of them prove accurate or inaccurate. The *process* we use to approach negotiation has as much impact as our words. Any aspects of process that might generally be classified as "gamesmanship" probably give us a worse negotiating relationship. Gamesmanship is a contest to assert the upper hand. Some people feel a compulsion to engage in this sort of behavior, but there's no evidence that it leaves them better off. Consider the familiar put-down of deliberately making the other person wait. The objective is to communicate that the other person is relatively unimportant to you, and this supposedly makes the other person more willing to make concessions. It doesn't work that way: offending the other party is more likely to lead to resentful stubbornness than to concessions.

The way you open the negotiation can say a lot about how you construe the relationship. Suppose, for example, that you're a seller and you open the negotiation with a high asking price. Your motive may be to leave a lot of room to make concessions. But the tactic may make you seem an adversary—and you'll probably be treated as one.

Or suppose that you're a purchasing agent and you start off the negotiation process by issuing an invitation to make bids. You're communicating to suppliers that you're indifferent as to who gets your business. Loyalty means nothing to you, nor does past service: you'll give the business to whoever puts the best offer on the table. The implied relationship is purely transactional and instrumental, and has none of the alliance characteristics that bring benefits to value chain partnerships. So, by issuing a request for bids, you may be limiting the relationship that's possible with the supplier before you ever begin face-to-face negotiations. Suppliers may give preferential treatment to alternative buyers who treat them more like partners.

Issuing a draft contract as the first step in negotiation can likewise have a negative effect on the relationship. You may have good intentions. You may wish to streamline the negotiation process by giving the other party a "discussion draft" so as to focus the conversation on the points where you don't agree. But the draft contract can give the impression that you don't intend both parties to have an equal say in shaping the agreement. Many negotiators with competitive personalities like to lead off with a draft contract because they think it gives them "a first-mover advantage." But this approach can hurt the next phase—information gathering.

The general point is that *a poor process during the relationship-building phase will reduce the negotiator's effectiveness in all subsequent phases.* Allow me to reiterate that relationship building isn't a step a negotiator can "skip": the relationship *will* form with or without the negotiator's conscious management of it. In fact, not seeming to care about the relationship is a powerful signaling device in itself. It says that the relationship is purely instrumental, and that the other party can expect to be treated accordingly.

Phase 3: Information Gathering

PHASE 1	PHASE 2	PHASE 3	PHASE 4	PHASE 5	PHASE 6	PHASE 7
preparation	relationship building	information gathering	information using	bidding	closing the deal	implementing the agreement

Negotiation involves information processing by both parties. They consider what they want from the interaction, and what's possible to achieve given the needs, resources, and constraints of the other party. This is the essence of interdependent decision-making, one of the three fundamental objectives of negotiation. If the preparation phase was done well, they'll have gathered some general background information. Now it's time to get specific information, which must come directly from the other party.

The relationship between the parties is likely to have an enormous impact on the ability to gather information. If there's high trust, the other party will feel more comfortable disclosing information, because there'll be less fear of being exploited. If the negotiators like each other, and see each other as allies rather than competitors, they're more likely to be motivated to take care of each other and will pursue joint gain opportunities. In contrast, if there's a narrow-scope role relationship (the sense that "this is strictly business"), communication will be guarded and constrained to a narrow, task-oriented information exchange. If there's a competitive dynamic in the relationship, the parties will be focused on winning, and will withhold information for fear that it could be advantageous to the other party.

The success of information gathering is affected by the process as well as by the relationship. Information gathering is more difficult when negotiators depart from the ideal sequence I've been describing.

Suppose, for example, that a negotiator begins the interaction with an opening bid. By asking a lot, or offering a little, the negotiator initiates an adversarial process early on in the interaction. As the negotiation unfolds, he or she begins to wonder whether the *timing* of the deal may be a source of value to the other party. It's difficult to obtain that information in the context of the adversarial relationship that has developed. The other party will be anxious about how information he or she supplies will be used. That's why it's best to postpone bidding until information gathering is complete.

For the same reasons, starting the negotiation by issuing a draft contract makes information gathering harder. A draft contract is another form of opening bid. But focusing the other party's attention on the contract introduces a new complication. Contracts can put the discussion within the realm of legal wrangling rather than problem solving. The legal realm is concerned with rights, obligations, and penalties. These tend to define and dominate the working relationship between the negotiators. The natural inclination is to begin arguing. That's what you're supposed to do when interacting over legal matters—contest the other party's wording and substitute wording that'll favor you. Legal processes are adversarial by design.

Arguing is incompatible with trying to discover each other's underlying needs. Suppose you're a supplier of furniture to the hotel industry, and a hotel chain has begun negotiations by issuing a draft contract for custom furniture that contains stiff penalties for late deliveries. Your natural response will be to have your lawyer argue with their lawyer about how the contract clause is worded. Lawyers are professional arguers: they're not negotiators. Your lawyer will want to put in restrictions that limit when the penalties apply—such as when there's a natural disaster, when the buyer changes some specifications, when the buyer doesn't give enough advance notice of schedule amendments, and the like. These clause amendments allow the lawyers to earn a living, but they're unlikely to help the negotiations. Arguing is not information gathering. It involves talking, not listening. Your lawyer will never discover that the hotel chain would be willing to buy one of your *existing* furniture lines, which would be cheaper to buy and more profitable to sell because you've already amortized all the development costs. And doing so would make delivery delays unlikely, because you keep a large inventory on hand.

Sometimes it's negotiator personalities—rather than poorly chosen tactics or impaired relationships—that inhibit information gathering. People who are shy or introverted tend to be less comfortable asking for information: it makes them feel awkward. And some individuals are hesitant to probe because privacy was emphasized in their upbringing. In high-privacy cultures (such as British upper classes), social norms discourage revealing information about yourself, and it's considered "nosy" to ask about other people's situation and needs. If you have these predispositions and simply accept them as things you can't change, you'll probably be less effective as a negotiator. You won't learn to distinguish between "prying" into the other party's personal life and asking enough questions to facilitate sound joint decision-making.

Some other individuals are disadvantaged because they can only think of negotiation in zero-sum terms, as a result of having a competitive personality. Competitive people tend to see negotiation as a game to be won. This perspective makes them hesitant to give up information, because they don't want to give the "opponent"[4] an advantage. Because the competitive negotiator is obviously hesitant to give up information, the other party—

following norms of reciprocity—becomes suspicious and guarded, and doesn't give information either.

Furthermore, the competitive negotiator who does happen to get information is likely to distrust it, because false information is part of many competitive games and struggles (such as gambits in chess, feints in football, and diversionary or disinformation tactics in war). Thus, for many reasons, a predisposition to construe a negotiation in competitive terms gets in the way of the information-gathering process. Recall from Chapter 2 that competition is a *negative* relationship dimension.

When distrust seems to be inhibiting information gathering, it may help to *give* a little information in the hope of getting some in return. If you're giving information, you're signaling some degree of trust, which may get the other person to reconsider how exploitative you really are. Taking the first step also sets up pressure to give information, due to the norm of reciprocity: people feel a compulsion to return a favor. Of course, you need to be cautious. If the other person doesn't reveal anything after you've supplied some information, be wary of further disclosure. You might have no choice but to handle the negotiation as an adversarial process.

Why Information Gathering Is So Important

Information gathering is vital in terms of deciding whether an agreement is feasible. Figure 6-2 illustrates the overlap of needs that arises in the classic negotiation situation. If we're analyzing the case of a buyer and a seller negotiating, the circle on the left represents the buyer's constellation of needs; the circle on the right, the seller's. Note that there's some overlap in the two sets of needs. This indicates that the seller has something to offer that the buyer needs, and the buyer has the cash that the seller needs.

Let's look again at why it's wise to follow the ideal sequence. Suppose you want to buy something. If you haven't gathered adequate information about the other party, you'll be in the dark as you begin the bidding process. You won't know whether you're offering much more than the seller was hoping to get, a price so low that the seller is insulted, or something in between.

Failure to gather enough information creates the predicament of the *unaware negotiator.* There are four possible negotiation situations shown in Figure 6-3; they're very different, and they need to be handled differently. If

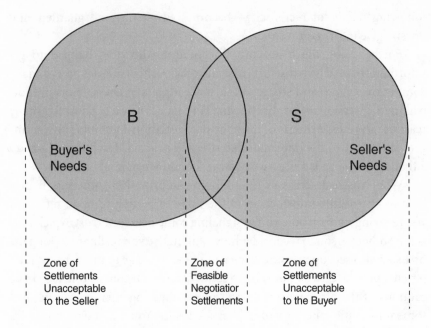

Figure 6-2 Feasible Negotiation Zones as Defined by Respective Needs

you're only aware of your own situation and needs, you're clueless about what the joint situation is and how best to approach it.

We've thus far been discussing a Type II situation in which there's a small overlap of needs. The focus of the negotiation is on how much of each party's needs get met. But you *have* to learn about the other person's needs if you're to approach this interaction effectively.

The Type II situation is the classic negotiation scenario that scholars tend to write about. It's not the most common one we encounter in the real world, but it has been popular among academics because it's an easy one to study in the laboratory. Information gathering involves assessing the feasible range of settlements, the other party's underlying needs, and alternative ways to get these needs met.

If you're a typical manager,[5] the most frequent type of negotiation you'll encounter is the Type I situation. Here, the overlap of needs is enormous. You're trying to work out a joint decision with someone you interact with regularly, either inside or outside the business context. It's important that you decide *something*, and that the process by which you get there doesn't strain the ongoing relationship. In close relationships, information

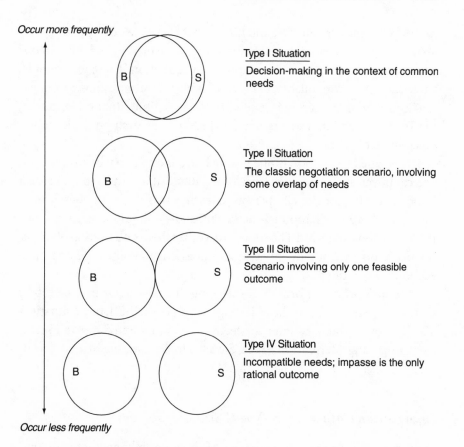

Occur more frequently

Type I Situation

Decision-making in the context of common needs

Type II Situation

The classic negotiation scenario, involving some overlap of needs

Type III Situation

Scenario involving only one feasible outcome

Type IV Situation

Incompatible needs; impasse is the only rational outcome

Occur less frequently

The unaware negotiator's problem

1. Not knowing whether a deal can be struck at all
2. Not knowing whether a deal is a good one or a bad one

FIGURE 6-3 Alternative Negotiation Situations

gathering is often construed as a sign of caring. Imagine a negotiation with your significant other in which you didn't bother to even ask what was important to him or her. At best, you'd seem inconsiderate.

In the Type III situation, there's only one feasible outcome—or, more precisely, there's only one point at which needs overlap. This occurs, for example, in saturated markets in which all the sellers have the same cost structures. Cost structures converge when competitors benchmark against each other, discover and adopt industry best practice, then compete on price to the point where there's very little profit margin for anyone. Buyers, meanwhile, study the market and know what everyone's charging. So they aren't going to pay more than the minimum. Information gathering in this situation involves learning about nonprice negotiation issues: for example, value can come from quality, delivery schedules, customization, or financing. Information gathering is used to confirm that the situation is, indeed, the Type III situation it was assumed to be,[6] and to search for the less obvious sources of value.

The Type IV situation is one in which needs don't, in fact, overlap. If I, as a car buyer, stop to admire a new Rolls-Royce at an auto show, the most important thing for the salesperson to learn is that the Rolls doesn't meet my needs. It's too big, too fuel-inefficient, and—I should have mentioned this first—too expensive! The sooner we realize there's no overlap of needs, the better off we both are, because an impasse is the only outcome that's economically rational.

Without proper information gathering, the negotiator may be totally unaware of whether he or she is dealing with a Type I, II, III, or IV situation. This will make the negotiator ineffective in judging outcomes and inefficient in getting there. In fact, there isn't a logical argument that can be made *against* information gathering. Why *wouldn't* you do it?

Information Gathering in Type II Situations

Let's assume you've gathered enough information to know that it's a Type II situation—there's some overlap of needs, but each of you wants something that comes at the other's expense. This divergence of interests is a basic dynamic in Type II negotiations, and economists have done a good job of helping us analyze these interactions. Let's use economists' diagrams—utility graphs—as we explore the beneficial effect of good information gathering (see Figure 6-4).

Assessing the benefit to each party. The vertical axis of Figure 6-4 shows the value of various outcomes to the seller. Let's say, for illustration, that a successful executive is moving to New York City and needs to sell her house on the outskirts of another major city. Values on the vertical axis can range from zero to maximum value. She'd get zero value (S_{zero}), shown at the bottom of the vertical axis) if she *gave* the house away. She'd get maximum value (S_{max}) if she found a buyer who loved the house, was so rich

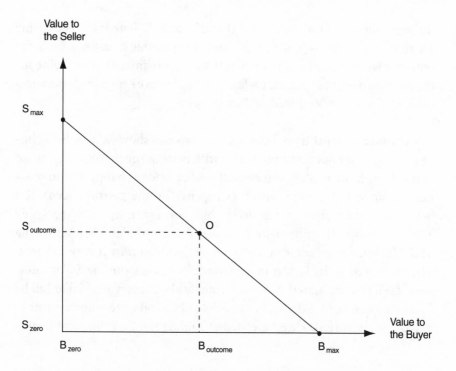

FIGURE 6-4 Assessing the Benefit of a Negotiated Outcome to Each Party

that he or she didn't care how much it cost, and was desperate to conclude the deal before someone else bought it.

The horizontal axis shows the value to the buyer. The maximum value for this party is shown on the right (B_{max}). Getting the house for free—as in the case of an inheritance—would be the best conceivable outcome. The worst outcome, on the left of the horizontal line (B_{zero}), is paying an outrageous price in an inflated market. Its value is zero because the buyer has spent so much on the house that there isn't enough money left to buy furniture, and there's no hope of regaining the investment when it comes time to resell the house.

Now let's look at the diagonal line that connects the two maximum points, S_{max} and B_{max}. All the points on that line are feasible negotiation outcomes. That is, they have more than zero value to each party. Let's look at the value to each party of point O. The figure shows that point O has a value of $S_{outcome}$ to the seller and $B_{outcome}$ to the buyer. In fact, the value of any outcome can be calculated simply by looking at the equivalent point on the vertical (seller's) or horizontal (buyer's) axis. Different levels of value are shown in Figure 6-5, which depicts three possible outcomes. O_1 is the outcome we looked at in Figure 6-4. It has approximately equal value for the buyer and seller. Outcome O_2 favors the seller more than the buyer; outcome O_3 favors the buyer rather than the seller.

The marginal utility of benefits. The two axes show value as being linear. Linearity implies that an outcome with twice as much value (e.g., twice as much profit to a seller) will make the seller twice as happy. But in practice, the appeal of certain outcomes depends on the person's needs. If a homeless person finds a ten-dollar bill, for example, he is probably extremely happy. If a billionaire finds the same ten-dollar bill, it's not a big deal. The value is the same, in dollar terms, but the *utility* is very different. The concept of utility factors in how much you care about the dollar value. Now the homeless man doesn't care equally about every ten-dollar bill he finds. Suppose he found a trail of ten-dollar bills, one after another, within a five-minute period. He'd be elated at finding the first one, and simply

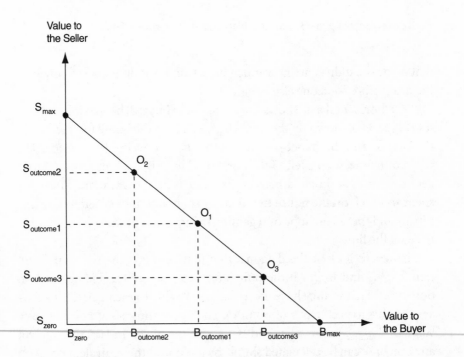

FIGURE 6-5 The Benefits to Each Party of Different Outcomes

pleased to find the tenth one. Economists refer to this phenomenon as the marginal utility of benefits. Marginal utility, essentially, is how much happier you are with each incremental unit of value.

Information gathering should include an assessment of the utility of various levels of outcomes to the other party. If you know how the other party will react to various offers, you'll know how best to make concessions when you get to the bidding stage. You may also learn *what else* the other party values. Maybe there are concessions you can make that don't cost you anything but the other person values highly, such as immediate cash, the right to buy an item back within thirty days, delayed delivery, and so on.

Assessing the cost of disagreement. In most negotiations, the cost of disagreement is high. Imagine reaching an impasse with your boss, a customer, a family member, or a neighbor. The continuing disagreement hurts the relationship. In these situations, there aren't good alternatives to negotiated agreements.

But suppose the situation is an unusual one in which the negotiation is an isolated transaction rather than an event in a long-term relationship—or, worse, that you're dealing with someone who buys into old-paradigm approaches to negotiation that advocate threatening impasse in order to "claim" a favorable settlement.[7] In either situation, you'll have to be prepared for the possibility that the other party will threaten to walk away and it will be prudent to figure out what the other party will have to settle for if a deal can't be reached with you.

Let's look at how we need to modify Figure 6-4 in order to take the cost of disagreement into account. Figure 6-6 shows that both parties have deals they can fall back on if the negotiation fails. We can continue to consider the same case of an executive selling her home to show what happens to the analysis when we factor in alternatives.

The horizontal line drawn just above the horizontal axis shows the level of value the seller will have to settle for if she can't make a deal with the present buyer. Imagine that a local real-estate speculator has made an offer that has some appeal, but the seller is negotiating because she thinks she can do better selling the house privately. The speculator has left the offer open, so she knows that she can make a sale that will yield value at level S_{alt} if the negotiation with the present buyer falls through. Economically, this means that it would be irrational for her to consider offers below S_{alt}—what she'd get if she simply sold to the speculator.

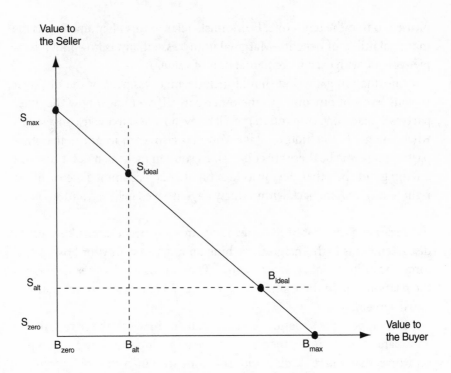

FIGURE 6-6 The Benefits to Each Negotiator of the Alternatives

The buyer, meanwhile, has looked at several houses in the area and can buy an equivalent house for B_{alt}. So if he can get a cheaper price from her, his value will be greater (i.e., his outcome utility will be to the right of B_{alt}). It would be economically irrational for him to pay more than B_{alt} for the house: he'd be spending more than he needed to.

If we consider both parties' alternatives, we see that the economically rational set of outcomes has shrunk. The range is not from S_{max} to B_{max}; it's from S_{ideal} to B_{ideal}. The buyer won't pay a price higher than S_{ideal} and the seller won't take a deal lower than B_{ideal}. The point S_{ideal} is so labeled because it's an ideal outcome for the seller, given the buyer's alternative. It's the most she can hope for in a Type II transaction in a relationship with a stranger. At S_{ideal}, the buyer is economically indifferent between owning this house and buying the other one he's been looking at. For similar reasons, B_{ideal} is the best feasible outcome for the buyer.

By this time, it should be clear why information gathering is so important in Type II situations. If you know what the other person's point of indifference is—and you have a relationship that makes you unconcerned about how she or he fares in the transaction—you can make an offer that's only slightly better than the alternative and thereby maximize your outcome. But if you haven't done information gathering adequately, you're in the dark, and you're likely to "leave money on the table."

Let me emphasize that an analysis that factors in no-settlement alternatives is only relevant to Type II negotiations in unimportant relationships. (Most negotiation texts don't point this out, and give you bad advice as a result.) For example, suppose you're negotiating with your spouse/partner over where to take a midwinter vacation. You want to go to the mountains to ski, while your partner wants to go to the Caribbean to dive. You're dealing with a Type I situation in a relationship you value. Therefore, it's not a good idea to consider the alternative of taking another "honey" on vacation with you, even if you've had an attractive offer.

In Type I negotiations—the most common type we encounter—the analysis needs to be conducted without considering an *alternative* to a successful negotiation. It's silly to consider alternatives to coming to an agreement with your partner, your boss, business associate, joint-venture partner, colleague from another department, major supplier, or customer. And these are the people you usually negotiate with. These negotiation situations aren't transactions, and the cost of disagreement is likely to be high.

Unilateral Information Gathering

It should be obvious that it's always a good idea to *get* information. But it's not always a good idea to *give up* information. If the relationship is adversarial, if you can't trust the other party, or if he or she is treating the interaction as a game, then get the information you need but be careful what you disclose. If you're successful in getting all the information about the other party, while revealing none yourself, you can use this information to arrive at a deal that's very good for you. But even when you feel a need to be fair in the particular situation, this doesn't change the advice that you should always *get* information. How can you *know* you're being fair if you don't gather information?

Multiattribute Negotiations

Thus far, we've discussed only simple Type II negotiations, where there's only one issue in dispute, such as price. But in real life, there's rarely just one issue. Suppose you want accommodations for a one-week vacation in the Florida Keys, and you're negotiating with the owner of a condominium. You evaluate the asking price in the context of which week the renter is offering. If the week is during Spring Break from school, a high price may be acceptable to you. But the same price is less acceptable in August when Florida is uncomfortably hot and humid. So you assess value by simultaneously considering *two* factors (or attributes), price and timing. This is a basic multiattribute negotiation.

Now let's add in two more attributes. Suppose the landlord actually owns two condominium units in the same building. One provides a magnificent view of the ocean. The other is on the opposite side of the building, overlooking a busy highway. Suppose also that the landlord has really good windsurfers stored in the basement, and could either make these available for your use or not. This further complicates your decision process, because now you have to consider the utility of various combinations of attributes. Suppose you had the following five alternative offers on the table. Try rank-ordering them from most appealing to least appealing.

A. High price, ocean view, no windsurfers, week of July 4th

B. Low price, no view, windsurfers, Christmas week

C. High price, no view, no windsurfers, Spring Break

D. Low price, ocean view, windsurfers, middle of August

E. High price, no view, windsurfers, early January

Your ranking of these five possible offers will tell you something about your own preference structure. Maybe you'll learn that price is the most important factor to you at this point in your life. Or maybe the opportunity to do unlimited windsurfing is so attractive that you don't care where you sleep at night so long as you can be on the water all day. Perhaps you're a romantic who likes ocean sunsets, and will trade off a lot of things for a great view. Or maybe your schedule is so important that the most important thing is to take the vacation at the perfect time. In addition to learning your preferences, you'll learn how you're willing to make trade-offs among them.

Most people have compensatory preference structures. They can tolerate giving up one thing they like if they get other things to compensate for its loss. But everyone's unique, so trade-offs will be idiosyncratic. Information gathering is vitally important because this is where the negotiator learns about the other party's idiosyncratic preference structure. Some attributes are more important to one party than the other. Often, it's possible to make trade-offs in a way that both parties get what they value most highly. The negotiating process is a means of integrating their respective needs—therefore, scholars refer to it as *integrative* negotiation.[8]

Let's see how the analysis becomes more complicated—and the negotiation becomes easier—when there are several issues to be considered as part of an outcome "package." Let's imagine that a fictitious landlord and a vacationer might rank-order outcomes A through E as follows (1 means first choice, therefore high value):

	LANDLORD'S IMPORTANCE RANKING	VACATIONER'S IMPORTANCE RANKING
A. High price, ocean view, no windsurfers, July	2	5
B. Low price, no view, windsurfers, Christmas	4	1
C. High price, no view, no windsurfers, Spring Break	1	2
D. Low price, ocean view, windsurfers, August	5	3
E. Low price, no view, no windsurfers, January	3	4

We can plot these outcome values on the same type of diagram we've been using. This has been done for you in Figure 6-7, which shows an array of points that do not fall on a straight line connecting two maximum-value points.[9] Because outcome "packages" consist of several attributes, different outcome packages have different combinations of benefits. This can be seen clearly in Figure 6-7.

Look particularly at outcomes A, B, and C in Figure 6-7. A clearly favors the landlord at the vacationer's expense. B does just the opposite: it favors the vacationer at the landlord's expense. C seems to be the best overall solution because it meets a lot of each party's needs—it yields high value to both parties, and not at each other's expense. D and E seem to be inferior solutions because both parties can do better (by agreeing on C) without sacrificing much value.

Now let's state a general point about integrative negotiations. If the negotiator is interested in discovering the best solution *for both* parties, the objective is to move in a direction away from the origin (the origin is the point where the two axes meet, at L_{zero}, V_{zero}).[10] Good integrative outcomes are those above the zero-sum line, in a region where *both* negotiators are better off. But this is very difficult to achieve unless there's adequate information gathering. The negotiator needs to know what's important and unimportant to the other party, in order to combine this information with

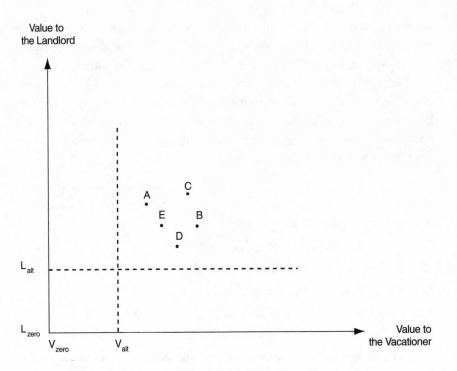

FIGURE 6-7 Possible Outcomes of a Simple Multiattribute Negotiation

what's important and unimportant to himself or herself. But remember—negotiators have to have a trusting relationship in order to be effective at information gathering.

You probably noticed that the landlord-vacationer example was highly simplified. We looked at only five sample outcomes, when in fact there may be thousands of possible outcomes. For example, we considered only "high" and "low" price, but there's an array of intermediate prices between these extremes (and some prices beyond, that aren't feasible). We also considered only five different weeks, and there are fifty-two weeks in a year. As a result, the real set of *possible* outcomes is more like what's shown in Figure 6-8.

Now let's leave behind the landlord and the vacationer and consider the generic case of two parties involved in a Type II negotiation. This is shown in Figure 6-9. The two parties are referred to as X and Y. It can be Brad and Janet, the sales group and the manufacturing group, or the United Steelworkers Union and US Steel.

The most important feature of Figure 6-9 is the Pareto-optimal fron-

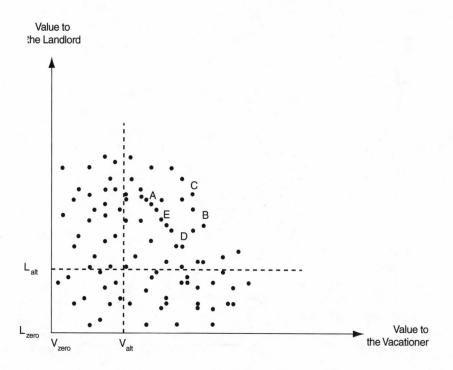

FIGURE 6-8 The Set of Outcomes of a Realistic Multiattribute Negotiation

tier. This is the set of outcomes that can't be improved upon, from a *joint gain* perspective. There may be outcomes that will benefit one party more at the other's expense, but none that will leave both of them better off—or one of them better off at no cost to the other. Outcomes behind this line (i.e., closer to the origin of the graph) are economically inferior, because at least one of the parties could have done better. Thus, a negotiation that achieves an outcome at point N is better than one that results in point A (where both parties "left money on the table").

Why, some ask, should a negotiator be concerned with achieving joint gain rather than individual gain? The answer goes back to the premise of this book. Most of our negotiations—even Type II negotiations—are with people with whom we have a long-term relationship, in both our business and personal lives. In transactions—isolated interactions in which the relationship has no history or future—perhaps relationship quality is less of a concern. But many people have a value system that emphasizes fairness, even in transactions: they believe that we shouldn't allow ourselves to be

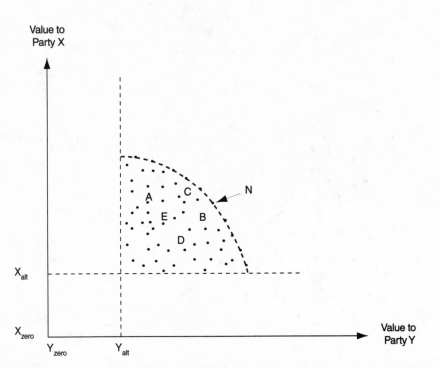

Note: The curved dotted line shows the Pareto-optimal frontier. There are no outcomes beyond this line that leave either party better off without making the other worse off.

FIGURE 6-9 The Pareto-Optimal Frontier

exploited, but neither should we exploit others. Besides, there's nothing *wrong* with seeking joint gain wherever possible, even in transactions with strangers. And the other party is more likely to agree to an outcome that benefits him or her as well as you.

Phase 4: Information Using

PHASE 1	PHASE 2	PHASE 3	PHASE 4	PHASE 5	PHASE 6	PHASE 7
preparation	relationship building	information gathering	information using	bidding	closing the deal	implementing the agreement

Information gathering is a vitally important phase of negotiation because it involves learning about the other party's needs. You already know your own needs. So if you can gain knowledge about the other party's needs, this puts you in a position to figure out what outcomes will be acceptable to her or him. The next phase, *information using*, involves persuading the other party to agree to your proposed solution.

Persuasion needs to be based on the information you gather because individuals have some motivation to meet *their* needs. This may sound pretty obvious, but it's surprising how many people approach negotiation as an argument rather than as a persuasion task. They seem to believe that once the other party recognizes the merit of the argument, he or she will agree to the outcome, making whatever concessions are necessary. This approach neglects the other party's motivation to take care of her or his *own needs*. Therefore, pointing out the "merits of the case" is seldom as persuasive as showing how the proposed solution leaves the other party better off.

The importance of the information-using phase is emphasized in sales training. Sales representatives are taught to gather information about the customer's needs, resources, and constraints, and then to position the sales appeal in terms of that information. The classic "line" of the stereotyped U.S. used-car seller, "Do I have a deal for you!" illustrates the point. The key words are *for you*, indicating that the appeal is couched in terms of the buyer's needs. A "sales pitch" that doesn't focus on the customer's real needs is largely a waste of time, and may even be an annoyance.

Furthermore, sales representatives are taught *never* to argue with customers. Arguing is discouraged because arguments don't tend to result in agreements. And even if a deal is struck at the conclusion of an argument, this process is an unpleasant experience for the customer that can have repercussions for the long-term relationship. Experienced negotiators realize that if a settlement is reached in the context of arguing over terms, the settlement is likely to have been achieved *in spite of* the arguing, not as a result of it.

Information using is also the basic process in *problem solving*. Many conflicts can be resolved without one party having to make a sacrifice (to make a concession, or agree to a compromise). But to do this, the parties must be able to share enough information so that they realize that options exist for meeting the other party's needs as well as their own.

In the negotiation we considered earlier (over the Florida condominium rental), let's suppose that the parties agreed on a particular vacation week, gave up the ocean view in exchange for use of the windsurfers, but couldn't agree on price. The landlord was holding out for a high price, and the vacationer was unwilling to pay it. But suppose the vacationer discovered that the landlord's financial concerns involved paying for his daughter's wedding without going further into debt. The vacationer might solve the landlord's cash flow problem by *prepaying* the condominium rental at the lower rate. That would leave both of them with their needs met. This is an example of where information using makes the negotiator more effective.

Psychologists call information using "empathic persuasion." Empathy involves understanding a situation from the other person's perspective. In using empathic persuasion, negotiators tap into the other party's thought processes and help *them* make the case for why they should accept the proposed outcome.

Here's where it really helps to have done a good job of relationship building as well as information gathering. In broad-scope relationships, you know more about how the other parties think and what's important to them. This helps you figure out what kind of appeals will work best. Strong relationships also involve high trust. This really helps you at the information-using stage. It's hard to persuade people who distrust you because they wonder whether your message is manipulative and self-serving.

Phase 5: Working Out the Details

PHASE 1	PHASE 2	PHASE 3	PHASE 4	PHASE 5	PHASE 6	PHASE 7
preparation	relationship building	information gathering	information using	bidding	closing the deal	implementing the agreement

Suppose you've done a really good job of preparation, relationship building, information gathering, and information using. You've proposed a course of action that meets your needs, and shown how it also meets the other party's needs. In an ideal world, the other party would simply accept it. But in real life, the other party may want to make some adjustments and may offer a counterproposal. This engages you in an interactive decision process. This might involve choosing one proposal or the other, a compromise between the two, or a creative solution that achieves the objectives of both proposals in a way neither of you had envisioned beforehand. How well this process goes will depend on the relationship you've created.

The bidding process is the interaction that moves negotiators from initial positions to a joint decision. Let's consider the case of the Type II, zero-sum conflict diagrammed in Figure 6-6. Scholars call this *distributive nego-tiation*. Compromise is necessary because one's gain necessarily comes at the other's expense. When both negotiators are making concessions, we call this a *two-pole bidding process*. The negotiation range is anchored when the two negotiators make their opening bids; the two-pole bidding process involves converging on an outcome both negotiators will accept.

The Two-Pole Bidding Process

We can use a classic buyer-seller example to illustrate the basic dynamics of two-pole bidding. The same dynamic occurs in a range of situations—such as when your boss wants a report by the end of the day and you want the rest of the week to finish it, or when your joint-venture partner wants to spend less on research than you think is necessary. But we'll use the buy-sell situation for our example because it's simple and familiar.

Figure 6-10 shows the sequence of events in the bidding process. The negotiation begins with the seller announcing an asking price of S_{asked} and the buyer offering $B_{offered}$. After some attempt by each party to justify why his or her position is the more reasonable, the seller makes a concession, offering to reduce the price by \$100 (S_{asked}-\$100). The buyer protests that the seller is still asking too much money, and continues to argue for the rea-sonableness of $B_{offered}$. The seller, feeling that the \$100 price reduction is a show of goodwill that needs to be reciprocated, says, "Hey, I've come down \$100 but you haven't moved at all."

The implicit—yet well-understood—point is that it would be *unfair* of the buyer not to make a reciprocal concession. The buyer bows to this social pressure, and raises the offer to $B_{offered}$ + \$100. But they're still \$400 apart. The seller makes another \$100 concession in asking price, which is again reciprocated by the buyer after some prompting. Now the parties are very close to each other's last bid, and it's time to split the difference at O, an out-come that's midway between the two starting points: S_{asked} and $B_{offered}$.

This simplified illustration is characteristic of the two-pole bidding process we expect to see in Type II distributive negotiations within adver-sarial relationships. Each party makes an opening bid. We should note that the less reasonable the opening bid seems, the more difficult it is to get a deal rather than an impasse. Extreme positions and unyielding stances cause relationship strains.

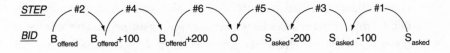

FIGURE 6-10 Steps in the Bidding Process: An Illustration of Distributive Negotiation

But even when people are being reasonable, negotiation is stressful and time consuming. So why do it? Why not look at the opening bids, ascertain that they're both reasonable, pick the midpoint, and save the time and anguish of making all those concessions? There's actually a good reason. *The bidding process is primarily a means of managing expectations.* The seller asks for more than the item is worth *as a signal* that this isn't a "distress sale"—that is, he isn't so desperate to sell that he'll take a low price. Likewise, the buyer offers an unrealistically low price to signal that she isn't so obsessed with buying this particular item that she'll pay more than it's really worth.

The ritual concessions foster convergence because they're guided by norms of reciprocity ("If I concede that amount, it's *only fair* that you do so too"). There's also a norm that you can't simply take back a concession once it has been "put on the table."[11] The split-the-difference norm that facilitates the final settlement is also based on a sense of fairness. Thus the process is predictable. This is why the midpoint of the opening bids is the best guess as to what the outcome will be.

Persuasion often involves helping the other party to come up with a rationale for abandoning a stance she or he has previously taken. As you know from your own experience, sometimes people say things to support a particular argument that aren't really true, aren't relevant, or overstate something. Later, what has been said can get in the way of reaching a settlement. You can't turn back the clock, and have them not say it—so you have to help them back away from the statement without embarrassment. The negotiators are cooperating to devise a face-saving strategy for making concessions.

In addition to helping the other party save face, a good negotiator will also advocate flexibility. If it's possible to prevent the other party from locking into a position, this helps maintain the flexibility that may be needed for subsequent concessions. The trick is doing this without getting into an argument: *how* you deliver your message can be as important as its actual content.

The One-Pole Bidding Process

Two-pole bidding isn't your only choice. An alternative is one-pole bidding. Here, the whole focus is on *one party's* position. Let's look at the process of buying a new car to illustrate this process.

Suppose a potential buyer goes into a dealership and is interested in a car on the showroom floor. The buyer balks at paying the $30,000 list price shown on the car's window sticker. The salesman offers to reduce the price by $1,000, but she still balks. After considerable discussion, the salesman knocks another $1,000 off the price. The buyer now displays more interest, but won't agree. So the salesman, "as a final concession," knocks yet another $1,000 off the price, and this is enough to close the deal at $27,000 (outcome "O"). Figure 6-11 illustrates the steps in this process.

The important difference in the one-pole bidding process is that one party—the seller in this case—takes the initiative and retains it throughout the interaction. This confers a great advantage, because any adjustment of bids is relative to the opening bid, and the salesman alone is deciding whether to grant or refuse concessions. Because there's no counterbid, there's no social pressure for the salesman to make equal concessions; therefore, the buyer has little power in the interaction: all she can really do is make arguments based on benchmarks, or threaten to walk away from the deal. The salesman, meanwhile, needs only to make enough concessions to ensure that she accepts the deal.

One-pole negotiations are often the result of tradition rather than a bidding strategy. For example, when you buy real estate, get a job offer that states a starting salary, receive a list of union demands, or get an assignment from a professor that has a due date, you're being lured into a one-pole negotiation. You should look for other examples in the world around you: you need to be able to instantly recognize this tactic.

In many cases, you can turn a one-pole negotiation around, to your advantage. For example, you can conduct your own one-pole negotiation, even in a new-car showroom, by starting from what you'd be willing to pay right now. Let the salesperson talk you up, and treat the list price as irrelevant. You can get a lot of information about the dealer's cost from the Internet during the preparation phase.

It might seem that you're always better off engaging in a one-pole bidding process. But there's a hazard. Once you've made your opening bid, if the other party is really clever and assertive, you'll be facing a counterbid

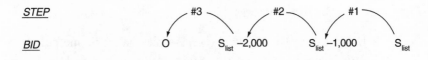

$$STEP \qquad \#3 \qquad \#2 \qquad \#1$$

$$BID \qquad O \qquad S_{list} -2{,}000 \qquad S_{list} -1{,}000 \qquad S_{list}$$

FIGURE 6-11 Steps in the One-Pole Bidding Process

that you can't ignore. The counterbid might establish a midpoint that's disadvantageous to you. Then, in order to arrive at your target outcome rather than the midpoint, you'll have to persuade the other party to make concessions that are larger than yours. This isn't impossible to accomplish, but it's not easy because it runs counter to fairness norms.

Bidding in Multiattribute Negotiations

Many business negotiations involve several attributes that must be considered simultaneously. If the attributes are independent, negotiators can deal with them one issue at a time. When you're changing jobs, for example, you might first negotiate compensation, then how large a support staff you'll have, then how soon you'll be eligible for promotion. It's unlikely that there'll be significant interaction between these decisions. You probably wouldn't, for example, settle for a smaller support staff if there's a shorter time before you're considered for promotion, so it doesn't matter that you're settling these issues one at a time.

But suppose instead that you're supplying a component to a manufacturer of telecommunications equipment. You're offering just-in-time delivery, collocation next to the manufacturer's final assembly operations, a cost-plus price, and asking for a long-term exclusive supply agreement. It would be very risky to deal with these issues in isolation from one another. Guaranteeing just-in-time deliveries may impose serious costs on your business if the manufacturer is lax about production planning. Cost-plus pricing will motivate the manufacturer to plan operations in a way that minimizes the disruption of your own business. Collocation benefits the manufacturer by minimizing delivery costs and maximizing flexibility. But you wouldn't go to the expense of collocating unless you had a long-term agreement. Otherwise, you'd be stuck there if the contract were put out to bid at the end of the year. Thus, your stance on any one issue depends on the agreement on the other issues.

As a result, *in multiattribute negotiations, it makes sense to bid packages.* To make package offers, you need to figure out what you want, and what you're willing to trade off. If you and the other party make a series of choices between alternative packages, you'll learn a lot about the other party's preference structure. This supplements what you already know about your own preference structure. If you assess the utility to each party of a wide range of possible settlements, you'll be able to map feasible outcomes on the two axes shown in Figure 6-9. The final decision should involve selecting a point on the Pareto-optimal frontier, otherwise at least one of you is "leaving money on the table" unnecessarily. If the process is a good one—not distorted by "gaming"—you should arrive at the solution that's best for both parties[12]—Point N.

You need to have a negotiation *process* that'll allow you to get to an optimum solution. Obviously, information gathering is the easiest way to come to understand how the other party values the various attributes being negotiated and makes trade-offs among them. But what you can't learn through direct inquiry you can figure out from the pattern of choices that the other party makes when considering trade-offs.

Serial Bidding

In longer-term relationships (rather than one-time transactions), issues can come up *in sequence* that need to be resolved through negotiation.

Suppose two issues come up over time that are completely independent of each other. For example, two co-workers may be negotiating over which of them will represent the department at an industry association meeting in Maui. A month later, the same two managers may be negotiating over who'll get to use the summer intern. There's no logical linkage between these issues, so it's different from the classical multiattribute negotiations we've been describing. The Maui decision must be negotiated, and *then* the intern decision must be negotiated. If these negotiations become linked, then we have serial negotiation. One manager may say, for example, "If you let me go to Maui, you can have the summer intern to yourself." Serial negotiation is described by several colloquial phrases—such as "logrolling" and "You scratch my back, I'll scratch yours."

In serial negotiation, the negotiators take into account other interactions in the series. Sometimes, you don't know what the future negotiations will involve, but nevertheless you can make concessions knowing that the other party will owe you in the future. You'd be relying on universal norms of fairness and reciprocation. Your generosity makes the other party indebted to you. Thus, you can keep a "running scorecard" of who has made concessions. This only works in certain types of relationships. There has to be enough continuity that you're sure you'll be dealing with the other person again. And there has to be enough trust so that you're confident you won't be exploited.

There's a lot of serial negotiation in close relationships, but the motive is different. You tend to give in easily when an issue is important to the other party, and the other party does the same for you. It's an expression of caring rather than indebtedness. In practice, the series of negotiations is often so rich and intertwined in close relationships that the parties *couldn't* keep track of the equity balance. In fact, an attempt to balance equity in the closest personal relationships is often a sign of relationship instability.

Avoiding Impasses

An impasse occurs when the parties break off negotiations. An impasse is the rational thing to do in a Type IV situation (see Figure 6-3) because there's no overlap of the two parties' needs. But if an impasse occurs in a Type I, II, or III situation, something went wrong with the process. Process problems most often occur during the bidding phase, so let's try to understand them better.

Earlier we noted that *bidding primarily involves managing expectations.* You need to help the other party accept that the final outcome will fall short of his or her expectations. That's what's really going on in the bidding and counterbidding process. It's a way of signaling what's achievable. The idea is to dampen the other party's optimism about getting a better deal than you can afford to give.

But even while you're making the other party more pessimistic about the outcome, you must maintain the other party's optimism that the effort will result in a deal. The bidding process is tiring and stressful, so you need to motivate the other party to hang in there and continue with it. Negotiators are more likely to give up if they see the situation as hopeless, so it's very important to reassure them that their efforts won't be wasted. This eliminates a favorite tactic of unsophisticated negotiators—threatening to walk away. Of all the negotiations that ended in agreement after use of this tactic, I've yet to see one that concluded successfully *because of* this ploy: those negotiations seem to have come to a successful conclusions *in spite of* the use of the get-up-and-leave tactic.

When you think about it, all you're really doing when you threaten to walk away is balking at making another concession. There are different—and better—ways of doing this. The obvious alternative is to simply say, "Look how much I've conceded already. I want to make a deal, but not at any cost. Help me out here." Most people prefer polite resistance to a threat. And even if the negotiation ends with an impasse either way, the ongoing relationship will be stronger if you don't get up and leave: that's *rude.*

The get-up-and-leave tactic is subtly encouraged by some negotiation texts that put undue emphasis on figuring out your "walkaway" point, and then using this to gain leverage in the negotiation. In most of the negotiations you'll ever do—in your business or private life—you won't have the option of making a deal with someone else instead. So you're better off focusing on concluding the deal, even if the other party is resisting. It takes a lot of skill to keep a negotiation going and make progress toward an agreement. But any idiot can get up and walk out.

Tactics for Avoiding Impasses. Let's take this one step further. You want to avoid an impasse, and you know this requires keeping the other person motivated to continue. It's good advice to never say *anything* negative about the progress of a negotiation. Say something positive instead. Emphasize what you've accomplished rather than what still divides you. It really makes a difference in terms of motivation. If someone has spent the last hour making concessions, and all you can talk about is how many more concessions still need to be made, it's easy for the person to get discouraged.

Professional negotiators—such as sales representatives—emphasize the positives even when the situation seems hopeless. You can say, "We're not that far apart: let's hang in there and make a deal. I'm sure we can do it." That's much better than saying "Looks like I'm wasting my time here. Why don't you call me when you get serious about this deal." It should be obvious that you can't negotiate unless you keep interacting. Positive statements foster further discussion; negative statements are likely to shut the conversation down.

Impasses sometimes result from frustration rather than clumsy bidding tactics. Frustration is an emotional reaction that arises when you feel blocked in pursuing an objective. The feeling wells up inside you when you can't make any progress and you experience an impulse to escape from the stressful situation. An impasse won't let you achieve your goals; but if you've come to believe that the other party isn't going to let you achieve your goals anyway, an impasse provides an escape from the frustration.

Knowing this, a component of bidding is managing the other party's frustration without making concessions that'll hurt you. If you sense that the other negotiator's frustration is mounting, you may need to do something to alleviate it. Perhaps you can make a small concession that doesn't cost you much, but gives the other party a sense of progress. In multi-issue negotiations, maybe you can move on to talk about another topic where you *can* make some progress, and come back to the frustrating topic later, in a new frame of mind. Negotiations that break off because of frustration tend to damage the relationship, so if there's a way to ease the frustration without "giving away the store," you're usually better off.

Sometimes impasses result from the other party's tactics. Perhaps the person is being overly aggressive, insulting, or rude in interrupting you. You feel your anger and resentment rising, and your impulse is to be equally nasty. Self-control can be helpful here because an impasse may deny you the benefits you hoped to gain from negotiating.

An alternative to impasse is to "take a time-out" and discuss the process that's evolving. There are, of course, good and bad ways to do this. If you say, "I'm not going to discuss this any further until you stop being such a jerk," this won't help the process. It's better to say something like "Look, I'm not comfortable with the direction this conversation is taking. You seem to be getting annoyed, and I'm getting frustrated because we ought to be making faster progress toward an agreement. I know it's in both our interests to make a deal here. So can we start again? I'll do my best not to irritate you, and hope you'll do the same." In effect, you'd be taking the role of a facilitator. Facilitation often helps when the process is going awry, and there's no requirement that the facilitator be an outside party. Negotiators can do this for themselves.

Bidding in Other Negotiation Situations

Much of what we've discussed thus far has concerned Type II situations—those where there's a small-to-moderate overlap of needs. The reason for the emphasis is that the bidding phase of negotiation is more important in Type II situations than in other types. But we should briefly make note of the kind of bidding that occurs in Type I, III, and IV situations.

In Type I situations, the most common type, there's great overlap between the parties' needs, usually because these negotiations occur in complex, ongoing relationships. In relationships that are very close, the parties' needs are largely inseparable, so the focus is on *commonwealth interests* rather than the self-interests of each party.

Nevertheless, negotiators sometimes do go through a bidding process in Type I situations. They exchange proposals for how to deal with the situation at hand. *Proposals* are very different from *positions* taken by opponents: the tone is one of offering ideas rather than issuing demands. Exchanging proposals creates a menu of alternatives for addressing the problem. The negotiators discuss the pros and cons of each, generate new alternatives, and then pick either the best one or the best combination. Done well, this process can strengthen the relationship as well as deal with the problem that was straining it.

In Type III situations, there's only one feasible outcome. But negotiators usually don't know this *for sure* when they begin negotiating. Quite often, people have some room to move that isn't immediately obvious. For example, store managers sometimes have latitude to give discounts, even when prices are posted and bar codes will ensure that cashiers ring up the posted amounts. It isn't easy to take advantage of this discretionary power of store managers, because they're worried about setting a bad precedent: they wouldn't want it generally known that the nonnegotiable prices aren't as fixed as they seem. But they may "bend" to make a sale. Try negotiating next time you're booking a hotel room, for example. You'll be surprised how negotiable the fixed rate can be. Hotel managers hate to have unoccupied rooms.

In Type IV situations, you shouldn't be spending much time negotiating at all. But this assumes that you're 100 percent certain it's a Type IV situation. You may want to test your *assumption* that there's no overlap of interests, to see if it's a valid one. There's an old saying—"There's no harm in asking"—that rings true here. You or the other party may have misunderstood the situation.

One good reason for making overture bids in apparently hopeless situations is to insulate yourself from remorse. Suppose you see your dream house and you're certain you can't afford it. For the rest of your life, you might be second-guessing yourself. What if the owner had been desperate for immediate cash? What if you misunderstood the market and sellers were starting out asking silly prices in the hope that a naive buyer would come along and buy at that price?

Think of it this way: if you don't make an offer of any sort, there's a 100 percent chance you won't get the deal. If you do make an offer, at least there's a *possibility,* even if it's highly unlikely. And you'll be able to tell yourself, "At least I tried."

Manipulative Bidding Tactics

Bidding is a persuasive process. You have to persuade the other party that the deal you're offering is an attractive one and that she or he isn't going to do any better. Persuasion is therefore *the means* of managing the other party's expectations. There are three basic persuasion approaches used in the bidding process:

1. Convince the other party that he or she can't get more than is now being offered.
2. Explain that the other party is actually getting more value than she or he realizes.
3. Transform the other party's thinking to get him or her to see your offer in a new light.

Each persuasive approach involves making statements implied to be true. This leaves open the possibility of misrepresentation, which involves a broad spectrum of tactics:

a. *Withholding unfavorable information* involves misrepresentation by omission. The negotiator isn't making false statements, but neither is she or he telling the whole truth. The withholding tactic distorts the truth by presenting one-sided arguments when the negotiator is aware of there being two sides.
b. *Obfuscation* involves telling the whole truth but presenting it in such a way that the other party has difficulty understanding what's really being said. Sometimes the other party will use technical jargon without adequate explanation of what you need to know. Sometimes important information is concealed in footnotes or buried in pages of "boilerplate" contract language.
c. *Spin doctoring* involves framing the issues in their most favorable light. All communicators have a choice of how they construct persuasive arguments and what vocabulary they use. When spin doctoring has the effect of misleading the other party, then we're really talking about misrepresentation.

d. *Dissembling* goes beyond spin doctoring. It involves making the situation seem different from what it really is. Suppose a salesman is negotiating for advance payment for a large order of essential parts. He justifies his request by saying that his company has a high cost of capital, and upfront payment allows him to offer a lower price. In practice, the supplier is on the brink of bankruptcy and needs cash to solve short-term liquidity problems. The salesman is dissembling in the sense of making the situation look like a good-faith effort to integrate the supplier's and customer's interests, when he knows this is not the case.

e. *Lying* involves making statements that are known to be false. In the bidding process, the intent of a lie is to get the other party to make decisions about concessions based on false information. For example, many people lie about what their alternatives are. Suppose you tell a potential buyer, "Someone else already offered me that much. But if you're willing to pay me a thousand more, you and I can make a deal right now."[13]

Lies may be very serious, as in the case of selling something that you know to be a bad deal—a defective product, a company that's about to be involved in major litigation, or real estate that's contaminated with toxic wastes. Or they may be mild, as in the case of saying "It's been nice doing business with you," or "You got the best of me in this deal" when neither statement is true. Negotiators are *always* aware when they're telling bad, rather than harmless, lies.

RELATIONAL ETHICS IN NEGOTIATION

The bidding process offers many opportunities to be less than honest in your persuasive appeals, as well as to use other tactics that will bias outcomes in your favor. Therefore, you have to decide whether your tactics are ethically acceptable.

There are several traditional approaches to thinking about whether your behavior is ethical. But a *relational ethics* approach is probably more appropriate for making decisions in the types of situations managers most often encounter.

The basic idea of relational ethics is to figure out what is appropriate behavior in the context of the relationship. If someone is your best friend, certain tactics are appropriate as you negotiate. If the person is a sworn enemy, other, self-protective tactics are appropriate. In business contexts, the other party may be a peer-rival, one of many suppliers of a commodity, a merciless purchasing agent, a value-chain partner, a colleague from another functional area, or a potential ally. *Different relationships create different implications for what's ethically acceptable in the bidding process.*

If there is strong competition, you can expect the other party to use tactics like withholding information, obfuscating, or putting a self-serving spin on how information is presented. If you wish to join in the competition, you might do the same. The two of you are jousting for advantage. The winner is the one who can come up with the cleverest deceptions. This may be done tongue-in-cheek, or with an outward display of sincerity. The ethical test here involves awareness. If the other party knows you're distorting your persuasive appeal, and can appropriately discount your message, then what you're doing isn't much different from playing poker.

In fact, some negotiators construe their interaction as akin to playing poker. When this happens, deception and bluffing are elements of the contest, so dissembling and lying are viewed as permissible tactics, and the only constraint is whether you can get away with it. *Game theory* implies this kind of relationship exists between negotiators, and such behavior is acceptable. Economists describe negotiators using exploitative tactics as "opportunistic," while others might call them dishonest. To game theorists, underhanded negotiating tactics are all part of the game—they're no different from faking a pass in football or trying a deceptive gambit in chess. The game is amoral.

But a word of caution is in order here. You have to judge the appropriateness of tactics from two perspectives—how you construe the relationship, and how the other party construes the relationship. If *both* of you view the relationship as involving two rivals playing a game, then game tactics may well be ethically acceptable. But if the other party is expecting you to be sincere and honest, it's hard to justify being dishonest. This is the essence of relational ethics: negotiator behavior that's acceptable in one relationship may be unthinkable in another.

Phase 6: The Close

PHASE 1	PHASE 2	PHASE 3	PHASE 4	PHASE 5	PHASE 6	PHASE 7
preparation	relationship building	information gathering	information using	bidding	closing the deal	implementing the agreement

At the conclusion of the bidding process, the negotiators will have arrived at an outcome that they've tentatively agreed upon. Now it's time to close the deal.

A simplistic view of the closing process involves getting the other party to actually sign the agreement. But really good negotiators know that getting a signature is the least important aspect of concluding the negotiation—that there's something much more important to attend to.

The basic objective in closing the deal is to build commitment to the agreement. When the parties finish the bidding, the agreement they have is still *tentative.* They've repeatedly taken positions and then abandoned them. The negotiated outcome is nothing more than the last position they took, so they need to become committed to it. Without commitment, they may not honor the agreement when it comes time to implement it.

The most important factor that holds negotiators back from making a commitment is anxiety. Thus, during the closing process it's important to separately consider what people are *saying* and how they're *feeling.* A major source of anxiety is worrying about whether the other party has taken advantage of you. Here again the relationship you've created will make a difference. If the relationship has been competitive, you'll be more worried about being exploited. If there's high trust and a sense of alliance in the relationship, you'll worry less.

Even in positive relationships, anxiety arises from postpurchase dissonance (also known as "buyer's remorse," or "the winner's curse"). This is where we second-guess ourselves: "Why is the other party happy with the deal? Did I not gather enough information to know what's a fair deal? Did I settle for too little? Am I leaving money on the table?" The bigger the decision, the more stressful it is.

For example, people are both happiest *and* most miserable when they buy their first house. Let's say you found "the perfect house" but the real-estate agent had listed it at a price that was high for the local market. So you made a counteroffer 20 percent below the asking price. That put you below the price of comparable properties, but you had the funds to come up a little in subsequent rounds of bidding. You were surprised when the owner immediately snapped up this offer.

Objectively, you got the perfect house at a price below what you were willing to pay. So why did you end up feeling miserable? Because the close was a poor one. The realtor got in the way of forming a relationship with the owner. This prevented you from gathering information about the owner's needs, and what the owner's alternatives were if she or he didn't make a deal with you. So you were in the dark. You didn't know whether the owner was desperate to sell and gave you a super deal, or whether the owner was thinking, "There's a sucker born every minute." The seller, by the way, would have been just as upset if you had immediately agreed to the full asking price.

A general point here is that the *process* of negotiation tends to make people feel anxious when the bidding comes to a conclusion. The real-estate agent was running an impersonal, faceless process. You were spending more money than you'd ever spent in your life, and you were denied all the assurances that you and the seller were equally satisfied with the outcome. You'd have been spared all that stress if you'd been able to meet with the seller and learn why he or she had accepted your counteroffer. You needed reassurance. (See "A Painful Close" below.)

A Painful Close

I have a bad history of making purchase decisions that don't make total sense to my wife. Her diagnosis is that I have low impulse control, especially when there's an opportunity to acquire an adult toy. I, on the other hand, have always viewed myself as finding creative ways to meet family needs. Take, for example, the lawn situation. We have a very large lawn at our summer home on the coast of Maine. In August, the grass dries out and turns to straw because the fog and drizzle of early summer give way to a month of drought. But the lawn is on the shore of a lake. So here I am, looking at the lawn here and the water there, figuring out what would be the most efficient way to sprinkle water on the lawn without running our well dry.

To make a long story short, one day I went out with my friend Fred and came home with two fire engines. I got a fabulous deal because I bought the pair—a volume discount of sorts. Readers with lawns should note that if you shoot a fire hose straight up into the air, you can make it rain on your lawn. It's really fun. You can even water flower beds with a fire hose after a little practice. (The first flower bed was blown into the neighbor's yard: I used too much pressure. You also have to be careful when washing windows with it. They break pretty easily, and the dining room can get ankle deep in water within seconds. That doesn't go over big in any household.)

But my wife wasn't impressed with the wisdom of this purchase. Maybe it was driving up to the front of the house with lights flashing and sirens wailing that got us off to a bad start. Whatever the reason, she never was convinced that I had bought legitimate irrigation equipment rather than two more toys. Here's where my history reduced my credibility. She didn't think I really needed more than five motorcycles. Or a 1922 Indianapolis racer to drive to the office during good weather. The result of this history is that I'm not allowed to make any purchases without adult supervision.

OK, that's the context. Now here's the situation. We'd been paying a local contractor to do some shoreline landscaping for us. The workman was using a very large (twenty-ton) excavator to move dirt around. I sat and watched him work for a couple of hours. It's amazing how much work you can do with one of those large machines, especially if you're used to moving soil with a spade and a wheelbarrow.

As he was leaving to take a lunch break, the workman commented on my apparent interest and asked me if I wanted to operate the excavator while he was at lunch. Of course I did! But I was concerned. The machine was huge and immensely powerful, and could obviously do a lot of damage. I said to him, "What if I screw something up?" His response was honest, if not comforting. He said, "What do I care? It's *your* property." So I got into the machine and after a few minutes of instruction, ran it for an hour. That was *really* fun.

Turn the clock ahead eight months. I came across this flyer announcing an auction. Featured at the top of the flyer was a picture of the biggest, most beautiful excavator I've ever seen. A large contractor was going bankrupt and all of his equipment was being sold off to the highest bidder. I took the flyer home. As soon as I put it on the table—before I opened my mouth—my wife said, "No!" using that same tone of voice she uses when the kitten is about to climb the curtains to stalk a fly.

An hour later, I meekly asked, "Can we at least talk about it?" This brought on a stern lecture about the "toys" I already owned—a tractor (well, three, if you count the antique and the log skidder), a bulldozer, a backhoe, a skid-steer loader, a dump truck (well, OK, two, if you count the smaller one, which hasn't been sold yet, and the two pickup trucks don't count because they aren't dump trucks), a giant wood chipper, and a few more gardening tools—big ones, admittedly, but this is a thirty-acre property. And I did eventually sell the two fire engines, most of the motorcycles, and the 1922 Indy car. Plus the boat. Sometimes you have to make sacrifices to make room for more toys.

The next morning, I announced that I could probably make a business case for buying the excavator. We had a budget of $20,000 to pay contractors to do major earthmoving. (Our 30 acres is actually a wildlife refuge, and we've been digging ponds for waterfowl, otters, and beavers, as well as undoing the damage that had been done by strip-mining in the mid-1900s.) Creating and restoring wildlife habitat is a big undertaking. So I argued that we should be indifferent between paying that much to a contractor and buying the machine, doing the work ourselves, and then reselling the machine. Eventually she consented to let me go to the auction. I had to agree to an absolute $20,000 limit, that she'd accompany me, and Fred would stay home.[14]

So we showed up at this auction. I knew I was out of my league right away. Everyone except me was a construction-company owner. They were going from machine to machine, making insightful comments about this and that, talking about what each one was worth. (I was clueless.) They even looked different. I was the only one *not* wearing one of those baseball hats with a logo on it—John Deere, Detroit Diesel, Caterpillar, Budweiser. I had just come from the office and was dressed like an Ivy League professor. And my wife was the only woman there.

But nevertheless, I was prepared. I had done some research on the excavator. It was a Caterpillar 235, which had an industry reputation as the best large excavator in its class. The dealer offered to sell me a new one for around $350,000, and said prices for used ones were all over the map, depending on the machine's condition, the state of the used-equipment market, who else was bidding that day, etc. He was skeptical that it could be bought for $20,000. They'd be looking for at least $50,000. But then he added, "Hey, you never know. An auction's an auction."

The excavator was the last item being sold that day. This means I had to keep quiet while they sold off all this *beautiful* equipment that we really could have put to good use had I not been threatened with bodily injury if I opened my mouth. So I really had an appetite when the excavator lumbered forward in front of the crowd. It was magnificent, I thought. It's too big, my wife pointed out. OK, so it weighed fifty tons and was bigger than our house. And it was too large to move over public roads without those silly pickup trucks with the flashing lights that go in front of and behind a huge tractor trailer. But it would do a lot of earthwork, very fast . . .

The auctioneer started out, "Here we have the last item to be sold today. It's a Caterpillar 235, the Rolls-Royce of excavators. You all know what it's worth, so who'll start the bidding at $50,000?" I was crestfallen. The Caterpillar dealer was right. This machine really was out of my range.

But there was silence in the room, and more than 100 construction-company owners were shuffling about, talking quietly.

The auctioneer resumed, "All right, who'll give me $35,000?" Again there was silence. Next he said, "OK, who'll give me *anything* for this Caterpillar 235?" Sensing opportunity, I blurted out, "I'll give you five thousand." The auctioneer peered at me, as if in disbelief, then said, "OK. We have to start somewhere. Who'll give me ten?" The man next to me looked me over, curiously, and then said, "I'll give you six." Someone else said, "Seven." So I said "Eight" in a resolute tone, hoping to signal that it was pointless bidding against me. But someone else said "Nine" and the man next to me bid "Ten."

Two minutes later, the man next to me had bid "Nineteen" and I had one chip left to play. I jumped in with "Twenty" before someone else did. My wife's grip on my arm had crossed the threshold of pain. She isn't always subtle when communicating with me. There'd be no latitude on the $20,000 limit I had agreed to, and I already had welts developing.

But a curious thing happened. There was silence in the room. The auctioneer said, "OK, we're at twenty. Who'll give me twenty-one?" After more silence, he said, "Come *on*, people. This is a Cat 235. Who'll give me twenty-one?" After more silence, he repeated, "I can't believe this. Who'll give me twenty-one?"

Well, I couldn't believe it either. The experience had become surreal.

I was having a panic reaction. The color had drained from my face, my mouth had become dry, my hands cold and sweaty. I hoped this was a bad dream. The auctioneer's voice sounded distant as he said "Going once . . . going twice . . ." I was hoping the ground would swallow me up, or that I could magically turn back the clock and start the day again. I was suddenly rescued from the depths of my despair by a brilliant idea. The man next to me had bid $19,000. Why not give him $1,100 so he could outbid me?

But before I could make the offer, the gavel came down, and the auctioneer said, "Sold! To the gentleman in the tweed jacket. Thank you for coming, folks. The next auction is in two weeks at . . ."

I didn't hear anything else. I was in shock. It had dawned on me that here I was, a rank amateur, who was willing to pay more than everyone else in the room—people who knew the construction business and the market for used heavy equipment. In a daze, I paid for the excavator. As I walked through the parking lot, my panic attack blossomed into clinical depression. It lasted for two days.

Now let's look at what the problem was. It was *the close*. Instead of just saying "Sold!" the auctioneer could have said, "Sir, you just got yourself a hell of a deal. The only reason you paid so little for this machine is that the construction industry is currently in recession. You bought the best machine in the world at a fraction of its true value. If all you do is park this and then sell it when the recession's over, you'll make a lot of money. You're lucky to have had $20,000 to *invest* today."[15] But he didn't. Auctioneers don't close deals. They simply terminate the bidding process. They really ought to think about the close as a means of providing greater value to buyers.

The point here is that postpurchase dissonance is so powerful that you're not immune to it even if you expect it and understand it. Hey, I *teach* this stuff. And I treat people who suffer from anxiety and depression. But I couldn't help myself. Objectively the purchase was a bargain, but still I couldn't help reacting to the heartless close.

We should note that postbidding dissonance arises primarily in isolated transactions. There's less anxiety if the current negotiation is one event within a longer series of interactions, because you usually have less to worry about. Even the least-ethical competitive-type negotiator is going to be hesitant to exploit you if it risks retaliation. And if you're engaged in *serial negotiations,* the norms of reciprocity will give you some protection: if you get a really bad deal this time, the other party will be obliged to make it up to you in subsequent dealings. In short, your worst fears arise when you know you may never see the other party again. Thus, a strong ongoing relationship is your greatest comfort.

Reassurance Tactics

With this understanding of how postbidding anxiety arises, let's now return to the process of closing the negotiation. Your objective is to reassure the other party that her or his anxiety is unfounded. You can actually say that you got less from the deal than you hoped for, or expected. You can say that she or he negotiated well when dealing with you. You can draw comparisons to other negotiations to provide reassuring external benchmarks. Almost anything you say along these lines will be better than total silence.

The best reassurance tactic is to restate specifically why it's a good deal for both parties. Your ability to do this will depend on how good a job you did of information gathering. You have to really know whether it's a good deal to be credible in persuading the other party that it meets his or her underlying needs.

The importance of the relationship-building phase is very obvious when it comes time to close the deal. The relationship that has developed will influence how vulnerable the other person feels. If she or he feels a strong bond and trusts you, confidence in the constraining effect of relational ethics will reduce anxiety about being exploited.

A useful reassurance tactic is to emphasize continuity of the relationship. Anxiety is highest in isolated transactions. So it can be helpful to make the deal seem less isolated in time and space. An executive can say, for example, "Hey, we're both in this industry together, and everybody knows everybody. You and I both have reputations to maintain, and both of us will look back and be proud of what we agreed on today. We've done our best to come up with a package that seems to make the most sense for both of us. What more can we do?"

There's also a piece of advice for negotiators who have competitive personalities. *Never gloat about how well you did, even long after the negotiation is over.* This is obvious to most people, but people who like to compete sometimes go beyond simply doing better than the other party: they point out that they won and the other party lost. This degradation ritual may be acceptable in certain macho sports contests, but it's the *worst* way to close a negotiation. Not only does the other party feel bad about settling for too little, she or he also has to endure humiliation. In business dealings, the result can be disastrous, because the other party will avoid doing business with you in the future, seek revenge, or find excuses not to implement the agreement.

Thus far, we've discussed how you use reassurance tactics to alleviate anxiety in the other party. You may also need to alleviate your own anxiety. You won't always be lucky enough to be dealing with someone who's sensitive enough to understand the problem and use a reassuring process. But you can usually take someone with you who will make you feel good about your decisions. Many people do this instinctually. They invite a friend to accompany them on shopping expeditions (where they may buy nonroutine items). The motive to seek companionship is obvious; the motive to seek reassurance is less obvious but often more powerful.

Phase 7: Implementing the Agreement

PHASE 1	PHASE 2	PHASE 3	PHASE 4	PHASE 5	PHASE 6	PHASE 7
preparation	relationship building	information gathering	information using	bidding	closing the deal	implementing the agreement

It's a big mistake to assume that the negotiation is over and done with after the contract is signed. The negotiation isn't really complete until the agreement has been put into effect. If the process has been a good one, the negotiators are more likely to follow through on what has been agreed to. If the process has been a bad one, they'll have little personal commitment to making the deal a reality.

The implementation problem is very obvious in U.S. labor negotiations, where contract negotiations are seen as different from contract administration (what we're calling implementation). If contract negotiations have been bad, contract administration will be a nightmare. The union will contest every questionable action by managers and will flood management with grievances—protests that need to be addressed by means of a formal conflict-resolution process. The costs are very high: grievances consume managers' time, cost money to arbitrate if the union won't accept management's proposed resolutions, and impede work flow.

U.S. labor negotiations usually founder at the relationship-building phase. The parties maintain an adversarial stance toward each other, and this influences all of the negotiation process. The agreement therefore usually ends up being a reluctant compromise that union members are resentful about. Not surprisingly, they have a stronger motive to be a nuisance to management than to ensure that work proceeds in the best interests of the company.

Or think about negotiating a pay raise. The most favorable time for you to bring up the issue may be when you're approaching a deadline in delivering a project to a client. Let's say you did most of the work, and at this point in time, your input is crucial to finishing the project on time. If you demand a 10 percent raise, you may get it. But your ultimatum may haunt you during the implementation phase. Your boss may give you less responsibility in the future, for fear of being so dependent on you. You also may be denied promotion opportunities, and given poor assignments and low performance ratings. Remember that human beings are emotional creatures, and they react in emotional ways.

CROSS-CULTURAL DIFFERENCES

Our model is normative—it specifies how a negotiation *should* proceed, ideally. But negotiators from different cultural backgrounds tend to approach negotiations differently. Let's contrast two cultures, to see how different approaches can lead to compatibility problems. Let's look at how American and Japanese men[16] approach a business negotiation, then draw some lessons from the contrast.

The biggest difference is in how much emphasis negotiators from each culture give to the different phases. Figure 6-12 portrays the approaches taken by "typical" U.S. and Japanese businessmen. Note that each negotiator departs from the "ideal" model in culture-specific ways. The emphasis is different and the sequence is different.

As you can see, stereotypical U.S. businessmen emphasize bidding. This is largely due to the emphasis on economic thinking in U.S. business education. Preparation tends to focus on bidding tactics (what's the best opening bid, what's the fallback deal in the event of an impasse, at what pace and in what increments should concessions be made, etc.) and on developing arguments to support one's own position and refute the position the other party takes.

Notice that U.S. businessmen tend to engage in information using

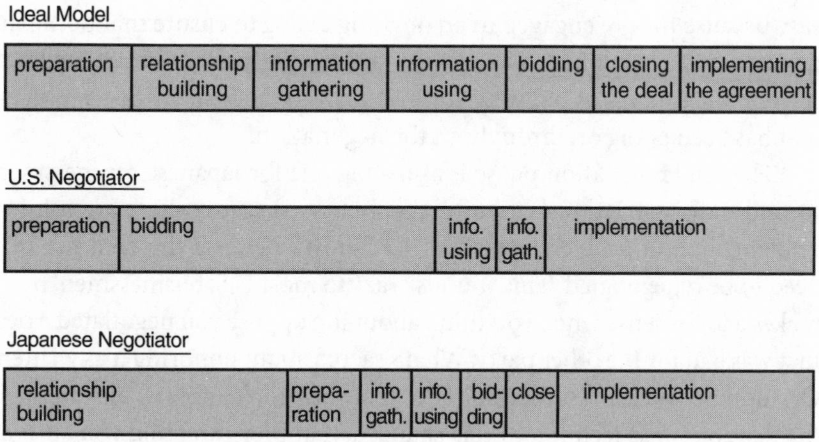

Ideal Model

preparation	relationship building	information gathering	information using	bidding	closing the deal	implementing the agreement

U.S. Negotiator

preparation	bidding		info. using	info. gath.	implementation

Japanese Negotiator

relationship building		prepa-ration	info. gath.	info. using	bid-ding	close	implementation

FIGURE 6-12 Cultural Differences in Approaches to Negotiation: Stereotyped U.S. and Japanese Businessmen

before they do their information gathering. I know this sounds silly, but here's why it happens. In the preparation phase, negotiators try to come up with a "sales pitch"—a persuasive speech that justifies the position they're pushing for. Of course, the speech won't have much motivational value unless it's based on the other party's needs. The negotiator soon realizes this and starts asking questions in order to craft stronger arguments. But it's hard to get information at this point, because it's obvious to the other party that any information divulged would be used against him or her.

Notice also that there's considerable emphasis on implementation in negotiations by the U.S. businessman. This is because his approach usually leaves him with implementation *problems.* His bidding process tends to be adversarial, which results in an adversarial relationship as well as an unpleasant process. There's no close, except to get the other party to sign a legal document. So the other party emerges with little commitment to the agreement. If subsequently there's something to be gained by not living up to the terms of the deal, the other party will look for every loophole and ambiguity. This creates implementation problems.

Japanese businessmen emphasize the relationship-building phase. They may spend months—or even years—getting to know you. This forms the context in which they do their preparation. Preparation tends to be a collaborative effort with you. Information gathering is fairly easy, once a strong relationship bond has been formed: they already know a lot about you and can easily figure out what your needs are. Information using is also easy because they're engaged in an ongoing dialog to ensure that both parties' needs are being met. The close is ceremonial, and is simply the latest stage in the process of building commitment to the agreement—a process that has been going on throughout the negotiation.

The implementation phase is also a big one for Japanese businessmen, second only to relationship building—but not because there are a lot of implementation problems to solve. Rather, it's because the contract may need to be renegotiated. This sounds crazy to most U.S. businessmen, but it makes a lot of sense when you think about it. Suppose you negotiated a deal that was bad for the other party. What's sacred about honoring it as written? Or, suppose you learn something later that you didn't know when you made the deal. Suppose technology has changed, that they can build you an even better product, or they'll actually lose money on every unit they supply. If the contract doesn't make good business sense at the time of implementation, why *wouldn't* you amend it so that it's in the long-term best interests of both parties? So, to Japanese businessmen, implementation involves continuous improvement of all kinds—including the business deal itself.

These fundamental differences in approach cause misunderstanding and suspicion when Japanese and U.S. businessmen negotiate deals. The Japanese are suspected of stalling, to elicit concessions. The Americans appear to be trying to trick the Japanese into signing a contract loaded with unfavorable terms. Neither assessment is accurate.

CONCLUDING THOUGHTS ABOUT NEGOTIATION

In new-era organizations, negotiation is the principal means of getting things done. Bringing negotiations to a successful conclusion isn't easy. Nor is it fun, except in unusual circumstances. Yet it's necessary.

The first thing you need to do is to assess the negotiation situation. Most of the negotiations we engage in, in our business and our private lives, are Type I situations (see Figure 6-3). Here the objective is to get a high-commitment agreement while preserving the ongoing relationship. Most negotiation texts address only Type II negotiations, even though these are less frequent. In those, the objective is to reach an agreement that meets your needs—and you can do this only if it meets the other party's needs, too.

Type III negotiations have only one feasible settlement, and Type IV situations have none at all. The reason you negotiate in these two scenarios is to ascertain that your assessment of the situation is accurate. People often give up too easily, and miss opportunities to reach or improve a negotiated outcome.

Once you know what sort of situation you're involved in, you choose an approach that's suited to the situation and the relationship. This chapter has presented an ideal sequence. The single most important determinant of success in negotiating is information gathering. How good a job you do will determine whether you're shooting in the dark or working toward a clear objective. Your effectiveness in information gathering is most affected by the relationship you're able to develop with the other negotiator. The bidding process—which gets all of the attention in old-paradigm texts that have a narrow economics orientation—may not be important at all if the relationship is strong and information exchange thorough. Finally, the close is worth paying attention to because you need to be concerned about implementation.

This chapter has focused on negotiation between two parties, because this allows simpler explanation of core concepts. But managerial negotiations often involve more than two individuals. All of the points made in this chapter apply to the multiparty case, but there are additional factors to take into account. These are covered in the next chapter, which focuses on how managerial groups make joint decisions.

NOTES

1. See Irving Janis, *Groupthink: Psychological Studies of Policy Decisions and Fiascoes* (Boston: Houghton-Mifflin, 1982).
2. There are other forms of power, some of which arise from various relationship dimensions. A full discussion of these is beyond the scope of the book.
3. See, for example, *Negotiating Rationally* by Bazerman and Neale (New York: Free Press, 1992).
4. Some *writers* see negotiation in competitive terms, too, which doesn't help the situation. These authors refer to the other party as "your negotiation opponent" and describe outcomes in terms of the extent to which each person "won." They can't get beyond this vocabulary even when winning is irrelevant to the situation: in such cases they refer to outcomes as win-win, an obvious oxymoron. Their writing appeals to competitive types, but it doesn't really help them become better negotiators in business and other long-term relationships: instead, the writing reinforces tendencies that are getting in the way. We'll discuss this issue in more detail in the final chapter.
5. Examples of atypical managers, in this context, might include commodity brokers or other traders.
6. Sometimes negotiators are surprised to find out that what seemed like a Type III situation is actually a Type II situation, with a range of feasible outcomes. They'll never discover this if they skip the information-gathering phase of negotiation.
7. A key concept in these formulations is the best-case scenario if the parties won't agree to a negotiated solution. This approach reduces managerial effectiveness in most situations they encounter. It focuses on failure rather than success in negotiating, submission to power rather than commitment to an agreement, and competitive instincts rather than the quest for creative consensus.
8. Walton and McKersie articulated this approach to negotiation in *A Behavioral Theory of Labor Negotiations* (New York: McGraw-Hill, 1965). They also came up with the term "distributive bargaining," which we'll discuss shortly.
9. That only happens, economists point out, when the interdependence between the two negotiators is zero-sum—when one's benefit comes at the other's expense.

10. This is very different from trying to gain advantage in a zero-sum struggle, as we saw in Figure 6-5, when the seller tries to achieve outcome O_2 and the buyer tries to achieve outcome O_3.

11. And you certainly aren't supposed to "go backward"—i.e., follow a concession with a less generous bid. These "exploding offer" tactics are viewed as coercive—designed to punish the other negotiator, and they hurt both the process and the relationship.

12. Point N is called the Nash equilibrium, named after the mathematician/economist who proposed it. If you're interested in seeing his original work, see Nash, "The Bargaining Problem," *Econometrica* 18 (1950):155–62. If you're interested in seeing an application of Nash's theory to business negotiations, see Greenhalgh, Neslin, and Gilkey, "The Effects of Negotiator Preferences, Situational Power, and Negotiator Personality on Outcomes of Business Negotiations," *Academy of Management Journal* 28 (1985):9–33.

13. Some authors of negotiation books discuss "bluffing" as a tactic distinct from misrepresentation. I don't know what the difference is. If you're bluffing, aren't you communicating something you know isn't true?

14. This was a bit unfair. Fred is really creative at helping me find good reasons for owning various vehicles and pieces of equipment. But he had three tractors and at least nine cars at the time, so my wife thought he wouldn't be a good influence.

15. I also would have been better off if Fred had been with me. He can always put a positive spin on purchase decisions, no matter what lunatic thing you buy.

16. I'm deliberately contrasting the approaches taken by men in each culture because later in the book, we'll explicitly consider the different approaches taken by men and women.

CHAPTER 7

GROUP DECISION-MAKING

Western organizations gained their characteristic shape and internal operating mechanisms during the Industrial Revolution. Their evolution into impersonal, machine-like structures was shaped by managerial ideology that envisioned hierarchically organized roles, interchangeable people doing prescribed tasks, and individualistic motivation of role occupants.

Groups didn't fit into the picture at all. People were assigned to individual roles, from the CEO mapping out strategy to the hourly worker carrying out a job description. This perspective overlooked the central tendencies of our species to seek community, inclusion, and commonwealth. It also neglected people's natural drive to join groups, rather than operating alone. It placed people in an unnatural setting that tended to alienate rather than inspire them. As a result, organizations weren't very efficient, effective in sustaining competitive advantage, or appealing to high-potential employees.

The heyday of old-paradigm organizations has passed. Attention has focused instead on start-up companies and on organizations that have reinvented themselves (like General Electric). It's noteworthy that start-ups are structured and operate more communally than hierarchically. And the large businesses we admire have become more complex in ways that make collaboration essential.

This chapter recognizes that, in new-era organizations, people work primarily in groups. In many cases, group membership spills over organizational boundaries—the internal barriers that create silos, and the external barriers that hinder organizations from uniting as an integrated value chain. So managerial effectiveness requires competency in managing group processes.

We'll be looking at how *groups* in new-era organizations negotiate to arrive at *joint decisions*. We'll see that the groups can make decisions that are better than what even the brightest members can make individually—but only if the *process* is a good one.

THE COMPLEXITY OF ORGANIZATIONAL DECISIONS

As the business world has become more complex, so too have the decisions managers have to make. Let's take the simple "textbook" make-or-buy decision as an example. In the 1970s all you had to do was get the best price from an outside vendor, then calculate what would be the difference in your overall financial status if you manufactured the product or component yourself.

Today, the outsourcing decision is vastly more complicated. You have to address many more issues. Who has distinctive competency to supply that product or component? What kind of relationship do I want to have with the vendor (ranging from arm's-length supplier to value-chain partner)? How will outsourcing position me against global competitors? What quality level can I get from the vendor, and is that quality static, or are they involved in continuous improvement? Is the vendor helping me optimize design-for-manufacturability-and-assembly? Has the vendor reengineered operations *across* our organizational boundaries? Who will benefit from increases in efficiency attributable to learning-curve effects? What are the vendor's cost-drivers? What are mine? Will our union contract constrain outsourcing? Does my own organization *have to* outsource components—so as to have enough "local content" to be able to sell the finished product in an important host country? Can all the people who are affected by the decision be included in the decision process? I could go on, but I think you get the point. *Simple make-or-buy decisions are anything but simple in the new era.*

Complex decisions require input from multiple sources. In practice, no single person has the expertise to consider "all the angles." And seldom does one person have the authority to demand compliance from everyone involved in implementing the decision. Absence of authority has become a significant factor because organizations have become more decentralized, and extended enterprises—multiorganizational alliances—involve more than one power structure. Thus, decisions have to be undertaken *in collaboration with* other managers.

Because business decisions have become so complex, we have to use a different process to make them—and different criteria to judge them. Most people believe managerial decision-making involves sophisticated mathematical analysis. But despite the stereotype of MBA-trained managers evaluating choices on laptop computers, this rarely happens when decisions are of strategic importance. Because of the complexity, a whole spectrum of criteria is needed to evaluate a managerial decision.

CRITERIA FOR EVALUATING ORGANIZATIONAL DECISIONS

Suppose a management group was deciding whether to build market share quickly. The objective might be to establish a market presence, deter new market entrants, or create brand awareness that would pave the way to introduce the rest of the product line. A simple analysis of profitability might make a course of action seem economically unwise when in fact it's strategically important.

But in addition to making economic and strategic sense, decisions need to make communal and practical sense. That is, decisions need to be made in a way that strengthens the relationship between the decision-makers as well as their commitment to the decision. Strengthening the relationship is important because successful businesses depend on robust alliances—both within and between organizations. Strengthening commitment is important because decisions are usually worthless if they aren't properly implemented.

The criteria by which we can evaluate organizational decisions include economic, strategic, and communal factors. We'll see that *how* you go about making the decision will have an impact on its effectiveness. In new-era organizations, important business decisions are usually made within groups, and are usually negotiated. Therefore, what we're really talking about is how to evaluate a group negotiation. Let's look at the various evaluation criteria.

1. Commonwealth Benefit

Group members typically "wear two hats" when they participate in decision-making. They have a role in advancing commonwealth interests—the interests of the organization as a whole. But they also take on a role protecting the parochial interests of their own subunit.

When managers from different areas are invited to participate in "cross-functional" decision-making, for example, it's hoped that they'll give primary attention to commonwealth interests. But this doesn't always happen, as you know. Often, decision-makers construe themselves as champions of their ingroup: they act as if their mission is to prevail against outgroups in the contest for resources, power, and privileges. When this happens, the decision process involves a struggle between warring factions instead of collaboration to solve organizational problems.

The first criterion to apply, therefore, is did the decision-makers keep the focus on the commonwealth objective? Did they make a decision about what is good for the organization as a whole? If they pursued parochial interests instead, the resulting decision is likely to be suboptimal. That is, it's likely to be optimal for an organizational subunit rather than the organization.

2. Commitment

Commitment involves the degree to which managers are strongly resolved to uphold the agreement. A weak commitment means there's little psychological investment. A strong commitment means there's "buy-in": the person "owns" the decision, in the psychological sense. Managers who are highly committed to a decision are likely to put in extra effort to ensure that the decision gets implemented, even if problems emerge along the way. Under the same circumstances, managers with low commitment won't go out of their way to help: they won't care if the decision never gets put into practice. Likewise, when the decision is criticized, highly committed managers will defend it, while uncommitted managers will say nothing—or even add to the criticism.

Commitment is the most important factor in *implementing* real-world business decisions. In Chapter 6, we defined negotiation as a process of achieving commitment to a course of action. *Commitment is the essence of an agreement.* The terms "agreement" and "commitment" are used interchangeably in everyday language. You can say "I have a commitment from this company to do X" or you can say "I have an agreement with this company to do X" and you'll mean the same thing.

3. Ease of Implementation

A decision isn't a good one if it's difficult to implement. The whole point of making a decision is to get something to change. If nothing changes—as a result of *how* the decision was made—then the decision process hasn't been an effective one. Implementation difficulties can arise from low commitment. If negotiators feel forced into going along with a decision, for example, then it would be natural for them to be uncooperative—to "drag their feet."

Implementation difficulties can also arise from *what* was decided upon. Some people, for example, take the easy way out when negotiating a difficult situation—they end the negotiation by agreeing to something that isn't feasible. Let's take the example of Julie. She's negotiating with her boss, Stan, at the end of her first year on the job. Stan is offering her a 10 percent raise, because she's been doing a superb job and the company doesn't want to lose her. Julie wants more vacation time (she gets only the two weeks allowed by company policy for anyone with only one year of service), and is willing to take only a 5 percent raise in exchange for four weeks of vacation. Stan *knows* the human resources office won't allow an exception, but Stan is scared that she'll quit if they reach an impasse. So he says, "Julie, you've earned the 10 percent raise, and you shouldn't have to give up a cent of it to get more vacation. So *take* the raise I'm offering you. Now, here's what I'm willing to do about the vacation. I'll take the case to higher management and try to negotiate an exception. If they'll let me, I'll give you the 10 percent raise *plus* the four weeks' vacation. But you won't be able to talk with other employees about anything special we can come up with. Is that a deal?"

In this example, Stan is being evasive rather than explicitly dishonest. In fact, he *will* have the conversations as promised, but he'll be "going through the motions" rather than negotiating with any real hope of making progress. His settlement is acceptable to Julie, but it's not implementable. Therefore, it's not a good outcome.

4. Impact on the Relationship

Negotiations almost invariably take place in the context of an ongoing relationship, and this is especially true in group settings. How many instances can you cite in which a group made a significant decision but the members were strangers beforehand and they never interacted again? (I can't think of any, outside of the laboratory.)

Thus, an important criterion for decision-making is whether the relationships are better off in the aftermath of the decision. If you were able to sway a decision to your advantage, you might think you did well. But what if others don't like the way they were treated and want to avoid dealing with you in the future? What if they hold a grudge, and are waiting to take revenge? In Chapter 5 we noted the increasing importance of cross-functional collaboration within organizations and of strategic alliances between organizations. The success of these crucial organizational arrangements depends on the relationships between the people who interact face-to-face. Thus, it's obviously dangerous to sacrifice long-term benefit for short-term advantage.

5. Comprehensiveness

A good decision addresses all aspects of the problem. Sometimes it's easier to address only part of the problem, but this can be a mistake. For example, suppose you're part of a corporate task force and you decide on a plan that will increase sales. You won't have served the organization well if you haven't also addressed quality and profitability. If the increased sales require outsourcing to a supplier that can't work to the same quality levels, then this will cost you customer loyalty. Or, if the cost of the promotion campaign offsets the profits that come from it, you may be doing little more than "buying customers." The temptation to address only the easy aspects of the problem is common in management: we call a decision that hasn't been comprehensive enough a "quick and dirty" solution.

This doesn't mean that there's no advantage to tackling the various parts of the problem separately. To the contrary. It can be wise to parse big problems into manageable components. That way, you're not overwhelmed by the total task. But there's a difference between parsing (addressing different parts of the problem *over time*) and suboptimization (doing a good job on one aspect of the problem *at the expense of* the other aspects).

6. Consideration of Alternatives

Some creativity is desirable in any decision-making process. In an era of transformational change, you don't want to limit yourself to traditional solutions to problems. You want to consider a spectrum of approaches. So a good decision process is one in which you've been "thinking outside the box." Certainly there's some inefficiency to brainstorming, in the sense that some alternatives will turn out to be dead ends. But the advantage of discovering dead ends is that you now *know* they're dead ends, not overlooked opportunities.

Two tendencies limit the alternatives that decision-making groups consider. One is the tendency to draw on existing standard operating procedures to address organizational problems. This doesn't work well if the group is dealing with a problem the organization hasn't previously encountered. The other is Groupthink—the tendency of groups to censor divergent thinking about the alternatives. This process involves social pressure on members to think about problems the same way the rest of the group is thinking about them.

7. Fairness

There are two kinds of fairness: fairness of the outcome, and fairness of the process. Each must be taken into account in decision-making. A *fair outcome* is one that gives each party approximately equal benefit. A *fair process* is one that gives each party enough real input in the decision. Process fairness is more important than outcome fairness in group decision-making. But it's also important in two-party decision processes (see below). It's important because people will often be highly committed to an unbalanced outcome if they feel fully heard.

Process and Outcome Fairness in Couples' Interactions

Men and women tend to emphasize different aspects of fairness. Men tend to emphasize outcome fairness while women tend to emphasize process fairness. This produces an interesting dynamic when they interact. The following is typical of the interpersonal strains that get reported in couples' therapy sessions.

WIFE: Do you want to go to your parents' house for Thanksgiving this year?

HUSBAND (absent-mindedly): Sure.

WIFE (after thoughtful pause): Well, actually, I wasn't asking you to *agree* to a request. I thought it would be good for us to *talk* about it.

HUSBAND: What is there to talk about? I've already agreed.

WIFE: Well, *I'm* not sure we should go there again this year. We went last year.

HUSBAND (puzzled): If you don't want to go, why did you ask me to go?

WIFE: I didn't actually *request* that we go: I only wanted to bring up the issue for us to talk about.

HUSBAND (putting his newspaper down): OK, then. Let's talk about it. Where would *you* like to go?

WIFE: I don't know. We spent Thanksgiving with your folks last year and my folks were in the house alone. What are your folks expecting this year?

HUSBAND (picking up his newspaper again): I don't know. But I'll ask them when I call them later.

The next day:

HUSBAND (as he takes off his coat): It's all set. We're going to *your* folks' house for Thanksgiving.

WIFE (frowning): Slow down, honey. I thought we were going to *talk* about this.

HUSBAND: What is there to talk about? Yesterday you said it was your folks' turn to do Thanksgiving. So I'm agreeing with you.

WIFE: I didn't ask you to *agree* with me. I said we should *talk* about this. I'd prefer not to do Thanksgiving with my folks this year. My brother will be there and it's very stressful with his drinking problem. . . .

HUSBAND (looking bewildered): If you didn't want to go, why did you suggest it?

WIFE: I didn't suggest it; I only brought it up as an illustration of the things we need to talk about. Like how my parents will feel if we go to your parents' house again this year.

HUSBAND (showing some signs of frustration): OK, so now I have to call my parents back and tell them we're coming after all . . .

WIFE: No. Not yet. Can't we just *talk* about this? Maybe this is the year we should take a November vacation. It's the best time to get reservations and discount rates. Maybe we should go someplace warm. What do you think?

HUSBAND: I think I have to check the calendar at the office. I don't know whether it's even feasible to take Thanksgiving week off.

WIFE: OK. Let me know when you're ready to talk about it. . . .

The next day:

HUSBAND (beaming, as he takes off his coat): I stopped by the travel agent on the way home. Here are the tickets. A week in Puerto Rico. . . .

WIFE: Honey, what's this? I thought we were going to talk about Thanksgiving.

HUSBAND (looking dismayed): I thought you'd be delighted. Yesterday you said you wanted to go someplace warm for Thanksgiving week. So I made all the arrangements....

WIFE: Honey, that was just *an example* of how we might do something different. I said I wanted to *talk about* Thanksgiving. You're making decisions but you're not talking about them....

HUSBAND (very frustrated): What's the matter with you? Can't you make your mind up? I've been doing everything you asked me to do and you're still not happy.

WIFE: The only thing I asked you to do was talk about it.

HUSBAND: Aaaargh!

Outcome fairness is less important in managerial decisions because we know that we can't always "get our way"—that many factors have to be taken into account in organizational decisions, and sometimes, the solutions we favor won't be accepted by the rest of the group.

The process-fairness problem arises when our voices are silenced or ignored. If the response is "That's not what the rest of us think, so stop wasting our time," we'll be offended and resentful, and experience low commitment. An alternative response is "We've heard you out, and that's a legitimate point of view. It certainly addresses some of the problem, but it doesn't deal with other aspects of the problem. The rest of us believe we've arrived at a better overall solution, even though this isn't perfect either. The question is, can you live with it? We really need your support." Most people would feel better about how they were treated if members of the group used the latter approach. *Inclusion in decision-making is the essence of process fairness.*

8. Precedent

Organizational decisions aren't made "in a vacuum." They usually have consequences for other decisions. The reason for the spillover arises from widely shared norms of equity and consistency. Equity norms dictate that people be treated the same. Consistency norms dictate that if one situation is handled in a particular way, it's reasonable to expect similar situations to be handled the same way.

Consistency is such a strong expectation in Western societies that decision-makers must take into account the precedent their decision will set. In disciplinary cases, for example, decision-makers may prefer leniency in a particular case but will worry that this will mean they'll have to show the same leniency in all future cases. In collective bargaining, the management team may wish to be generous to the workers in a particular plant because of arduous working conditions. But they'll worry—for good reason—that all of the other plants will insist on the same level of generosity. In a range of negotiation situations, people expect consistency, so a good decision is one that sets a good precedent—or at least avoids setting a bad one.

9. Decision-Makers' Own Needs

Despite the emphasis we gave to negotiator needs in Chapter 6, this is not the number-one criterion for judging organizational decisions. You'll recall that we studied two-party negotiations in which the parties were acting *as principals*. In organizational decision-making, negotiators are supposed to be acting *as agents*—representing their organizations. Negotiators' own needs may not be the same as the organization's needs.

This is the *agency problem* in economics. Economists assume that self-interest is the dominant motive, and urge that incentives be set up so that the agent won't sacrifice the interests of the constituency. In real life, most of us are also influenced by a sense of responsibility and professional ethics—or at least fear of embarrassment if we get caught putting our own interests ahead of our client's.

Nevertheless, managers need to be aware of the motive to serve parochial needs. Decision-makers are people, and display all the complexity that comes with being human. They might well ask, "What's in it for me?" and this will need to be weighed alongside what's in it for the organization. They might also ask, "What's in it for my unit?" This is very likely to happen in siloed organizations with control systems that reward unit performance rather than total organizational performance, or with strong ingroup/outgroup dynamics. For example, sometimes the decision task will be, how do we customize to achieve greater market penetration without making the production manager's job a nightmare?

An extreme example will illustrate the danger of ignoring parochial interests. It's useful to involve workers in decisions about downsizing the organization. They can look at the basic economic factors and recognize that the organization can't survive and prosper if it's too large for its current scale of operations. But management can't expect them to be totally objective when faced with the decision to eliminate their own jobs.

10. Economic Optimization

Putting the economic wisdom of a decision in last place in no way diminishes its importance as a decision criterion. If the decision is simple enough and managers have the information available to apply a formula of some sort, they should go ahead and calculate the optimum decision. It's great if you know, for example, that deciding an issue one way will maximize net present value of the income stream—or minimize such factors as expenses, total distance traveled, time to market, or environmental impact. However, even when the economic effects can be calculated, other considerations usually need to be factored in.

STRONG AGREEMENTS

Significant business decisions usually rely heavily on commitment for successful implementation. As a result, managers are often better off focusing on strong agreements rather than trying to guess at what's economically optimal. This is because managers rarely have the data needed to accurately assess the impact of strategic choices; therefore, they can only find out in retrospect whether a decision was wise or stupid. But meanwhile, they have to do the best they can. There's a saying among seasoned executives that *an imperfect decision that can be successfully implemented is better than a perfect decision that can't.* So it's crucial to arrive at a strong agreement. Let's see what's involved.

We'll start by examining what it means to agree. A simplistic notion is that you have an agreement when everyone involved says "yes" to a proposal. But here's where the English language fails us. We have only one word for "yes," but the range in *levels of agreement* the word "yes" denotes is actually quite large.

The strongest meaning of "yes" is an unequivocal "I'm 100 percent behind this idea. Let's do it." The weakest is "Sure. I hear what you're saying. But you should be able to tell by my tone of voice that your latest proposal doesn't meet my needs at all. We're going to have to keep talking."

It's vitally important to understand subtle differences in level of agreement. This is especially true in group decision-making. A decision may be made at the group level, but it's experienced at the individual level. If there are five managers in a group, you may have five different experiences of how strong an agreement it is. One manager may be so highly committed that he or she emerges as the champion of the cause. Another may think it's a bad idea, but say nothing so as to avoid offending the champion. A third may be indifferent. A fourth may be generally positive about the decision but highly distracted by other concerns so that the commitment is superficial. The fifth may have deep reservations that are hard to put into words. Such diversity of agreement within a group is fairly typical, but it's to be avoided if at all possible.

This brings up a very important point about group decisions. *It's usually misleading to say that "the group" agreed to this or "everyone" decided that.* Those expressions overlook important differences within the group. While it would be going too far to say that a group agreement is only as strong as that of its least committed member, it's vitally important to assess—and manage—each member's commitment.

Although we don't have a handy vocabulary that describes the spectrum of agreement strength, we certainly can distinguish strong ones from weak ones. Figure 7-1 shows this range. If every manager in the group experiences a full sense of "ownership" of the decision, each manager's commitment is very robust and this bodes well for decision implementation. It's not quite as good when managers accept the decision but have reservations. In real life, this may be the best that can be accomplished given the dilemmas and trade-offs that can occur. As you know from your own experience, the more complex the decision, the more difficult it will be to make everyone happy and enthusiastic about it. For complex decisions, acceptance with reservations may be a good outcome. Indifference is less desirable: managers aren't opposing the decision, but neither do they have any enthusiasm for it.

You start to get into trouble when there's reluctant compliance. This means the manager is "going along with" the decision—in the sense of not opposing it—but is only complying because she or he feels at a power disadvantage. But the reluctance signals that there's no commitment to successful implementation. Thus, if circumstances arise that would excuse that manager's failure to implement the decision, he or she is likely to withhold effort. Even worse is muted opposition. Overtly, the manager seems to

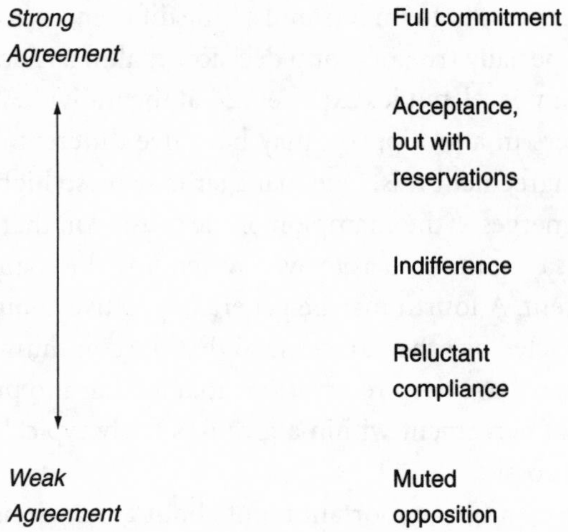

Strong
Agreement

Full commitment

Acceptance,
but with
reservations

Indifference

Reluctant
compliance

Weak
Agreement

Muted
opposition

FIGURE 7-1 Various Degrees of Agreement Strength

accept the decision; covertly, she or he does not. This manager *seeks out* excuses for not implementing the decision, or perhaps creates those excuses through subtle acts of sabotage.

Understanding the spectrum of agreement strength should complicate how we think about someone being fairly quiet during a decision-making process. Silence is often given false interpretations. There's a tendency—especially among Western men—to interpret the *absence of disagreement* as agreement. This is a big mistake. Agreement is a positive commitment. If someone is not expressing a positive commitment, this can mean a lot of things.

Silence sometimes means indifference. If you don't care either way about an issue, you may let others hash it out without much input from you. You may remain present to signal your general sense of solidarity with the group, but you may not be paying much attention to the conversation.

Silence can also mean intimidation. Sometimes it's not OK to disagree. A domineering boss, for example, may "brook no dissent within the ranks." Fearing punishment, subordinates may say nothing rather than express an honest opinion that would be different from what the boss thinks. Sometimes peers become resentful if you disagree. They take your different perspective "personally"—as disloyalty—and harbor a grudge. Being around such people feels like "walking on eggshells," which tends to silence people involved in group decisions.

Group conformity norms may be silencing dissenting members. Recall that ingroups focus on what members have in common, and emphasize how they're different from outgroups. The preoccupation with ingroup commonalties generates pressure on members to suppress their dissenting views. The penalty for being open and honest may be "the silent treatment"—ostracism: this can be so painful that people will allow their own opinions to be totally ignored rather than risk rejection and exclusion.

Of course, ingroups don't always discourage contrary viewpoints. For example, when a person has earned the group's trust and acceptance, and is viewed as an important contributor, he or she can "get away with" violating some group norms. Social psychologists refer to the notion of "idiosyncrasy credits" to denote the latitude given to a member whose loyalty and contribution are undoubted. The person has earned the right to be a nonconformist. But there are limits to the idiosyncrasies that are tolerated. The individual, for example, couldn't violate the core values of the group.

In addition to granting idiosyncrasy credits, groups may have explicit norms that *encourage* honest dissent. Managers who are broadly educated will know that Groupthink can constrain what gets discussed, leading to bad decisions. So group members sometimes impose specific speak-up norms to counteract the silencing effect of Groupthink. For example, the group members may have a process that *requires* each person to state any reservations that she or he is harboring. Or, a group member may be put in the "devil's advocate" role to ensure that someone raises opposing points of view. Perhaps outsiders—such as consultants—are brought in to give a perspective untainted by Groupthink.

Alternatively, cultural norms may be silencing dissenters. For example, some Asian cultures emphasize interpersonal harmony. In such cultures, it's considered impolite to contradict what someone has just said. Saying "I disagree" risks loss of face for the person you're disagreeing with. In face-saving cultures, the combination of silence and eye contact might signal disagreement, and give the person taking a strong position the opportunity to reconsider and then be the one to introduce a different perspective. In business environments where there's a diverse work group, someone who is not interculturally sensitive may misread the silence and lack of eye contact as indifference—which justifies ignoring the silent person. This is a mistake. The best way to deal with this situation is not to demand to know what the quiet person is thinking, but rather to draw out his or her views in a culturally sensitive way. The objective is to make the person feel *included,* not confronted.

Whatever the motivation for silent disagreement, good negotiators will make room for quieter voices to be heard. We've seen time and again that aggressive young managers enjoy the rough-and-tumble of a spirited debate. This tends to be more of a verbal competition than a thoughtful deliberation, and it *excludes* people who are being silent for whatever reason. There's no evidence that aggressive arguments lead to superior decisions. They usually lead to ego gratification, unbalanced decisions, and relationship problems.

THE PROCESS OF GROUP DECISION-MAKING

The degree of commitment can be the most important attribute of major organizational decisions. We'll now see that *the strength of an agreement is determined largely by the process by which the decision was made.*

Some ways of making decisions within groups generate commitment; others do not. Managers have three basic options. They can *use power* to force others to accept a decision. They can *argue* about the merits of one course of action versus another. Or they can *negotiate*—which involves building relationships, gathering information about underlying needs, getting creative in meeting those needs and being persuasive about why a particular solution is best, and building commitment to the chosen solution. Let's look at the impact of these alternative approaches on the strength of the agreement.

Power. Managers should avoid using power whenever possible. Nobody likes to feel that a decision has been forced upon her or him. People have a drive to be autonomous—to make up their own minds without being pressured—and resent being left with little choice. This motive arises during adolescence, as any harried parent of a teenager will testify. It persists, taking subtler forms, throughout a person's life. So it needs to be taken into account during group decision-making.

If we go back to the criteria we just listed for good organizational decision-making, we see that power fails on three principal criteria. First, the use of power doesn't build commitment. It may generate compliance, but this often leaves the person who must obey opposed but not openly resisting. When this happens, decisions are more difficult to implement. Power use also produces problems of fairness. Remember that the fairness of the process depends on whether you've had a fair say in the decision. This doesn't happen when you're being pushed around. Third, the future relationship may be impaired as a result of the use of power. Power use emphasizes domination and submission. It fosters resentment and avoidance. This doesn't mean that managers should never use power. The point is simply that the resulting agreements are usually stronger when power use is minimized.

Argument. We saw in the last chapter that arguing isn't a good approach either, because it doesn't get people to change their minds. We noted that when you lose an argument, you rarely become convinced to see the situation the way the winner does. More often, you've given up trying to reach an agreement—or even to be heard. Arguments are contests of verbal aggression. They usually waste time and irritate people. Occasionally, a persuasive message gets communicated successfully, but this happens *in spite of* using argument as the means of communication. There are better ways to have a conversation if your intent is to persuade.

If arguments are so counterproductive, why do they occur so frequently in Western business? It's largely because Western businesses tend to attract people with a high need for power and a competitive drive. In the presence of a perceived rival—peers automatically get perceived as such—someone with this personality profile feels an adrenaline rush and a strong impulse to argue. Primitive instincts take over and drown out mature business judgment. Don't you know people like this?

Arguing involves highlighting selective information—the information that supports the arguer's own point of view. It also involves discrediting information that supports the opposing view. Thus the information on which a decision could be made is limited, polarized, and often distorted. Arguers don't listen, in the sense of absorbing information from others: at best, they monitor counterarguments for the purpose of refuting what the person has said.

An argumentative process doesn't surface all the information necessary for a group to reach a thoughtful decision. Typically, in group deliberations, two people are arguing and the others are helpless bystanders. The argument interrupts rather than advances the decision process. So it fails on the criterion of building commitment to the decision. Argument also impairs relationships, because it's an adversarial process that creates distance. Arguments don't lead to comprehensive decisions because arguers address the subset of issues that lend themselves to spirited argument, and focus on simple, polarized choices: comprehensive decisions usually involve complex trade-offs. Furthermore, arguers don't do much brainstorming, because this requires open-mindedness and postponement of evaluation until all the alternative choices are on the table. Argument is anything but open-minded: the impulse is to evaluate and discredit competing choices instantly. And few people would consider argument a fair process—one that leaves them feeling fully heard. Thus, argument does not fare well when judged by most of the criteria for evaluating managerial decision-making.

Negotiation. Argument has superficial similarities to the bidding process in negotiation. Both processes involve taking a position and defending it. A principal difference is that in negotiation, the bidding process is couched in a multiphase process. When done well, bidding is preceded by relationship building and information gathering, so that the negotiator is able to assess needs and say how proposed solutions address those needs. Persuasion is empathic rather than argumentative.

Negotiation is a better group decision process because it involves *building commitment* to a course of action. This is precisely what managers need to achieve in any group decision, because the objective is to successfully implement a course of action. The relationship-building processes can actually strengthen future relationships, because strong relationships can override momentary disagreement. Negotiated decisions are likely to be more comprehensive, because the process—done well—surfaces creative alternatives. Fairness norms heavily influence the process and outcomes, so there's less resentment of the way you were dealt with. In short, negotiation succeeds on exactly the same criteria where arguing and power use fail.

The rest of this chapter provides details of how managers can use a negotiation process to make group decisions. Recall that a process is how you go about doing something. The main point is that irrespective of what the *outcome* of the decision is—strategy A or strategy B, for example—managers will be better off using a *process* that leads to a strong agreement.

We'll look at the various aspects of the decision-making process. As we do, we'll be evaluating whether managers' choices about how to proceed are likely to enhance or undermine the overall objective, which is to achieve full commitment rather than reluctant compliance. To make it easier to visualize the impact of each choice the manager makes, we'll consistently use a vertical scale (shown in Figures 7-2 through 7-8). At the top is full commitment—a strong sense of buy-in among the people involved in making the decision. At the bottom is reluctant compliance—where those people simply *give in* and cease resisting. Let's now consider each of the dimensions along which a decision process can be evaluated.

The Process of Managing "Airtime"

Conversations within a group can be more or less disciplined. If there are no rules at all, we have anarchy: people speak whenever they have an impulse to do so. The most verbally aggressive people will dominate— steering the conversation so that the argument will be on their terms, interrupting others, and shouting down competing views. The least aggressive will recede, perhaps dropping out of the conversation completely. Competitive personality types love anarchy because it offers them the opportunity to boost their egos. But those who are shut out don't develop a commitment to the outcome, and resent the people whose behavior excluded them.

A minimum process intervention is to impose a rule that lets people speak in turn. Someone might say, "Let's go around the table and have everyone tell us what they see as the problem and what they think we ought to do about it." This assures everyone at least an entrée into the conversa-

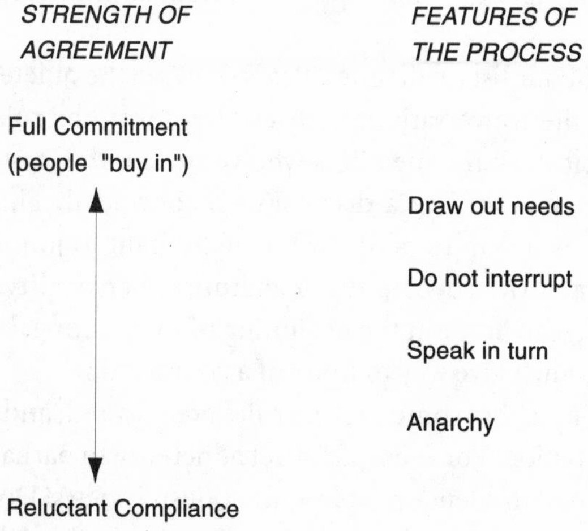

STRENGTH OF AGREEMENT	FEATURES OF THE PROCESS

```
Full Commitment
(people  "buy in")
        ↑                    Draw out needs
        |
        |                    Do not interrupt
        |
        |                    Speak in turn
        |
        ↓                    Anarchy
Reluctant Compliance
```

FIGURE 7-2 Reactions to Different Airtime Rules

tion. It doesn't guarantee anyone will feel heard, or that the speaker will be able to utter more than opening words. But it's better than anarchy.

The group can improve the chances of quieter members feeling heard by prohibiting interruptions while someone's speaking. This can be frustrating to argumentative types, but with nothing to do but listen, they might enrich their understanding of the issues. They may also consider alternatives that they hadn't thought of.

It's best to avoid imposing no-interruption rules that are *too* strict: simple clarification may be needed early in a monolog, and if it's not given, the listener may "tune out." So a good process rule is that you can't interrupt to refute a point of view, but you can ask questions for the purpose of clarifying the speaker's point. You can say, for example, "Excuse me. You just said we should outsource all the customer service functions. Did you really mean *all* customer service?" Of course, some people insinuate counterarguments in the form of questions. Thus, any question that begins with "Don't you think *that* . . ." is more of a statement than a question, and falls outside of the realm of requests for clarification.

We should note that people speak at around 200 words per minute, but can easily process information at 800 words per minute. So they can usually figure out what you're saying before you finish expressing your thought. In a lively conversation, some interruption is acceptable because it doesn't interfere with communication quality—that is, it doesn't matter whether you finish your sentence: you said enough to convey the message. What we're talking about here is interruption as verbal dominance, which is very different.

At the top of our list of airtime rules is drawing the quieter members of the group into the conversation. In its crudest form, the rule requires the group to explicitly ask the members who've spoken the least to say what's on their minds, long before a discussion is concluded. This mechanism communicates inclusion to people who are hesitant to join in the rough-and-tumble of a spirited debate, due to culture or personality. The competitive types are free to argue at the beginning of the meeting, but toward the end, the debate must give way to more of a conversation.

We should note that some process rules are misused, and turned into a means of domination. For example, strict adherence to parliamentary procedure can be used to silence people with opposing views. Doing this tends to make people feel excluded rather than included in the deliberations, so it's the opposite of what you want. Therefore such tactics are out of place in a management context. Airtime rules should ensure that everyone feels fully heard.

The Process of Dealing with a Dissenter

Suppose there are five managers in a decision-making group. Four are in agreement, but the fifth still has a different view about what ought to be done. How the group deals with the lone dissenter makes a big difference in how much buy-in the group gets from this person. Let's look at the range of process options available to group members, and the likely impact of each (see Figure 7-3).

Coercion is at the bottom of the list because it involves forcing the dissenting manager to concede the point. Typically, the dissenter is threatened with punishment of some form. The person may be told, "You can sandbag this decision if you want to, but let's not forget that you have a request in to increase your unit's budget for next year. Don't expect our support if you're going to hold out on us." Sometimes the coercion is much more subtle, involving nonverbal disapproval cues that threaten ostracism. Coercion isn't a good way to deal with dissenters because anyone who's been forced

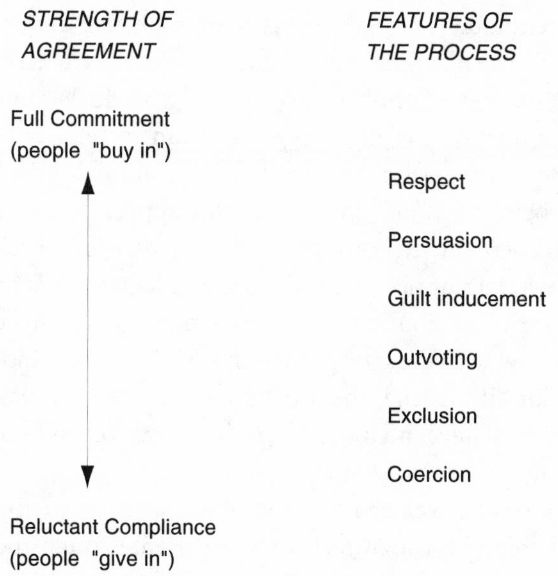

STRENGTH OF
AGREEMENT

FEATURES OF
THE PROCESS

Full Commitment
(people "buy in")

Respect

Persuasion

Guilt inducement

Outvoting

Exclusion

Coercion

Reluctant Compliance
(people "give in")

FIGURE 7-3 Reactions to How the Group Deals with a Dissenter

to agree doesn't *really* agree. The other group members don't hear the opposition, but it's still there, and will surface during implementation.

A dissenter can be silenced by exclusion rather than by coercion. This is done by not involving the dissenter in the ongoing conversation. Here's how it's done. People insert their voices in a group conversation by starting to speak. Whether they continue to speak or let their voice trail off depends on other group members accepting the interruption, which is signaled nonverbally, by means of eye contact and body posture. If others want you to speak, they'll encourage you to continue by looking interested in what you have to say. If they don't want you to speak, they'll ignore you. This mechanism can be used to exclude dissenters. If they aren't given eye contact or otherwise acknowledged, they'll fall silent, and the discussion will proceed without them. This tactic obviously doesn't generate buy-in.

Another mechanism for counteracting dissent is to outvote the dissenter. We'll discuss voting processes in more depth later in this chapter, and see that some ways of voting are much better than others. But for now we can observe that it's a better way to deal with a dissenter than coercion or exclusion, particularly when the dissenter agreed *in advance* that final disagreements would be settled by a vote. The dissenter at least feels that the group's process was a legitimate way of settling the issue.

Guilt inducement is a form of influence. The objective of the person using this technique is to make the dissenter feel bad about "holding out on" the group. The dissenter may be told, "Look, we've been discussing this for three hours, and all of us have other things to do. We know you're not 100 percent happy with what they rest of us can agree to, but we're not 100 percent happy either. All of us have to compromise a little, but *you* don't seem to be bending at all." In general, this approach represents a better process than coercion, exclusion, or being outvoted, because the dissenters can choose whether or not to accede to the influence. This has a beneficial effect in terms of attributions. If the dissenters can say to themselves, "I *chose* to go along with the group," then they're likely to be more committed to the decision. If, instead, the attribution had been "I wasn't given any choice," then they'll feel no ownership of the decision and no obligation to implement it.

Persuasion is an even gentler form of influence. It attempts to "change the person's mind" through reason. The dissenter might be told, "Look, four of us think we ought to do it this way, and you think we ought to do it that way. We're all reasonable people here, so let's see why we come out with different conclusions. Why don't you try to persuade us and we'll try to persuade you—but however this comes out, we all need to be united in the final decision. OK?" Note that *persuasion, done well, is very inclusive in tone.* It also encourages open-mindedness, by modeling it.

The most relationship-enhancing approach to securing buy-in is to respect dissent. The dissenter might be told, "It's interesting that you come out differently on this issue when the rest of us are looking at the same information and wanting the same things for the company. At some point in the future, it may possible to look back and see whose view was better; but for now, we have to make some sort of a decision. So I'm wondering if you can live with the choice the rest of us think is the best way to go. We can't just do nothing, as you know. Can we count on your support?" This approach gives the utmost choice to the dissenter. So, if the dissenter does decide to go along with the group, he or she will be a willing participant. The dissenter feels heard, included in the group, and treated fairly, and doesn't suffer a loss of face that would strain relationships.

The Process of Voting

Let's continue to visualize a five-member group, but this time, imagine that each is a senior manager in charge of a functional area of the business (such as Sales, Finance, Research & Development, Production, and Marketing). Suppose they don't all agree on a course of action and someone suggests voting. Let's look at the implications of this process of resolving differences.

Figure 7-4 suggests that a simple majority vote is the least desirable way to achieve buy-in. This may come as a surprise to those who consider Western democracies the highest form of government. But when you think about simple majority votes in a business context, you see their downside. Suppose that three of these senior-level managers vote for a proposal and two vote against it. This means that two of them had the decision forced down their throats; they'll feel the process was unfair and not be enthusiastic about implementing it. This is a problem. For example, if the Marketing and Sales managers are balking, the new product or service may not be promoted adequately and the sales force may not devote special effort to make the initiative a success. Being outvoted tends to kill off commitment to a decision.

Continuing to negotiate until there's a strong majority—say, four out of five managers in favor—is better. The one outvoted manager will be

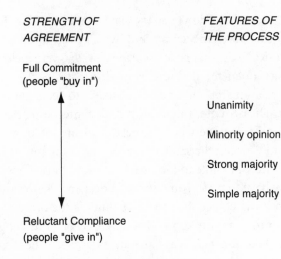

<small>STRENGTH OF AGREEMENT</small>   <small>FEATURES OF THE PROCESS</small>

Full Commitment (people "buy in")

Unanimity

Minority opinion

Strong majority

Simple majority

Reluctant Compliance (people "give in")

FIGURE 7-4 Reactions to the Voting Process

standing alone, without encouragement or allies. This makes it more diffi-cult to ignore group conformity pressures.[1] If the group *has* to use a voting process, gaining a strong majority minimizes its bad effects.

Promoting the minority opinion is a big step toward securing buy-in. Whoever is reporting the majority's decision also presents the views of the dissenter. The manager explaining the group's recommendation might say, "Two different opinions arose from our discussions. Four of us think that we should implement the plan I just outlined. But there's an alternative viewpoint that merits consideration, and here it is . . ." It costs the group nothing to make the report this way. And it may gain the group a lot. The dissenter will feel fully heard, respected, and included. If, subsequently, the majority's views are adopted—which is usually the case—the dissenter is likely to be more committed to the decision.

The ideal process is to keep working on the issues until there's unani-mous assent. There are good ways and bad ways to accomplish this. The good way is through inclusion and discussion—that is, the group keeps hashing out the issues until it's clear that they've arrived at the best option for the business. The bad way is to keep making compromises until nobody can object to the course of action. It's bad because what the group ends up with may be so watered down that it doesn't have the hoped-for impact.

There's also the danger of someone abusing the process of unanimous decision-making. If managers agree on a process rule that requires unanimity, someone who doesn't buy into the spirit of consensus can "hold the group hostage" in order to gain concessions. In effect, this involves withholding one's vote unless the others cater to his or her parochial needs. This tactic may produce short-term advantages to the individual, but the overall decision is likely to be less good for the business. Furthermore, the behavior of the person exploiting the situation will cause relationship strains.

Groups can counteract the tactics of a member who's exploiting the unanimous consent rule. There are subtle (and not-so-subtle) ways of reminding the individual that her or his relationship with the group is being risked. This has to be done very carefully, however: managers will walk a fine line between discouraging abuse and coercing compliance.

Unanimity is a lofty goal. In practice, negotiators don't always have enough time, enough patience and goodwill, and issues that are resolvable. But unanimity is possible to achieve in some circumstances. Let me reiterate that *it's important to strive for true unanimity, not the absence of dissent.* These are very different decision outcomes. Just because some group members are not actively opposing an option doesn't mean that they're in favor of it. The process may have silenced them. Unanimity means that everyone stands fully behind the decision.

The Process of Forming Coalitions

Coalitions are subgroups of people who are united in their stances or interests. They form spontaneously whenever there's a decision at hand. Such coalitions are informal, and often unspoken.

Let's go back to our five managers in a decision-making group. Let's say that three of them realize they're advocating the same course of action, but the other two want something different. A coalition is forming among the three managers. They have a choice of what *kind* of coalition forms, as shown in Figure 7-5. The managers can form an exclusive or an expansive coalition, and the process will be very different as a result of their choice.

An exclusive coalition involves three people overpowering the other two. The three, in effect, form a temporary ingroup that treats the other two as an outgroup—an opposing coalition. The three managers behave as a voting bloc that announces, at least implicitly, "Look, there's three of us, but only two of you; so it doesn't matter what you think. This decision is a done deal."

The exclusive coalition (so-called because it *excludes* outgroup mem-

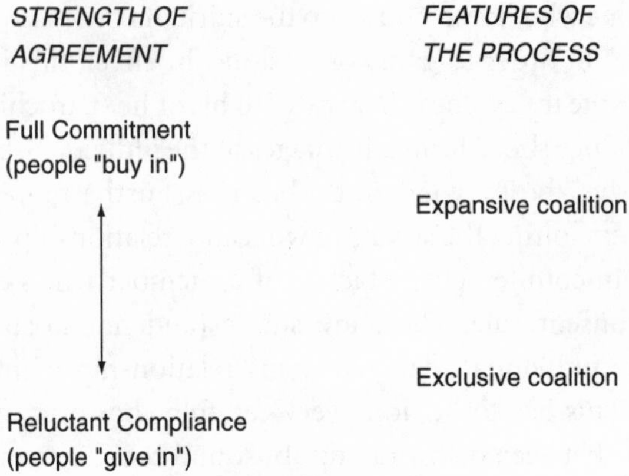

STRENGTH OF
AGREEMENT

FEATURES OF
THE PROCESS

Full Commitment
(people "buy in")

Expansive coalition

Exclusive coalition

Reluctant Compliance
(people "give in")

FIGURE 7-5 Reactions to Different Types of Coalitions

bers) operates as if the decision can be made by a simple majority vote. As we noted earlier, outvoting other managers doesn't foster their commitment. It also stirs resentment and thereby strains working relationships. Furthermore, exclusive coalitions raise the issue of whether a simple majority vote is a *legitimate* way to make a managerial decision, especially when that process wasn't agreed to in advance. *So what* if a course of action is popular among three of the five managers? If the decision doesn't make good business sense, the size of the voting bloc doesn't matter. As a result, the actions of exclusive coalitions can be dismissed as "organizational politics." Managers can say, "That wasn't a real decision. So I don't feel any obligation to implement it."

An expansive coalition operates very differently, and produces different results. Those same three managers, who discover that they're advocating a common position, set out to *recruit* others rather than to dominate them—hence the notion of an expansive coalition: it expands until it includes everyone. The three might approach the fourth by saying, "Three of us think this is a great idea. How would the proposal have to be modified before you could live with it?" The fourth manager would instantly feel included—that the others were reaching out to her or him—and might reply, "I could only agree to this proposal as a one-year experiment. If this program hasn't proven itself after one year, then we must abandon it." Let's suppose the three have enough confidence in the proposal that they can agree to these terms. Next, the *four-person* coalition goes to the fifth manager and says, "Four of us can accept this proposal as a one-year experiment. We'd really like to have your support. Is this enough assurance that the program won't be a disaster?" The fifth manager might reply, "My worry all along is that this might cannibalize our existing projects. I can't spread my people any thinner than they are now, and still be effective." The others might then agree that much of the development effort can be outsourced, and this might be enough to secure the fifth manager's commitment. It's certainly worth a try, because the coalition can always fall back on a vote if the effort at recruiting support fails.

Remember that the effort alone has a positive impact: simply by reaching out to the two skeptical managers, the three are communicating inclusion. They're signaling that they care about the relationship and the concerns of all members, and want the others to be fully heard. The other two will have a better attitude toward the decision than if they'd been dealing with an exclusive coalition. The agreement will be stronger because of the process that was used, even though the outcome is no different. And it costs the three managers *nothing* to approach the decision this way.

Honesty of the Process

One of the reasons groups—rather than individuals—make decisions is that the necessary knowledge is available *within the group.* It's rare that a single manager has the depth of knowledge—or breadth of perspective— to make a complex decision in a modern business. As a result, members of decision-making groups rely on others' inputs when forming opinions and drawing conclusions.

This raises the question of whether the information being contributed is biased. Distortion is more likely if group members construe the interaction as an argument, where the temptation to give biased information is strong: even basically honest people don't disclose everything if they're trying to win a debate. Information is unbiased when group members put all the information—positive and negative—on the table for the group to consider.

Managers react negatively to the suspicion that they're not being dealt with openly and honestly. And this affects the strength of the agreement. Figure 7-6 shows the various approaches managers can take in presenting information to the group. Falsifying information is a good way to sway an argument in one's favor. But there's a big downside risk. It's more likely that others will discover falsification than be successfully deceived.

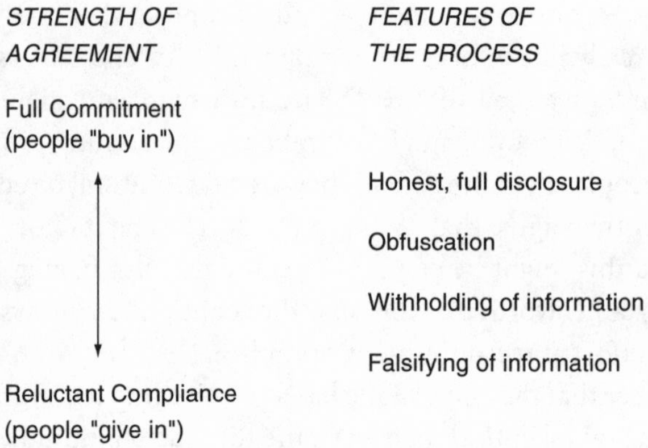

STRENGTH OF
AGREEMENT

FEATURES OF
THE PROCESS

Full Commitment
(people "buy in")

Honest, full disclosure

Obfuscation

Withholding of information

Falsifying of information

Reluctant Compliance
(people "give in")

FIGURE 7-6 Reactions to Degrees of Openness and Honesty

The first reason deception is unlikely to be successful is that most people are poor liars. They tend to give off nonverbal cues—from their face, hands, and legs—that put the others on alert. Each of us has picked up on such cues in dealing with others. We get a strong sense that the person isn't telling us the truth, even though we can't point to the exact gestures that caused the suspicion. Colloquially, we might say, "I got really bad vibes. I'm sure I'm not getting the whole story. I'm going to check out the information for myself."

The second reason deception is unsuccessful is that the truth tends to come out in the long run. You can win a formal debate by distorting information, and when the debate is over, the contest is ended. But real-life management situations are not games—and they're never "over." If information has been distorted, the deceit will usually become obvious over time. And when it does, those who had been persuaded by the falsehoods will become angry and resentful, damaging the ongoing relationship. They'll have a strong motive to undo the decision: it wasn't a legitimate one if it was based on falsified information.

For these reasons, falsifying information is at the bottom of the list in Figure 7-6. Just above it is withholding information. Here, the manager is telling the truth, but not the whole truth. This carries some of the same repercussions, but in Western societies, errors of omission (presenting only selective information) are less blameworthy than errors of commission (deliberately lying). Still, it's not a good way to build a strong agreement—or a strong relationship.

Neither is obfuscation—a fancy word for making an explanation so complicated that others don't really understand what you're telling them. This is less culpable than withholding information because, ultimately, you're telling the whole truth. But this tactic doesn't build strong agreements either. And it, too, strains relationships because it frustrates people and sounds condescending.

The ideal decision approach is to be open and honest. This means not having a hidden agenda, disclosing what your real interests are, stating your biases, and giving others all the information you have, whether or not it supports your interests. Ultimately, the decision will be a better one for the organization, and the other managers will be more committed to it because they won't feel they were duped. And your relationships and reputation will at least be intact, if not strengthened.

The Process of Recording the Discussion

There's a natural tendency for discussions to be unstructured. If people are speaking spontaneously, there'll be a hodgepodge of information "on the table." At some point, a group member will see a way to organize the information and provide structure to the discussion. If there's a flip chart or board available, he or she will write down the key facts and the key issues to be decided. This will evolve to include a summary of what has been agreed to. We call this process "recording the discussion."

Figure 7-7 shows two basic approaches to recording the discussion, reflecting biased or unbiased summaries of what has transpired and what has yet to be decided. The biased approach is manipulative record keeping. The manipulative manager writes summaries in a way that serves her or his interests. This may involve distorted facts, limited options, and issues polarized in such a way that alternatives seem absurd.

Taking command of the writing is a very powerful device for steering the deliberations. You know from your own experience that people have a natural curiosity about what's being written, and writing in a prominent place—such as on the flip chart in front of the room—gets people's attention. The manipulative recordkeeper takes advantage of this dynamic by writing things that will serve her or his personal agenda.

Manipulative record keeping takes different forms. The form most familiar to experienced managers is distorting the minutes of a meeting. The minutes are supposed to objectively summarize what went on and

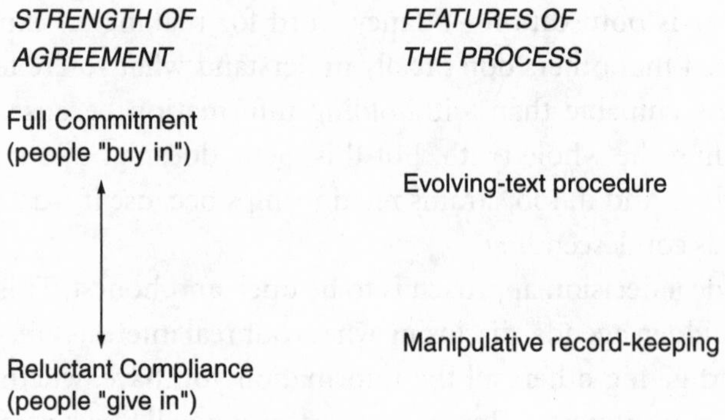

STRENGTH OF   FEATURES OF
AGREEMENT   THE PROCESS

Full Commitment
(people "buy in")
                                 Evolving-text procedure
        ↑
        |
        |
        |
        ↓
                                 Manipulative record-keeping
Reluctant Compliance
(people "give in")

FIGURE 7-7 The Process of Recording the Agreement

what was decided. This is an opportunity for unscrupulous managers to record half-truths and biased accounts. Suppose the meeting adjourned without reaching a conclusion. A manipulator who favored the initiative might write, "After considering various issues, the managers present saw the advantages to the company, but listed several issues that would need to be addressed before the initiative were actually implemented. These are . . ." Another manipulator who disfavored the initiative might write instead, "The managers noted a wide range of problems with this idea which, considered together, made them pessimistic that it could ever be implemented successfully. The problems are . . ."

People resent being manipulated, and can quickly figure out that the information is being distorted in a self-serving way. If a decision is reached as a result of this tactic, they won't feel bound to honor it, because it arose from an illegitimate process.

At the top of the scale is the evolving-text procedure. This involves a positive use of record-keeping. A discussion of complex issues often "goes around in circles" for a while, as people discuss the various factors that a good decision will take into account. Someone standing at a flip chart can list the issues, and the pros and cons of each option. This can be very helpful in focusing the discussion. Then the person can start drafting—for all to see—the key points of the agreement as it evolves.

The reason the evolving-text process works better is that it gives a stronger sense of process fairness. People can *see* that they've been fully heard if someone is listing the issues they view as important, their ideas for options, and the pros and cons of each. They also feel included. Furthermore, the decision made this way is likely to be comprehensive, and it's likely the group will have fully considered all the alternatives. In short, an evolving-text procedure fares well on most of our criteria.

The Process of Managing Time

We've been exploring an ideal model here—one in which the enlightened manager draws out every member of the group, tries to get unanimous agreement through an expansive coalition process, handles dissenters with the utmost patience and respect, is open and honest so as to get all the information on the table, and uses the flip chart to record everyone's opinions about everything. Needless to say, following the ideal model takes a lot of managerial time. This raises two questions in real-world management situations: (1) is the issue *worth the time* to "get it right"? and (2) is there *time available* to do it the ideal way? Figure 7-8 summarizes the trade-off.

If the initiative is extremely important and difficult to implement, managers are better off choosing a high-commitment process to make the decision. The time spent getting the decision right can be considered an investment that will pay a dividend in the future. Bad decision processes lead to implementation problems, which also consume a lot of time. Thus, in practice, the manager can either invest the time up front coming up with a strong agreement, or will have to spend time later dealing with imple-

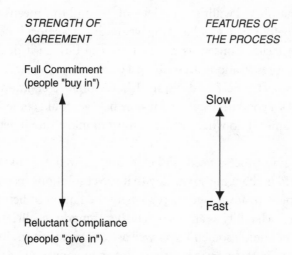

FIGURE 7-8 Time Demands of the Process of Decision-Making

mentation problems. Experienced managers know that it's better to invest time up front developing a strong agreement.

If there's no time available—such as during a crisis—then managers won't be able to follow the ideal model. The decision will have to be made quickly, and this usually means that whoever has power will use it. Experienced managers jointly consider how much time is available and how much time the decision is worth. Then they make their trade-offs and live with the consequences of the process they've chosen.

CREATIVE CONSENSUS

Let's summarize what managers are really trying to achieve when making significant business decisions. They need to take advantage of all the information that resides within the group. They need managers to feel ownership of whatever gets decided. They need to consider the broad range of alternatives, and come up with a comprehensive solution. And they need to arrive at a timely decision. A unanimous decision is ideal, but given the different experiences, personalities, and perspectives of different managers, they might have to settle for a creative consensus.

Consensus implies that everyone involved can live with the decision. There's no silent opposition, even though some managers may be more enthusiastic about it than others. All will be sufficiently committed to the agreement that they'll willingly implement it—and this means defending the decision before critics and making whatever extra effort is necessary to overcome obstacles. Consensus means universal buy-in; it doesn't mean that no one has reservations. Describing a consensus, a manager is likely to say, "No, this isn't a perfect decision. I have some reservations about it myself. But it's a good decision, and it's the best we could come up with. It makes sense and I'll do whatever's necessary to make sure it gets put into place."

The decision process needs to be creative as well as consensual. The business world is changing so quickly that novel solutions may be needed to gain competitive advantage. Here's where the notion of benchmarking can be as much a liability as an advantage. Benchmarking will let you know when you're not doing something as well as your competitors. But it won't help you find ways to do it *better*. If you want an unconventional solution to a conventional problem, you need to have a decision-making process in place that will bring out people's best ideas. Processes that are bogged down in "office politics"—particularly the operation of exclusive coalitions and manipulative record keeping—have a deadening effect on managerial participation. So it's important to develop and use a process that fosters creative involvement. It's also more *fun* to work under these conditions.

IMPOSING A PROCESS: THE LEADERSHIP FUNCTION IN GROUP DECISION-MAKING

We've seen that the strength of an agreement depends on the process by which it was made. This raises the question of who, within the group, will see to it that the best process is used. Someone has to suggest the idea of airtime rules, or of holding out for consensus rather than a simple majority vote. Someone has to get the group members to agree to the process, then monitor to ensure that it's being followed.

Taking on these process-management tasks is generally considered a leadership function, because it involves leading the group toward a creative consensus. Traditional notions of leadership—arising from old paradigms that emphasized individualism—saw one person leading a group. But several different group members can do process management. As a result, it makes more sense to ask who is doing the leadership tasks than to ask who is the group's leader. Leadership can—and, ideally, should—be diffuse. For example, it's easier to enforce a no-interruption rule if several group members are policing the process. And the quiet person will feel a stronger sense of inclusion if several people are drawing him or her into the discussion.

Appointing a leader or facilitator is not a cure-all for a faulty process. If there's a problem of domineering behavior by competitive types, simply appointing someone as leader or facilitator may not be sufficient to rein in the unruly behavior. It's better for the group to develop its own strong norms, and have a chorus of people enforcing them.

It's also hard to appoint a leader from within the group and expect her or him to be neutral in managing the process. Group members will always face the *temptation* to steer the process in self-serving ways—or worse, to use power to influence the outcome. Both of these tactics will reduce the legitimacy of the decision process in the eyes of others, and, as a result, group members won't feel obliged to uphold whatever gets agreed to. For this reason, groups sometimes get a neutral outside facilitator to help them run the process, and this works well under some circumstances. But the outside facilitator must get all the group members to agree to the process rules. It's another area where buy-in is important.

STRUCTURING THE PROCESS: USE OF AN AGENDA IN GROUP DECISION-MAKING

People don't come into meetings with a blank mind. They have points of view that they're eager to express. Usually, they'll find an opportunity to bring up these points no matter what the meeting topic is. This gives us reason to be skeptical about how beneficial it will be to impose a strict agenda.

James March and his colleagues[2] advocate providing "garbage cans." These are general topics to be discussed at the beginning of the meeting. The terminology is unflattering, but the general idea is sound: people aren't ready to settle down and talk about the main topic until they talk about the issues that are of pressing importance to them. But you don't want irrelevant issues to derail the discussion of the main topic for that meeting. So you begin the meeting with a broad topic that's tangential to the main issue that needs to be discussed. A cleverly chosen topic will allow everyone to say what's on her or his mind. Once they've had their say, the group members can leave that topic behind and settle down to the main decision task.

For example, let's say that our five-person task force has to decide whether to introduce a new product. If that's the only issue on the agenda, the decision-making process will be fairly unfocused until the discussion has been stretched to allow airing of managers' personal agendas. For example, the Sales manager might bemoan the low commissions being given to the sales force. The Marketing manager will put in yet another plug for a bigger advertising budget. The R&D manager will say that unless more engineers are hired, product development will proceed at a snail's pace. The Manufacturing manager will campaign for long production runs of uniform products. And the Finance manager will insist that all new products should be independent profit centers.

Each member of the group has heard these points made before, on numerous occasions. Nobody disagrees with any of the positions being taken. But, for example, if you spend money in one area, such as sales commissions, then you don't have it to spend on other things, such as the advertising budget. The lack of response doesn't discourage the managers from pressing their case at each opportunity. The challenge is to let managers express their views and concerns without derailing the meeting topic. Providing a "garbage can" is designed to accomplish this objective. Instead of having only the new product proposal on the agenda, there are two items: the garbage can issue and the new product proposal. The garbage-can issue is broad enough to accommodate everyone's issues. It might be something like "Can we grow the business without acquiring another company?" If 20 minutes is allocated and the objective is simply to begin to list the issues involved, this would allow all group members to air their views. Then they could concentrate on the new product discussion.

The 20 minutes allocated to the garbage-can issue isn't wasted time: the group will spend 20 minutes discussing what's on everyone's mind anyway, so why not provide a harmless forum for it? And that way, you wouldn't have to spend additional time getting a discussion *steered back* toward the new product proposal.

GROUPS AND TEAMS

Some managers refer to "groups" and "teams" interchangeably. This is usually a mistake. Teams imply opponents. This is a source of managerial problems that you can usually do without. Think about it: how could you have a team unless there were an opposing team? It would make no sense. If a basketball team never played anyone, would it still be a team?

Managers seldom want adversarial relationships between groups. Their success depends on collaborative relationships—both within the organization and within the value chain. If two groups construe themselves as teams, they're likely to behave like *ingroups* dealing with *outgroups*, and are unlikely to cooperate with each other. That makes it difficult to achieve commonwealth interests. For example, what if your "top management team" needs to interact with the "top management team" of a key supplier? There are already some oppositional dynamics in this relationship as a result of old economic models that construe buyer-seller relationships as inherently adversarial. You wouldn't want to add to the strain. You'll lose competitive advantage if the partnering is undermined by interteam competition.

The same is true within the organization. You wouldn't want your Sales team pitted against your Manufacturing team. This will discourage cross-functional collaboration within the organization—which is hard enough to attain on a good day. We learned earlier that the natural tendency of functional areas to form ingroups is reinforced by control systems that hold managers accountable for their own functional area. This in itself reduces cooperation. Add in a sense of interteam rivalry, and the organizational silo problem will be much more difficult to manage. These dynamics increase the difficulty of arriving at decisions that serve the organization well—those that would be highly rated on the commonwealth criterion.

This problem is surprisingly easy to fix. Instead of calling them teams, managers can call their groups "task forces" (or even "groups"!), and can mix in members from other functional areas and from value-chain partners. The teamwork can be saved for when it's really needed—when the business comes up against a rival value chain.

Notes

1. Note that this depends on the dissenter's relationship with the group. The group loses much of its influence over dissenters who've been alienated by the way the group has treated them.
2. See, for example, Cohen and March, *Leadership and Ambiguity: The American College President* (New York: McGraw-Hill, 1974).

CHAPTER 8

PERSONALITIES AND RELATIONSHIPS

Managing relationships is central to managing organizations. That's why relationships are shown at the heart of the model we discussed in Chapter 1 (see Figure 1-1). Ultimately, the most important relationships to manage are those between people, because even relationships between organizations are *experienced* and dealt with at the interpersonal level—in interactions between leaders or between organizational representatives.

Managing interpersonal relationships successfully requires skill in sizing up people. But the most important personality for managers to understand is *their own*. It shapes how they view human nature, how they construe the management task, how they prefer to organize the unit they're in charge of, and what kinds of relationships they form.

While it may be going too far to say that organizations are a manifestation of the leader's personality—as some authors have argued—the personalities of people in power certainly influence the culture, attract and motivate some employees (but not others), and, to some extent, determine how their unit is viewed and dealt with. Because the manager's personality can make such a big difference in personal and organizational effectiveness, managers really need to understand themselves well.

Managers most need to know whether their own personalities are shaping their unit in unhelpful ways. For example, those with certain personalities tend to gravitate to the old-paradigm ways of organizing and managing. The inclusive, consensual approaches to managing that are best suited to new-era organizations don't resonate well with these people, and are rejected or resisted by them as a result. In contrast, other personality types find the new-era approaches "very natural" and take to them readily.

But if managers understand themselves, and recognize the pathways to organizational effectiveness in the new era, they can override their own personality predispositions when the circumstances call for it. In other words, self-understanding is helpful to managerial adaptability.

The ability to size up people is also useful in managing the different individuals within the manager's unit. And *the more diverse the workforce, the more important it is for the manager to be good at dealing with different personalities.* In the old days, a manager could surround himself with people just like him. Minimizing personality differences in this way may have had some advantages in terms of surface congeniality, but it had disadvantages as well. In most people's view, it's unethical; in many organizations, it's inconsistent with corporate policy; and in most contexts, it's illegal. In any event, it's not a good idea: you can't have a simple, unidimensional workforce if you want to be successful at tackling complex, multidimensional business challenges. You need lots of different people with different ideas and approaches.

Integrating different personalities is a challenge because they form different kinds of relationships. For example, some managers have a pattern of greeting others in the office with a warm smile, and asking how they're doing in a way that shows they care about what the answer is. These managers will form relationships that are different from those of managers who just nod as they walk by quickly, shuffling papers and looking at the floor. We saw this difference when we contrasted the work experiences of Joe and Josephine at the beginning of Chapter 1.

The challenge of integrating different personalities is made more difficult by the tendency for personalities to have a reciprocal impact. Your response *to* me generates a response *from* me, based on my own personality characteristics. As the process of adjusting to each other continues, these personality-shaped interactions mold the relationship. You know this from your own experience. Some people bring out the funny side of you; others bring out the serious side. Some even get you into trouble that you wouldn't get into by yourself.

If the personalities are compatible, we're more likely to develop a strong, broad-scope relationship. If the personalities are incompatible, we have "bad chemistry." This happens, for example, when one person has a strong need to dominate (we might describe the person as a "control freak") and the other has a strong need for autonomy (recognized easily when they snap, "Don't tell me what to do!"). Understanding the personalities involved—and knowing how to distinguish between incompatible and simply different—is a critical part of developing good working relationships and dealing with the strains that arise in them.

As we delve into personality, we'll have to set limits on what we cover—otherwise the chapter could easily reach encyclopedia length. Scholars have identified thousands of personality dimensions (also known as *traits*). In this chapter, we'll confine our attention to two traits that have the most impact on relationship management in the organizational context: transaction orientation and relationship orientation.

Briefly, transaction-oriented people tend to focus on the situation and on gaining advantage from it. They tend to be individualistic, rational, action-oriented—and attuned to rights, rules, and power differentials. They tend to like the old paradigm. In contrast, relationship-oriented people tend to focus on the relationship—the bond between people—and what's needed to preserve and enrich it. They tend to be communal, inclusive, empathic, cooperative, and emotionally expressive. They feel "out of their element" in old-paradigm organizations.

These traits have been associated with gender, in that men tend to be socialized to one and women to the other. Because business—and the scholarly paradigm that legitimizes it—have been male-dominated for decades, transaction-oriented thinking has biased prescriptions for good management practice. We'll see in the final chapter that masculine thinking about management has become accepted as the norm, even though it makes organizations less effective in many circumstances.

In this chapter, we'll begin by looking at what the research on gender differences tells us about the two fundamental traits. Then we'll try to pinpoint how the traits impact managerial effectiveness.

GENDER DIFFERENCES

Almost everyone realizes there are strong differences in how typical men and typical women behave. Comedians have built careers on making light of the strains these differences create. So too have writers of self-help books. And, of course, marriage counselors make a living from sorting out gender-based misunderstandings. But despite widespread awareness that the differences are strong, few people are fully aware of what the differences are, and how they arise.[1]

The Effect of Child-Rearing Practices

A good place to start is by examining the differences in how Western white boys and girls are brought up. Let's recall that *Homo sapiens* is a social animal. This means there's something in the genetic code that makes people naturally seek out community membership and give a lot of attention to relationships. That is, men and women share the same species tendencies to be communal rather than individualistic, based on their DNA. But they get socialized differently, and, as a result, these basic tendencies are harder to spot in men's behavior. Let's see how this happens.

Babies of both sexes are treated the same way until they get old enough to interact with others—particularly with their parents and older siblings. Infancy is a rather enjoyable time of life for many people. Babies get most of their mother's attention, along with warmth, protection, and nourishment on demand. In fact, the bond with the mother is so strong that there's a blurring of identity: the mother feels the baby is part of her, and the baby experiences the mother as an extension of itself. Developmental psychologists call this *fusion*. But this period of bliss lasts for only a short time. As the infant develops, it gets trained to function in the family and in the world—that's what it means to be socialized. Here's where the differences start to arise: the training isn't the same for boys and girls.

Little boys are denied their mother's continuing comfort and protection at an early age, and taught to function individualistically. They're told they need to be independent, they're responsible for taking care of their own self-interest, and they must claim and defend their rights. They're taught to be rational: that is, to rely on logic rather than emotion, and to be able to explain their behavior in goal-oriented, cause-and-effect terms.

In addition, boys are taught to play competitive games where the objective is to beat the opponent and relish the victory. They're forbidden to violate the explicit rules of the contest (rules are enforced by a referee or by the other contestants, and they assure rights as well as imposing constraints). But boys are allowed—even encouraged—to use their ingenuity, guile, and skill to seize whatever advantage is possible within the explicit rules. Vague rules are opportunities to be exploited: cleverness and opportunism are legitimate elements of competing.

Little girls tend to be brought up very differently. They aren't pushed away from the mother the same way little boys are. They're allowed to continue the close relationship. In psychological terms, they don't experience the same separation and individuation. They learn—from the example set by the mother, supplemented by her tutoring—to maintain and nourish close relationships. This carries over into their games, where what they are taught is very different from what boys learn.

When girls play, the game can't damage relationships. If someone else is losing and feeling bad about it, either the game is stopped or the rules are changed. This makes perfect sense to little girls. A game is a pastime, not a chore—nor a trial in which their self-esteem is at stake. It's supposed to be *fun*. But it's not fun if someone else is getting hurt or feeling miserable. The little girl experiences her friends' pain as her own pain. She's sympathetic.

The same range of emotions arises in boys and girls, but boys are trained to suppress—or at least hide—the *expression* of these emotions, particularly negative emotions. Thus, boys aren't supposed to actually cry when they feel like crying. Girls are free to be as expressive as they want: they're not subjected to the same demands to be rational in an economic/logical sense. They can be open and spontaneous. Furthermore, they're free to be communal and inclusive in their dealings with other people, while this same drive is being supplanted by competitive individualism in boys. In short, *girls are encouraged to follow their natural species instincts, while boys are taught to deny them in preparation for life in a dog-eat-dog world.*

We should note how important play is in preparing youngsters for life. This is true of all the animal species we can adequately observe.[2] Puppies learn to be pack animals by romping with their siblings. Fox kits learn to defend themselves by playful fighting. Lion cubs learn to hunt by playing with their mothers and aunts as practice "prey." So it's not surprising that humans learn response patterns through childhood play that shapes how they approach situations as an adult.

The different socialization experiences give rise to profound differences in how the two sexes experience and deal with relationships. The general conclusion of developmental psychologists[3] has been that girls grow up to be concerned with interdependence, cooperation, and mutuality, while boys grow up to be concerned with independence, competitiveness, and individualism. Thus, girls are likely to look at a situation and wonder, "What's in it for *us*?" while boys are likely to wonder "What's in it for *me*?"

There are obvious parallels here to managerial tendencies to focus on commonwealth versus self-interest.

These contrasting orientations are attributed to the differences in early developmental experiences: females develop their identity through interdependence between mother and child; males establish their identity as a result of separation and individuation from their mother. This is probably consistent with your own experience: you've seen girls remaining very close to their mothers and other people describing it as a positive thing; but a boy who stays equally close to his mother is derisively called "a momma's boy"—or worse. The differing socialization experiences lead women to define themselves in relation to others, and men to define themselves in contrast to others.

The different early life experiences also lead males and females to develop a different conception of what rational behavior is. In particular, the utility-oriented rationality that many men respect is very different from the relationship-oriented rationality that seems more natural to many women. The difference in rational thought becomes evident during middle childhood.

Psychologist Carol Gilligan refers to the way traditionally raised females think about interactions and interdependence as "a different voice." When women and men encounter the same scenario, the women tend to pay attention to different features of the situation, focus on the long-term relationship rather than simply taking immediate action and moving on, tune in to their emotions, and think of how their responses express caring and inclusion. It's a different way of being and acting in the world. So even when women *say* the same things as men, they may *mean* something qualitatively different. This happens because they can experience the same situation very differently.

But women's behavior—both instinctual and learned—gets judged not on its own merit, but rather as a *deviation* from masculine behavior. That is, the question about gender differences typically gets framed as how are women different *from men*. Focusing on "different from men" implies that masculine thought and behavior are the standard. But think about this. Why aren't female thought and behavior the standard? This would make more sense if females are, indeed, doing what comes naturally to the species, and men are doing something different as a result of childhood socialization. It's really *men* who are expected to act "differently" in order to comply with Western social norms for masculine behavior. Only in unusual circumstances are they allowed to "be themselves"—for example, when they're around puppies and babies, or at particularly vulnerable times in their lives, such as when a loved one dies. Despite this, women are the ones who are made to feel inadequate because they don't live up to male standards, especially in corporate life.

Now, remember that we said these were *dominant* tendencies. It turns out that both men and women have typically masculine *and* typically feminine tendencies somewhere inside them. For example, we all start out being relationship-oriented, because we all begin our lives fully bonded to our mothers. But males are taught to suppress those tendencies. As a result, the tendency for relationship orientation may not become enriched with life experiences and evolve with maturity in typical men the way it does in typical women. Likewise, females learn to compete, to be aggressive, and to argue and fight for their fair share in a transaction. They needed to do this when they were young to avoid being overrun by their siblings. But further development of these skills tends to be discouraged as "unladylike." *Thus, men improve at getting the most out of transactions, and women get better at managing relationships.*

Transaction Orientation and Relationship Orientation

The male-female differences described here don't *always* emerge, even in cultures where this socialization pattern exists. Some men are raised to be very relationship-oriented, and other men develop this side of themselves through education and life experiences—often with the help of a woman coaching them. Likewise, some women are raised to be very transaction-oriented while others develop the approach out of necessity as they operate in male-dominated environments (such as business schools and many corporations). So it makes sense to switch from talking about men and women to talking about transaction-oriented managers and relationship-oriented managers. It's more useful to focus on the personality traits than on biological gender.

It's important to understand how these two traits impact managerial effectiveness. So we'll examine each of the knowledge and skill domains we've emphasized in this book and see how the two traits influence management.

Effects of Traits on Relationships

Traits affect the *kinds* of relationships that managers will form. Transaction-oriented managers' relationships are likely to emphasize exchange rather than a broader sense of communal affiliation. They will be thinking—and acting—as if the relationship is meaningful to them primarily as a means of obtaining benefit. This doesn't necessarily mean that they have a desire to exploit others—to "use" them. Rather, they tend to be indifferent to others except for what can be gained from their interactions.

A preoccupation with equity often provides the first clue that the manager is primarily focused on the benefits the relationship will bring. Transaction-oriented people often seem to be "keeping a scorecard" that tracks benefits received and benefits conferred.

Another clue might be discomfort when others do favors for them, and a sense of urgency to reciprocate such favors as soon as possible. At first glance, the urge to decline or reciprocate favors may seem to arise from a strong sense of fairness. But closer examination is likely to reveal motivation that is more complex. Both men and women have a concern for fair outcomes, but usually, their respective concerns are qualitatively different. The stereotypical man tends to be focused on *his right* to an equitable outcome, and will react strongly if his sense of entitlement is violated. The stereotypical woman tends to be focused on *what it means* to get an inequitable outcome. In particular, does it mean that she's being devalued? Organizational psychologists have largely overlooked this difference because they focus on the net effect—which is equal level of concern for equity by both sexes. Clinical psychologists see the difference easily because they focus on the manager's *experience*—on what a situation or event *means* to the individual.

The perceived time horizon of the transaction-oriented manager's relationships will typically be short rather than open-ended. This happens because they tend to construe relationships as episodes that are marked by "milestones." For example, the manager may visualize a business relationship lasting until a project is complete, a fiscal year has ended, or the next performance appraisal is due. The relationship doesn't extend beyond the milestone date/event, because it's defined by it.

In contrast, relationship-oriented people usually have a more open-ended perspective. They visualize the relationship as continuing indefinitely, although circumstances may change that will alter the frequency or nature of interaction. Relationship-oriented people are often disturbed by what they see as the transaction-oriented person's "inability to make a commitment." If they take it personally rather than viewing it as a personality difference, they may give up on the relationship as a result. In many cases, this will be the best outcome: they may have greater compatibility with someone who is more relationship-oriented. But here's where insight can be important. Attributing the other person's lack of commitment to the other's personality—rather than their own undesirability—keeps their self-esteem intact.

There's likely to be plenty of competition in the transaction-oriented person's workplace relationships. This will lead to a lower level of trustability, because this person will be seen as always looking for opportunities to gain an advantage. Advantage comes from striving hard to outperform a perceived rival (which may be good, from an organizational effectiveness standpoint) *and* from undermining the rival (which is usually bad). Sports training fosters both approaches to competing.

In contrast, the relationship-oriented person will be trusted more. She or he is likely to have evolved a sense of *relational ethics* that governs what's permissible and what's unthinkable in the context of the relationship. The motivating force in her or his relationships will be communal affiliation, and the focus will be on commonwealth benefits rather than on balanced exchange. In addition, these relationships are more likely to be open and candid, and this heightened level of disclosure contributes significantly to their overall strength. The sense of alliance will also be strong because it won't be impaired by inappropriate competition.

Managing Organizations in the New Era

Today's highest-functioning organizations are inclusive—they draw people into full participation, gain people's loyalty and cooperation, and accommodate an increasingly diverse set of workers. Relationship-oriented people tend to be more adept at making sure that this happens. Inclusion means caring about the relationships you form, and being aware of how some management approaches draw people together while others "keep them in their place."

Leadership. In old-style organizations, transaction-oriented managers tend to be better *administrators.* They're good at giving instructions, imposing rules, implementing policies, and installing control systems.

They can make the hierarchy run like a machine. In new-era organizations, relationship-oriented managers tend to be better *leaders*. Here, the architecture is flatter and decentralized, with rich, multiple bonds, and less-formalized communication and coordination. Leadership in these businesses requires real skill in managing relationships. These are often fast-moving start-up organizations in which getting the maximum contribution from each individual is critical to success.

Ironically, if the start-up organization is successful and grows, the common wisdom is that at a certain size, it will be necessary to bring in "professional management" to replace the informal coordination that had created the previous success. If the so-called professional manager who takes over is transaction-oriented and schooled in old-paradigm thinking, the organization will soon lose its vitality. The sense of commonwealth and inclusion will wane, resulting in an exodus of key personnel. The real cause of the slippage into mediocrity will probably go undiagnosed. The decline in performance will be attributed to "growing pains" or restless staff rather than an inhospitable and unwelcome shift in workplace relationships.

Value-Chain Partnering. Another crucial managerial role in the new era is forming and managing strategic business relationships within value chains. The bonds between the value-chain partners are strategic relationships—rather than hierarchies, markets, and contracts. Most of the coordination is lateral. Its success depends on the quality of the relationships between the people serving in liaison roles, between the groups that interact directly, and between the top-management groups of the value-chain partners. Within these networks, managers who are relationship-oriented tend to be better at building commitment, goodwill, and loyalty, as well as easing relationship strains.

Task-Centered Management. There's an even bigger effect at the interpersonal level. Relationship-oriented managers put time and effort into relationship preservation as an integral part of their jobs, and, as a result, they tend to form different kinds of relationships. Transaction-oriented managers tend to view the *task* as the primary focus. The basic bond between people at work, from this perspective, is accomplishing the unit's tasks; the only relationship issue that's important to them concerns role clarity. They figure that a clear organization chart and explicit job descriptions accomplish most of what's needed to manage relationships.

Transaction-oriented managers view broadening the scope of relationships as an irrelevant distraction. Broader relationships are "acceptable" if they don't significantly affect work performance; otherwise, they should be "left at the door." In contrast, the relationship-oriented manager views relationships as primary. They are the context in which the organization's work gets done. Work, from this perspective, is the outcome of joint effort—of cooperation and coordination in a commonwealth venture. The manager with this trait can have the same performance goals as the transaction-oriented manager, but sees a different pathway to achieve them. This manager sees high performance coming from having the web of relationships working well, and knows that when this happens, the workplace becomes a more attractive place to be spending time and, therefore, intrinsically motivating.

Leadership Styles. It's interesting to note that scholars who study management have been observing a fundamental difference in tendencies for decades. But until recently, they haven't looked at it in terms of relationship orientation. For example, researchers spent years contrasting "leadership styles" as being either task-focused or people-focused.[4] A leadership style, from their perspective, was the result of attitudes and beliefs about what makes a manager a successful leader. It was seen as a conscious choice about which way of dealing with others produces the best managerial results. With the benefit of hindsight, they might have seen the different ways of looking at the leadership role as an expression of underlying personality. Similarly, scholars who studied group dynamics contrasted people who were primarily concerned with the group's productivity with people who were primarily concerned with the group's process.[5] But they overlooked the linkage between these predispositions and childhood socialization.

Sociotechnical Systems. As a final example, the sociotechnical systems approach to designing work now sounds very much like the relationship-oriented view of how to create a work environment. The sociotechnical systems perspective is based on the premise that work should be organized in a way that's compatible with the social structures that naturally form. That is, you start with natural social groups and give them tasks to accomplish, letting *them* figure out how to organize and do the work. This was a revolutionary concept when it was introduced. But people have been operating sociotechnical systems for thousands of years. Unless management interferes, work gets integrated with the communal structure that forms naturally.

Managing the SPARSE Organization

Let's also briefly examine the effects of the two different personality types on management ability by referring back to the SPARSE organization we discussed in Chapter 1 (see Figure 1-1). All of the domains highlighted in that model must be managed to achieve high performance. Neglect of one domain leaves the organization dealing with problems of misalignment. We're going to see that the two personality types tend to have strengths in particular areas.

Strategy. Transaction-oriented types tend to have good strategic ideas because they are good at sizing up competitive arenas and pinpointing strengths and vulnerabilities. Where they tend to fall short is in the area of strategy implementation. They tend to downplay the need for strategic consensus. Some of them have told me, in so many words, that "strategic consensus is for wimps. What corporations need is a strong leader who'll set the direction and make sure everyone toes the line." Even when they've been taught the advantages of consensus in decision implementation, developing the skills to achieve this doesn't come easy. It's particularly difficult to dislodge the notion that the best argument will carry the day, and then rational people will do what's obviously best. Relationship-oriented people are much better at managing the decision process so that it's inclusive and doesn't lose sight of the commonwealth objective.

Processes. Transaction-oriented types tend to be good at the mechanistic side of decomposing and reformulating business processes. As a result, these are the people who tend to be drawn to consulting companies that specialize in business-process reengineering. Relationship-oriented types tend to be better at discovering what creates value for customers—which is what gives direction to process design. Their stronger sense of empathy makes them more attuned to how others see the situation. They tend to be drawn to marketing—the area of business that's primarily concerned with what creates value for customers.

Architecture. Transaction-oriented types tend to prefer the command-and-control mentality of conventional hierarchical organizations. They will say things like "everyone knows their role on the team" to explain their preference. They're less comfortable with the shifting network of relationships that constitutes an integrated value chain; but this is where relationship-oriented people are at their best. They live in a world of loyalty ties and understandings, rather than the more-traditional markets, hierarchies, and contracts. So they're more comfortable—and more skilled—at managing the set of relationships involved in an extended organization.

Resources. Transaction-oriented types are better at fighting for resources. They also tend to be good at managing nonhuman resources, because this is usually a rather mechanistic process. Relationship-oriented types tend to be better at managing people due to their empathic ability, sensitivity to emotional states and relationship dynamics, and their instinctive concern for inclusion. Transaction-oriented types tend to use power in managing people, rather than aligning motivation with commonwealth objectives. Relationship-oriented types are less likely to get stuck in chronic hostility with unions, because they tend to be uncomfortable with polarized relationships that exclude and demean outgroups.

Systems. Transaction-oriented people tend to be better at designing and operating *control systems;* relationship-oriented people tend to be better at creating and managing *communication systems.* The control system is a form of power: it allows the controllers to dominate the controlled. Communication is the basis of linkage between people, groups, and organizations. It's a relationship medium.

Empowerment. The two personality types visualize empowerment from different perspectives. Transaction-oriented types see it as delegation—as a means of leveraging one's own efforts. They consider empowered subordinates to be their agents. The degree of empowerment they will allow usually depends on the effectiveness of their control systems, because they fear "opportunistic behavior"—self-serving behavior that they, themselves, would consider. Relationship-oriented types see empowerment as freeing up communal groups to pursue commonwealth objectives, as best they know how. It's an invitation to take the initiative in continuous improvement. They tend not to think in terms of how much empowerment they will *allow,* but rather focus on the *practical limits* to empowerment.

Negotiation

Transaction-oriented people are better at some types of negotiations, while relationship-oriented people are better at others.

If the negotiation is a one-shot deal with someone you'll never meet again and there are no implementation issues, transaction-oriented negotiators tend to fare better. They tend to be more skilled at strong-arming the other party in a bidding contest, and better at using—and foiling—trickery. However, their ability to gather the information necessary to craft a good deal depends on the relationship they generate. If the relationship is adversarial (as it usually is), the other party will be hesitant to divulge information for fear of being exploited (a very real worry). Unable to gather good information, the transaction-oriented negotiator is operating in the dark. This means he or she doesn't know whether a hard-struck bargain is a great achievement or a defeat that leaves the opponent quietly gloating.

If the negotiation is an event in a long-term relationship, as is most often the case, relationship-oriented negotiators tend to fare better. That's what the research evidence shows.[6] Transaction-oriented negotiators tend to use win-oriented tactics, such as deception, interruption, and browbeating. They believe that their aggressive approach yields higher gains. This is objectively true if only the immediate payoffs are considered. But when the longer-term costs are factored in, the results often prove worse. For example, we've seen some exasperated negotiating partners make the concessions demanded by transaction-oriented negotiators, then vow never to do business with that person again. The victory was therefore a hollow one, because the negotiator got a small immediate gain but sacrificed a stream of returns stretching out into the future.

Today, the strategic success of a business often depends on building an integrated value chain that will compete against other value chains. In this context transaction-oriented negotiation is usually more of a liability than a benefit. The adversarial process is not a good way to deal with a partner.

The shortsightedness comes from the transaction-oriented negotiator's preoccupation with winning. Recall that people—boys in particular—get focused on winning during childhood when they're being socialized to beat others and then relish the victory. They learn to take advantage of others without actually violating explicit rules. Thus, when a negotiation is construed as a contest, it makes sense to deceive your opponent. After all, this is no different than faking a play in football, trying a gambit in chess, bluffing in poker, or mounting a diversionary tactic in war. It's a way to win that has brought social approval from like-minded people throughout their formative years. But a winning orientation is a zero-sum perspective that creates adversarial relationships whether or not *the situation* is one of zero-sum interdependence.[7]

Negotiations between the Two Personality Types

Despite the overall advantage that relationship-oriented negotiators have in managing long-term relationships, there are some predictable problems these managers encounter when negotiating with transaction-oriented managers. We can see the strains that arise by looking at what happened in a real, videotaped negotiation between a transaction-oriented man and a relationship-oriented woman.

> The negotiation began with the man's aggressive opening bid. The woman was taken aback by this approach because she had started the process with social interaction, aimed at building the relationship. Nevertheless, she accommodated his almost-rude interruption that said, in effect, "Let's stop wasting time and get down to business."
>
> If we look beneath the surface, his ability to control the process is not the result of her lack of assertiveness, even though many observers—typically, men—would make this attribution. During the debriefing she reported feeling caught in a double bind. If she stood up to him, they would engage in a contest-of-wills over how the interaction would proceed. This confrontation would make it harder to create the interpersonal relationship she was seeking: a cooperative relationship in which both parties sit on the same side of the table, facing the problem. If she didn't stand up to him, then his domineering tactics would prevail, and she still wouldn't get the relationship she wanted: they'd be sitting across the table facing off against each other, engaging in an adversarial interaction on his terms. Because she was relationship-oriented, she chose to avoid confrontation for fear that this might foreclose subsequent opportunities to improve the relationship.
>
> He answered her inquiries about his needs evasively. So, to model the response she wanted from him, she told him what her situation and constraints were. But he didn't reciprocate the information sharing, as she'd expected. Instead, he launched into a sales pitch that detailed why she

should accept his offer and be grateful for it. Her attempts to turn this into a dialog were rebuffed by his interruptions. He was clearly treating the conversation as an argument that he was determined to win.

He threatened her by reminding her, several times, of what alternatives he had if the two of them didn't reach a negotiated agreement. His aggressive style made her feel anxious and motivated her to end the interaction as soon as possible.

At the same time, his unrelenting stance made her wonder whether the outcome was so important to him that she really ought to accommodate his needs this time. This would be a sacrifice for her, but her generosity would be an investment in their future relationship.

So she gave in to his demands.

He congratulated himself on a successful negotiating performance, attributing his success to winning the argument and leaving her convinced that his way is the best way. He didn't understand what actually went on, because he interpreted the chain of events solely from his own—in this case a traditionally Western white male—perspective. In effect, he learned the wrong lesson from what transpired: he didn't *get it.*

The next time these two negotiated, she reminded him of her generosity in the last interaction. He looked baffled—sincerely so—and then dismissed her point as a negotiating ploy, telling her that whatever happened last time was irrelevant to the current conversation. She once again accommodated his almost-rude interruption that said "Let's stop wasting time and get down to business." She had a strong sense of *déjà vu.* Her reaction was one of sadness, frustration, and betrayal. But instead of blaming him for being exploitative, she blamed herself for being unassertive: that's what she had been told was her problem.

Now, the man in this scenario wasn't acting in a mean-spirited way to bring about these events. To him, the first negotiation was a transaction in which both parties would do their best to maximize self-interest. It was a game, and she wasn't a very good player. But that was *her* problem. His perspective was: "If you're playing tennis, you don't play badly just because your opponent isn't as good as you are. You play your best game and if they lose, they lose. It's no fun competing against someone who isn't trying: you can't learn from that, so you'll never get better yourself. So, in the second negotiation, this woman brings up the concessions she made the week before. An interesting ploy, but this was a whole new game. I wasn't going to fall for that. She lost the second negotiation too.

She had a long face, but it was obvious she hadn't learned a thing from the first negotiation. I don't enjoy negotiating with her."

The challenge for this woman—and for other relationship-oriented people in similar situations—is to persuade the other person to construe the situation as an opportunity to collaborate in joint problem solving, rather than as a game. But if she can't get the man to abandon zero-sum thinking and tactics, then she may have to adopt them herself so as to avoid being exploited in the short run. She needs to understand that from his perspective, the short run is all there is. Everything's a transaction; everything's a game of sorts.

Ironically, forcefully countering his competitive tactics may be the only pathway open to her for establishing a relationship. In fact, she has the skill set to do this very effectively. If she displays those skills, there's a chance he'll at least respect her, and this gives her a foothold from which to broaden the scope of the relationship. It wouldn't be her preferred way of developing a relationship, but it may well be her only alternative.

Her ability to switch from a relationship-oriented approach to one that's more transaction-oriented reminds us of an important point. Personality predispositions are *tendencies*—they represent what comes naturally. A person can choose to act differently if the situation calls for a different approach. Having said this, *it's usually easier for relationship-oriented people to switch to a transactional-oriented approach than vice versa.* Two factors are primarily responsible for this. First, relationship-oriented people are likely to have well-developed empathic skills; second, the transaction-oriented approach is considerably more amenable to training in the sense of a learned ability to perform a set of behaviors. Relationship orientation relies much more on a change in perspective and insight.

Achieving Creative Consensus in Groups

Relationship-oriented people tend to be much better at negotiating in group settings. The objective of a group negotiation is to achieve commitment to a course of action—to build as strong a consensus as possible. Transaction-oriented negotiators tend to turn group negotiations into debates. It's the winning thing again: group meetings become contests to see who can outargue the others. And, as we saw, winning the debate doesn't generate *buy-in:* it usually means the others have decided to just *give in*—that is, they've given up trying to be heard and simply want to end the unpleasant interaction. Relationship-oriented people, in contrast, have a strong sense of who's fully participating and who's feeling left out. They have a desire to draw everyone into the conversation, arising from the motive to foster inclusion.

Transaction-oriented people tend to consider the group a *team,* and this can lead to adversarial relationships with other groups within and beyond the organization's boundaries. We've discussed ethnocentrism at several points in this book. This is the tendency for ingroups to see outgroups as inferior, to look down on them with derision, and to treat them as enemies of sorts. This tendency increases ingroup solidarity, but it does so at the expense of the relationship with the outgroup. Team imagery fosters this harmful tendency: a group can only be a team if there's an opposing team, as we've already noted. The other group may be another division within the same company, or a group within a value-chain partner organization. In either case, it won't be good to construe the group as an opponent. Doing so makes decision implementation difficult, because groups that are treated like opponents tend to act like opponents and not cooperate.

Relationship-oriented managers tend to be better at figuring out the appropriate process for achieving a group decision. Transaction-oriented people want to appoint a leader with authority to run the meeting. In contrast, relationship-oriented people prefer a neutral *facilitator* rather than someone who'll use power to control the group. The difference makes sense, considering the origin of transaction orientation in early life experiences. Teams have appointed leaders vested with some authority, and they have coaches calling the plays from the sidelines. In contrast, relationship-oriented people visualize a network of bonds that make it easier for the group to manage its own process. They believe that the best answers can be discovered through dialog.

Many women, in particular, have group-management skills that seem to come naturally. Some of these are probably developed as the result of maternal modeling. Think of how mothers manage their extended families. These are extremely complex units to manage. They will likely include a set of kids with unique personalities, complicated relationships, and incompatible needs; a husband (or other life partner) who has a different personality, needs, and relationships; her own parents making demands of her; her in-laws making different demands; and various relationships she has to maintain within the community. Despite this complexity, she's able to achieve a dynamic balance.[8] And this is the group-process model that relationship-oriented people often have in mind.

Transaction-oriented managers aren't as good at fostering inclusion, largely due to their preoccupation with individualism and winning. The result is that some people become peripheral group members, with little loyalty, low commitment to the group's decisions, and nothing to keep them from deserting the group if a better offer comes up. Inclusion tends to be a low priority for win-oriented people. This stems from their socialization. Reflect on your own thinking as you read the following case situation.

> A 15-year-old girl had to relocate from the East Coast to the West Coast due to an illness in the family. She had left behind her entire circle of friends, and had to form relationships over again in the small high school. This proved difficult to accomplish during (ninth grade) classroom interactions: everyone seemed to already have a tight circle of friends that had carried over from the middle school. So she wanted to participate in extracurricular activities where she could find people she'd have a lot in common with. She was a natural athlete, so she decided to play soccer. But this wasn't her decision to make. She had to *try out* for the girls' soccer team. All but the best players would be excluded.

Now let's examine what kind of personality you'd need to have in order to think this arrangement makes sense. The purpose of a high school is to help students learn, mature, and prepare themselves for adult life—including the role of being a community member. Almost everyone would agree with this broad mission statement. So how is a system that requires students to try out for soccer consistent with these goals? How does someone *learn* to be good at soccer if one already has to be good at soccer to participate? How are people supposed to develop mature social relationships if the system prevents them from associating with people with like interests? How is the school helping the community to assimilate marginalized people—thereby preparing them for adult life—if its policies do nothing to help integrate them?

The coach doesn't see a problem. Neither do the principal and many parents (more precisely, many fathers). They're focused on winning. The most important outcome for them of having a girl's soccer team is that it wins games. Now let's put the situation in perspective. This is not a professional athletic team that depends on a winning record for gate revenue, for success in attracting television-advertising revenues, and for sales of team-branded products. It's a group of ninth-grade girls from a small urban high school that nobody has heard of beyond a five-mile radius.

Furthermore, to show how dysfunctional this approach is, we should note that the winning-oriented system doesn't even work well within "the chosen few" who make the team. When the team wins, the team can't rejoice as a communal entity. Instead, the "most valuable player" is singled out and given most of the credit. This preoccupation with individualism serves to alienate everyone else on the team. These other players made an indispensable contribution to the team's "commonwealth" success.

A relationship-oriented person would look at the same situation and would figure that any ninth-grade girl who wanted to play should be allowed to do so. Maybe the team wouldn't win every game, but so what? Why is it more important to win the game than for girls, at a vulnerable age, to suffer the misery of being excluded—and be told, in effect, that they aren't worthy of associating with the others? And why is one individual singled out as MVP? Objectively, the girl designated MVP was simply the *last* person to kick the ball on its journey into the other team's goal. The real challenge was getting the ball close enough that scoring a goal was feasible, and the MVP had no role in that process. She was simply in the right place at the right time.

So, you see, this is not about soccer. It's about personality. Transaction-oriented people see the world very differently from relationship-oriented people. One reason they tend not to be as good at managing group process is that their obsession with winning blinds them to the more important issue of inclusion. *A high-performing group is a highly inclusive group.* Motivation is maintained at peak levels because of the sense of membership and commonwealth. It's the effectiveness of the group that counts, not the contribution of any one member, and the process of managing the group needs to reflect this.

Gaining and Using Power

At the beginning of Chapter 6, we noted that in new-era organizations, managers need to use negotiation—rather than the power that comes with their position—to achieve results. Managers have to resort to power use when the relationship is bad and they don't have good alternatives for accomplishing managerial objectives.

The biggest difference between the two personality types lies in their willingness to use power. Relationship-oriented people are more hesitant to use power because it can easily damage relationships. Transaction-oriented people tend to be relatively insensitive to relationship damage.

Recall that the early life experiences of transaction-oriented people focus them on rights and rules. This predisposes them to enjoy using authority. Authority is the *right* to tell other people what to do, either by telling them directly, or by making or enforcing *rules.* Relationship-oriented people are less comfortable with this form of power because the hierarchical role relationship tends to crowd out other relationship bonds. That is, to use authority, you have to remind people who's the boss and who's the subordinate. Emphasizing "who's power-up and who's power-down" has a distancing effect that interferes with their larger goal of forming a broad-scope relationship. Transaction-oriented people seldom have such qualms about relational distance. Instead, they tend to *emphasize* social distance by surrounding themselves with symbols of authority—choosing an office lay-out, wardrobe, and terms of address that bluntly assert "I'm higher-up than you." It's a sign that they've won. You've undoubtedly met such people.

Transaction-oriented people also tend to be quite comfortable using reward-and-punishment power. These are people who were brought up to believe that dominating others is a good thing: after all, that's what competition is all about. So they have fewer qualms about the use of incentives—or threats—to achieve the outcomes they want. In contrast, relationship-oriented managers prefer to get results through a strong sense of common identity and commitment to a course of action. That's why they prefer to achieve negotiated agreements.

Both personality types engage in social exchange and use it to influence others' behavior. But there tends to be a qualitative difference in *how* it's used. Relationship-oriented managers use exchange as a carrot. They point to the commonwealth gains available from working together, along with the interpersonal benefits. Transaction-oriented managers use exchange as a stick. They demand reciprocation of benefits and threaten to discontinue the exchange if terms aren't met. When they "do favors," it's not a sign of caring; it's an opportunity to create indebtedness as a source of future power. And they're not apologetic about it, either. So their negotiation tactics tend to be heavy-handed. Concessions are debts, not gestures of goodwill.

Of course, if the relationship is already ruined because of the way the unit has been managed, heavy-handed tactics might not create any more distance. Indeed, managers may have little choice but to use them. But the potential for false learning is enormous under such circumstances. Many macho managers congratulate themselves on being tough enough to take on hostile workers, unions, suppliers, and customers, and put them in their place. They don't see their own role in creating the hostility they now have to deal with. And they don't see what might have been possible.

THE BEST OF BOTH PERSONALITY TYPES

Because each of these personality types may be better in certain managerial contexts, it's important to be skilled in both. These traits are, after all, only tendencies, not physical characteristics. They're primarily *learned* responses, so if you've only *learned* one approach, you need to learn the other.

More specifically, both men and women have the potential to be transaction-oriented or relationship-oriented. They differ in what tends to get used on a day-to-day basis.

If you find one of the approaches comes more easily to you than the other, then you can develop the alternative approach by practicing. The first step is, of course, self-assessment. What are your natural tendencies? (If you aren't sure, ask someone who knows you well and who's comfortable being honest with you.) The tendencies you already have are strengths, so all we're talking about is building upon them by broadening your repertoire.

This complementary-skills model seems to be what people are talking about when they extol the virtues of "the androgynous manager." This individual has all the strengths of the stereotypical male and the stereotypical female, and can emphasize one skill set or the other depending on the situation.

It's usually better to start out with a relationship-oriented approach and then revert to a transaction-oriented approach if the other person is acting aggressively and exploitatively—or if it's a crisis situation and you need to intervene quickly and forcefully. It's less promising to begin with a transaction-oriented approach and then switch to a relationship-oriented approach to heal the damage that's been done.

By developing a comprehensive managerial tool kit, you'll be increasing your ability to tailor your approach to the exact needs of the situation.

NOTES

1. Before we get into the details, let's note that most of the research on gender differences investigates dominant tendencies in white, Western cultures. The

research findings don't claim that every man or woman in these cultures was socialized in a traditional way, or that he or she fits the stereotype. In fact, there's as much variability within the sexes as there is between the sexes. However, this caveat doesn't render the generalizations false: it simply cautions us to be very careful applying what may be generally true *to a particular person.*

2. Even ants have been observed playing a game that looks like "tag."

3. See, especially, the work of Carol Gilligan (*In a Different Voice,* Cambridge, MA: Harvard University Press, 1982), and Nancy Chodorow ("Family Structure and Feminine Personality" in M. Z. Rosaldo and L. Lamphier, Eds., *Women, Culture, and Society,* Stanford, CA: Stanford University Press, 1974).

4. Examples would be found in the classic works of Fleishman and of Blake and Mouton. For further details, see E. A. Fleishman, E. F. Harris, and R. D. Burtt, *Leadership and Supervision in Industry* (Columbus: Ohio State University Press, 1955); and R. Blake and J. Mouton, *The Managerial Grid* (Houston: Gulf, 1964).

5. Scholars referred to these differences in terms of "task functions" and "mainteneance functions." See, e.g., I. D. Steiner, *Group Process and Productivity* (New York: Academic Press, 1972).

6. For further details, see Greenhalgh and Gilkey, "Effects of Relationship-Orientation on Negotiators' Cognitions and Tactics," *Group Decision and Negotiation* 2 (1993): 167–78.

7. See Greenhalgh, "The Case against Winning in Negotiation," *Negotiation Journal* 3 (1987): 167–78.

8. In managing the extended family, she's likely to seek the counsel of her community of women. This provides social support as well as the wisdom of people who've dealt with similar problems. She gains comfort from the sense that she's not "in it alone."

CHAPTER 9

RETHINKING MANAGEMENT

This book has emphasized the need to develop new knowledge and skills if we're to be effective managers in new-era organizations. We especially need to be competent at managing ongoing relationships. But our previous education—formal and informal—may not have prepared us for this challenge. Much of what we've read, been taught, or observed has emphasized the transaction-oriented approach to managing. This produces two problems: first, we've only been given half the managerial toolbox we'll need; second, we haven't been warned about the limited applicability of the half we got.

How, you might well ask, did the situation get this way? Some of the brightest scholars in the West have devoted their careers to studying organizations. Yet the progress they've made in the last hundred years hasn't been very impressive. Granted, work situations that used to be intolerable are now merely demoralizing or uninspiring. That's a dramatic improvement. But it's possible to do a lot better.

We ought to be particularly concerned that an increasing number of highly talented young people are drawn to start-ups rather than to larger conventional organizations. The work environments in start-ups are more exciting, more fulfilling, and more fun. They bring out the best in people. It ought to tell us something that they're usually run by people who haven't been schooled in the conventional wisdom. If they'd been trained in old-paradigm thinking, they'd have set up organizations that inspire workers to watch the clock until quitting time.

Overlooking the importance of relationships, inclusion, commonwealth, and consensus is very understandable—and predictable—if we recognize the bias in the old-paradigm way of thinking. Our theories, concepts, and models portray organizations *as a transaction-oriented person sees them.* They don't incorporate the perspective of relationship-oriented people. Because they present a one-sided viewpoint, they leave managers poorly equipped to take on the challenges of the new era.

Let's try to understand why the strong masculine bias in theory and research arose, and see how it has distorted management practice. Then we'll be in a position to see what most needs to be added to our managerial tool kit.

Biased Roots

Business education—whether delivered through books, courses, or training programs—is biased. That happened because it's based on biased theory and assumptions. The theory began to emerge during the Industrial Revolution. As business grew in importance, there was an increase in the need to understand what was going on, and how organizations could be made more effective. Large-scale business enterprises were a new phenomenon that called for a new scientific discipline. Instead of developing new theory tailored to the new phenomenon, scholars borrowed old theory from military science and economics, and adapted it to fit business enterprises.

That old theory was—and still is—heavily biased toward the transaction-oriented perspective, making it very "masculine." It emphasizes individualism, self-interested pursuit of utility, walking away from the relationship if you can get a better deal from someone else, economic exchange as the basis of interconnectedness, winning, rights, rules, and power. The theory has shaped business education, ranging from how you create organizational architecture to how you negotiate. It's not wrong. But it tells you only half of what you need to know.

The bias isn't surprising if you remember who was writing virtually all of the foundational theory—it was men[1]: usually, Western-educated white men from affluent backgrounds. And they were writing from the perspective of their own life experiences, which were shaped by the masculine socialization traditions we outlined in the previous chapter.

Now it's fine to have been brought up in a masculine way and to live a transaction-oriented life. But it's not OK if you're a scholar and allow this worldview to distort your theory of how to manage. When research is based on biased theory, it too will be biased because it will only address questions that arise from that theory.[2] It won't test alternative perspectives that might give you better insights about what approaches are best under varying circumstances.

Biased Knowledge

Left unchallenged, the "findings" arising from the biased research of the old paradigm will continue to mislead some managers. Those who aren't trained to critically evaluate scientific research are likely to conclude that research findings show how managers ought to manage. In scientific terms, the biased research findings will become *normative*—that is, they'll set the norms for what managers are supposed to be doing.

This problem is compounded when authors write textbooks extolling the virtues of the masculine-biased, transactional approach, citing all the research evidence that supports it, without cautioning readers about the biased nature and limited applicability of the research findings. This will leave relationship-oriented people—particularly women and many people of color—feeling that their natural instincts can't serve them well and concluding that they've been going about managing all wrong. In many cases, the exact opposite will be true.

This scientific bias is nowhere more evident than in the case of negotiation, the principal means by which relationships—and therefore new-era organizations—get managed. The personalities of scholars who established the field half a century ago seem to have shaped the conceptual foundations of what gets studied, written about, and taught. The resulting body of knowledge represents good advice in a few circumstances and bad advice in most others. Therefore, you need to be a critical consumer of what you're being given to learn. As it turns out, some of the most familiar material has the most limited applicability.

Winning

The most obvious evidence of masculine bias is an emphasis on winning. Boys are raised to believe that they're doing well when they're winning. Girls, however, are taught that they're doing poorly when they're winning *if the long-term relationship is put in jeopardy.*

Negotiation theorists have devoted almost all their attention to the masculine approach. The purpose of negotiation, one is led to believe, is to win. Look at the titles of various negotiation texts and training programs that talk about games, winning, and power. The people who wrote these books and designed these programs came from a generation educated in Western masculine paradigms.

Furthermore, negotiation theory is largely founded on game theory. *Game* theory. It's the economic point of view that visualizes interactions as contests that the participants—referred to as opponents—are trying their utmost to win.

Now, even the most traditional theorists recognize that there are situations in which both parties can come out better off if they cooperate rather than strive to take advantage of each other. And there are situations that create costs for both parties if the dispute festers rather than getting resolved. We might call these mutually beneficial situations and mutually problematic situations, respectively. But masculine-biased writers call them win-win situations. Just think about this term for a moment. Suppose you're fighting a duel, and you win: the other person is dead. But if the other person also wins: that means you're dead, too. You have a win-win situation—and you're both dead. The term is an oxymoron, and a symptom of the problem of masculine bias.

The inability to get beyond win-oriented thinking and vocabulary produces some serious distortions in what people learn. For example, one negotiation-training videotape portrays a win-win outcome as beating your opponent (using an exploitative approach) but concealing your victory and making him think *he won.*[3] Or, some scholars view win-win as taking turns coming out ahead. They call it logrolling: "You can win on this first issue, if I can win on the second." Another approach I read recently is that *any* settlement is a win-win, because the dispute has been resolved rather than allowed to fester.

Now, all of these points make some sense in certain contexts, but the win-oriented vocabulary keeps us locked in the masculine domain, and thus never very far beyond self-interest and adversarial relationships. A more-balanced approach would take us on an intellectual journey that reveals the other half of the picture—the relationship-oriented half. It gives us broader insights, and a broader response repertoire. And it's more inclusive: it values the perspectives of thoughtful people who don't happen to be traditionally socialized Western white men.

Game Theory

Similarly, game theory can get in the way rather than help us understand. It models only one type of negotiation situation. This was shown in Figure

6-6. It's a Type II situation in which there's a small overlap of interest that makes it worth the parties' time to negotiate.

Game theory is individualistic and win-oriented—hence the name. The challenge is to maximize your own utility in the game.[4] Your opponent can prevent you from getting your payoff by not agreeing to the outcome, in which case you'd have to settle for whatever utility comes from your best alternative.

The degree to which you win depends on how high the settlement is when projected onto your utility axis. You have several options for getting the other party to agree. These include trickery, misrepresentation, power use, or a creative solution that also gives your opponent high utility. Note that the motive for allowing the opponent to get a good outcome stems from your own self-interest: doing so will motivate him or her to let *you* get a good outcome.

It's a way to win.

The biggest shortcoming of game theory is that it can't be used to model a Type I situation—the type we most frequently encounter. *Game theory ignores commonwealth interest.* There's an axis for your interest and an axis for the other party's interest, but there's no axis for the interests *of the relationship.*

Commonwealth interest is qualitatively different from either party's individual interest, as we'll see next: it's more than the sum of the respective parties' interests.

Commonwealth

We'll begin by looking at some examples of Type I negotiation drawn from everyday life. These will illustrate the strengths and shortcomings of game theory and its derivatives.

> We first meet Anne as a single woman living in a condominium. She has a mortgage that's partly paid off, but interest rates are dropping, so she wants to renegotiate the interest rate. This shapes up as a classic two-party distributive negotiation. The banker has an interest in getting as much profit as possible from her loan; Anne wants to pay as little as possible. Models from game theory (and its offshoot, transaction-oriented negotiation theory) are useful here: it's a single transaction in which the interests are distinct and measurable.
>
> In fact, Anne never does refinance the condominium. While the

paperwork is being processed at the new, agreed-upon rate, she meets Nathan, marries him, and after the honeymoon they buy a house together. They didn't "live happily ever after" because this isn't a fairy tale. They did, however, "resolve conflicts constructively ever after" because they're real people with real differences, and they deal with their relationship strains promptly and effectively.

Let's move the clock ahead. Twenty years later, the mortgage is paid up, and the house has evolved into an attractive home due to the remodeling and landscaping this couple has done. They're happily married, have good jobs, and now have a teenage daughter, Sandra (and, of course, a dog).

Anne negotiates with Nathan almost every day about the house. But the negotiations don't involve interests that are conceptually separable. A transaction-oriented scholar might *posit* certain rights and interests (or financial equity) that she has that are distinct from his, in order to make the old paradigm seem to fit her reality. But Anne doesn't experience the negotiating situation that way. It's *their* house and *their* financial equity—and this is the context in which she negotiates. Anne would say that in concept, *their* house is no different from *their* daughter. The teenager can't be divided into his daughter and her daughter: neither can the house (or the dog). Thus, while they may not always agree on what's in the best interests of the daughter, house, or dog, they have a shared—or collective—interest in the welfare of each.

Anne is blissfully unaware that old-paradigm scholars might consider her inept, naive, and vulnerable. She hasn't been trained to consider each party's individualistic interests, decide what's her best alternative to negotiating with Nathan if they hit an impasse, and manipulate information to gain a favorable settlement for herself. So she follows an approach that comes naturally to her.

She negotiates over the house, the daughter, and the dog, and never even considers that she might have interests that old-paradigm theorists consider to be hers alone. Her focus is on the relationship; the focus of transaction-oriented theorists is on each individual party—the "opponents" in the negotiation.

Despite her benighted state, she does a good job negotiating. Issues get resolved in a way that leaves the couple satisfied and committed to the decision, with no relationship damage. So let's examine some of her specific negotiations, and evaluate the adequacy of transaction-oriented theory to model them. We'll see that without the notion of commonwealth—a concept that is intuitively obvious to relationship-oriented negotiators—we're at a loss to describe, understand, and predict her (and Nathan's, for that matter) actions in the negotiation.

A current negotiation is whether to put new wallpaper on the dining room. Anne wants to change the decor. Their tastes and style of entertaining have changed over the years and the wallpaper is the only part of the room that doesn't reflect these changes. She has good instincts about creating the right ambiance and knows that the old wallpaper—with its Revolutionary War themes—is getting in the way. Nathan, on the other hand, while just as concerned about the comfort of their guests, thinks it's fine just the way it is. He remembers the last time they put on wallpaper. It was stressful and frustrating and they ended up angry with each other. He doesn't want to put the relationship through that strain again so he suggests painting over the wallpaper. However, Anne has her heart set on a floral wallpaper she saw when she went to visit her sister last Christmas, and has found a similar pattern in the local wallpaper store. They get an estimate of what it would cost to pay someone to do it and find it more expensive than their budget will comfortably allow.

After weeks of intermittent negotiations, some short and some lengthy, in which they've exhausted all the reasonable options without finding an acceptable solution, her enthusiasm for wallpaper persists. So Nathan offers to put in extra overtime at work so they can afford to pay someone to hang the wallpaper for them. Anne really believes the redecoration is important to the family, so it makes sense to make sacrifices to do it. She's on salary, so she can't earn extra money from working longer hours. He gets paid by the hour, so he puts in the overtime.

Now, let's note her account of what they decided: "it makes sense to make sacrifices to do it." It makes sense to them—Nathan and Anne—not just to her. This is commonwealth rationality. Although Nathan is the one who puts in the overtime, the sacrifice is *theirs*. And they both agree to make the sacrifice, not for each other, or themselves, but for the relationship.

While the wallpaper issue is being deliberated, a second negotiation is underway involving Sandra, their teenage daughter. She wants her parents to grant an exception to the normal 10 P.M. curfew so that she can stay to the end of the school dance. Nathan has opposed it, and Anne is still thinking about it. The two parents negotiate, on and off, over several days. She is able to discern, and help Nathan understand, that the curfew issue masks the real discomfort, which involves his approval of Sandra's boyfriend. Maybe it's the boyfriend's green hair, or perhaps the safety pin he wears through his eyebrow, but Nathan isn't comfortable with this dating situation.

They discuss alternatives. If they say yes, it might set a precedent that would push the curfew back an hour for all dates. If they say no, Sandra may react very strongly: she's at an age when parental authority is problematic and they're already seeing some passive-aggressiveness in her. They don't want to precipitate a crisis. They reluctantly agree to the 11 P.M. curfew, but present it as a special exception that sets no precedent. Throughout their discussions, Anne and Nathan work to meet their communal interest in the welfare of their daughter and their relationship with her.[5] While their ideas of *how* to reach this differ at times, the need itself is shared at all times.

Even the dog is the subject of negotiation. The 6-month-old border collie is rambunctious, and they need to train it to restore some order to the household. The trainer wants them to use a toothed training collar rather than a smooth choker chain. Nathan thinks the toothed collar is a good idea, while Anne recoils at the thought. Nathan recounts what the trainer told him: when one pulls on the traditional smooth choker chain, this momentarily stops the dog from breathing but otherwise creates little discomfort. As a result, it doesn't provide an effective deterrent stimulus. The toothed chain, by contrast, simulates the feeling of an alpha dog dominating an errant pack member. The toothed choker functions as a deterrent because of the dog's instinctual response to the sensation of teeth around its neck. Training, by this method, is very efficient and painless.

But Anne isn't convinced by this sociobiological reasoning. The toothed collar looks to her like something the Marquis de Sade might have designed for weekend entertainment. She doesn't believe it's not painful. Nathan convinces her to try it around her own neck. She does, and finds it isn't as painful as she imagined because the teeth are well rounded and the pressure even. She and Nathan make some jokes about kinkiness but she refuses to let him take a Polaroid photograph. They decide to use the new collar to train the dog. Here again, throughout the negotiation, the need or interest at stake was a communal one—curbing the dog's disruptive behavior in an effective and humane way.

These examples should illustrate that the two-axis model isn't very helpful in understanding commonwealth negotiations. There aren't two parties. There is *one* party. Although in each of the illustrations Anne and Nathan started out with their own individual points of view and needs, their search was for something that would be in accordance with their relationships (to each other, to their daughter, and to the dog). The answers they found expressed and depended not on competition but on caring—an underlying characteristic of inclusion and therefore of commonwealth relationships.

This phenomenon isn't unique to couples. Equivalent examples exist in corporate settings. Consider a true joint venture, which we discussed in Chapter 5. It has needs and priorities that are distinct from those of either organization that sponsored it. The JV's chance of survival and prosperity is highest if it's given freedom to operate adaptively in its niche. But the failure rate of Western joint ventures is disturbingly high. We're learning that the quickest way to put a JV out of business is to operate it in a way that serves the interests of each sponsoring organization, rather than of the new entity that they created. That is, the managerial focus needs to be on commonwealth interests.

Or, consider a high-tech start-up company that's a true partnership, in which everyone participates in profit sharing—including those who do the daily work, those who manage, and those who simply invest. Negotiations over how much of the revenue will be reinvested rather than distributed are one-party commonwealth negotiations. These will be very different from negotiations in old-paradigm hierarchical organizations. There, two opposing camps—labor and management—would have struggled over the same revenue-allocation issue. Labor-management negotiations tend to follow the prescriptions of transaction-oriented theory, even when the parties' interests are objectively inseparable. Sadly, the adversarial process that ensues saps the organization's competitive advantage, and both the union members and managers come out worse off. Thus, there's much to learn from how the high-tech partnership handles what's basically the same issue. The focus on communal interests increases people's motivation to contribute to the organization's success.

Or, consider the integrated value chain. The fortunes of each of the contributing businesses rise and fall with the success of the extended enterprise. Therefore, their interests are largely commonwealth interests. As a result, models that focus on *system optimization* will be more informative than models of bilateral and even multilateral negotiation. For example, managers can learn a lot from how central figures in extended families are able to maintain dynamic harmony.

Clearly, we need new theory that takes us far beyond the existing transaction-oriented concepts and models. As a step toward imagining what that theory would be like, consider the new insights that come to light if all we do is add a third axis to our traditional game-theory diagrams.

Figure 9-1 shows how adding the payoff *to the relationship* (shown on the vertical axis) enriches our theory. This allows us to accommodate Type I negotiations as well as Type II negotiations.[6] It complicates our thinking in important ways—that is, in ways that begin to add in the relationship-oriented manager's perspective. In that sense, it lays the groundwork for developing a more inclusive theory, as well as a more comprehensive one.

To illustrate the usefulness of this approach, let's look at how it applies to Japanese supplier relationships, which we discussed in Chapter 4. As you'll recall, the assembler organization—let's say it's an auto manufacturer, such as Toyota—seeks out sources of supply for a key component.

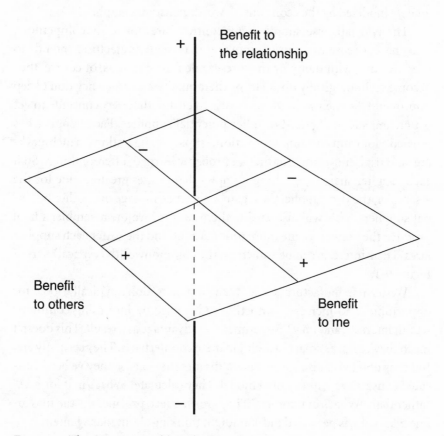

FIGURE 9-1 The Commonwealth Utility Graph

This involves a comparison of offered value (consisting of price, quality, reliability, design-for-manufacturability, just-in-time delivery, and continuous-improvement processes). The assembler then picks the best *two* suppliers. They're told they can share the supply business on the condition that they also share all their trade secrets.

This would be a preposterous request if it came from a traditional Western manufacturer (who would have put the supply contract out to bid, and given the whole contract to the low bidder). But even in the event that the manufacturer split the supply business between the two lowest bidders (to ensure that a source is available if one supplier is shut down because of a strike, fire, or earthquake), the two suppliers would remain adversaries. The next time the contract was put out for bid, they would again be competing to make sure they ended up as one of the two finalists. There's no commonwealth interest in the relationship the manufacturer creates between the two suppliers. Their interactions would therefore be adequately modeled by the economists' two-dimensional graph.

The two Japanese suppliers, by contrast, are not really competitors. They have a sense of security, knowing that the manufacturer intends to keep working with them for the foreseeable future (unless, of course, they become technologically obsolete, or their quality and efficiency don't keep improving). So their *mutual objective* is to ensure that they continue to get better, and stay well ahead of other potential suppliers. Each supplier has learned a lot from constant innovation, employee suggestions, benchmarking, and trial-and-error. But they've probably learned different things. So if each supplier shares everything it knows that creates greater value for the assembler, the two suppliers will gain a bigger advantage over other potential suppliers. This will also enable them to improve the assembler's final product: the better it is, the more product sold, and the better each supplier fares. Their interests can be shown on the commonwealth (vertical) axis of Figure 9-1.

Western manufacturers and their suppliers don't typically look for opportunities to increase competitive advantage by increasing commonwealth interests, and they lose competitive advantage as a result. This doesn't mean they're not as smart as their Japanese counterparts. They certainly are. But they don't visualize commonwealth interests because they've been educated to use a two-dimensional model. They calculate "What's in it for me?" rather than "What's in it for us?" They are, in effect, prisoners of the masculine bias that has pervaded old-paradigm thinking about management.

Conflict Management Styles

We noted in Chapter 8 that people's different personalities predispose them to use certain approaches rather than others. In reality, many different traits affect behavior when relationships are strained by conflict. But scholars who've been steeped in transaction-oriented ways of thinking tend to focus on people's tendencies to end up in a particular section of the game-theory matrix. The alternative "styles" are shown in Figure 9-2.[7] The styles are masculine-biased categories. That is, the aspect of personality that's stressed is the extent to which they pursue self-interest in the context of the other party's interests.

Competing personalities, according to this schema, tend to maximize their own self-interest with no regard for how the other party fares. It's the same, undiluted masculine approach that underlies Utility Theory. But people who have a competing orientation are usually not pathological narcissists. Rather, they've taken to heart the early-life training that says something like "You have to look out for yourself in this world. That's how meritocracy works: the fittest survive and prosper." Thus, people with com-

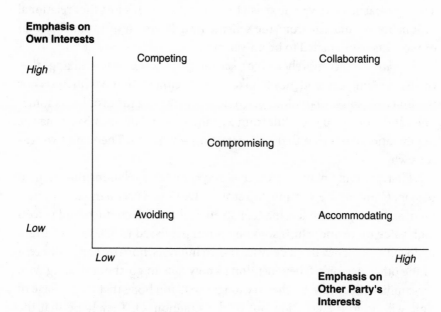

FIGURE 9-2 "Styles" of Conflict Management: An Attempt to Summarize
    Personality Dimensions

peting personalities don't consider themselves selfish. They're simply taking care of themselves in a context in which others are believed to be doing the same.

Accommodating personalities sacrifice their own interests to take care of the other party. From an economic utility perspective, this is irrational. Now here's where the depth of the masculine bias really shows itself. Old-paradigm economists figure that people like Mother Teresa who seem to be doing things for others are not acting out of a sense of community. They're acting out of self-interest, because following their religious convictions makes them feel good. Exchange theorists—economists' sociological cousins—figure that anyone who's acting in a caring manner is really building up indebtedness. The mother instinct, from this perspective, is a myth: all Mom is really doing is ingratiating, to keep herself out of a nursing home.

Without the distortion of the masculine bias, we can recognize accommodation as behavior that arises naturally among people who are relationship-oriented. They aren't making *sacrifices:* they're motivated by a sense of caring and are acting because they're in a position to make a difference. Said another way, they're doing things *for the relationship,* and they probably aren't distinguishing self-interest from the needs of the relationship. This approach, as we've noted, isn't irrational at all. It's just that relational rationality is different from the self-interested version of rationality that economists have posited to be universal.

Avoiding is incomprehensible to economists as well as to exchange theorists. Avoiding is a tendency to take care of neither your own interests nor the other person's. Masculine-oriented scholars view the avoider as someone who "won't step up."[8] But from a gender-neutral perspective, it may be highly rational—rather than self-defeating—behavior. There are two reasons why.

First, avoiding may be a rational response for a relationship-oriented person. Conflicts are relationship strains. Dealing with them takes quite a bit of skill. People who feel inadequate in dealing with conflicts and place a high value on relationships sometimes feel paralyzed to act: they're afraid to do *anything.* They don't deny their own interests, nor are they indifferent to the other person's. They just don't know *how* to go about dealing with the conflict effectively. So they try to ignore it and hope that the passage of time will drain the emotion out of the situation. Or they hope that the other person has a higher level of interpersonal competency and will take the lead in healing the strained relationship.

Second, avoiding may be the result of trauma. For example, a surprising number of avoiders come from family situations in which there's been a divorce. As the avoiders delve deeper in understanding the psychological roots of their predisposition, they often relate vivid memories of their parents squabbling over a protracted period. When their parents later got divorced, they "learned" that conflict leads to abandonment, and developed a phobic reaction to disputes. This is hardly a surprising outcome given how upsetting it is to experience a family breakup, especially when you're at a vulnerable age. The avoidance behavior is highly rational given the person's objectives and expected outcomes, even though it isn't self-serving in an economic sense.

Compromising is the predisposition to meet the other person halfway in zero-sum interactions. In some situations (such as pure distributive bargaining negotiations) compromising makes perfect sense: you split the difference in order to get a settlement that will be viewed as fair. In other situations, compromise is simply a time-saver. As you know, it takes time to search thoroughly for integrative solutions and evaluate each one; and often, the issue isn't worth the time. Under these circumstances, people may compromise so that they can move on to other issues that are more important.

When compromising becomes a trait rather than a situation-specific decision, we need to understand it. Here again, the explanation may involve early life experiences. When parents—particularly mothers—are dealing with a set of siblings, they tend to use compromise to resolve the endless disputes that arise from sibling rivalry. "OK, you can play with the toy first today, but your brother can play with it first tomorrow." If the child sees compromising modeled over several years, he or she is more likely to adopt this same technique as a primary mechanism for resolving conflicts.

Transaction-oriented people tend to visualize compromise in terms of a game that can't be won by either contestant—like a stalemate in chess, a no-score soccer game, or perhaps even a military confrontation that has become a standoff. If you can't win this one, they figure, you may as well settle it somehow and move on. For others, compromise can be another form of conflict avoidance: the person is "taking the easy way out" to avoid further relationship strains.

Collaboration is the predisposition to seek mutual gain. Transaction-oriented people see collaboration as the pathway to self-gain. They need to find ways to get the opponent to agree to a compromise that has high utility for themselves. If they don't have the power to claim value by forcing a solution, they can come up with solutions that also yield high payoffs to the other. This search for creative solutions often becomes a game in itself—much like a puzzle. It challenges their ingenuity. Relationship-oriented people aren't doing this at all. They are more likely to be engaged in a shared quest to come up with a solution that benefits the relationship (they're visualizing the vertical axis in Figure 9-1, not the upper right quadrant of Figure 9-2). The process of seeking solutions to mutual problems is often as important to them as the outcome: that is, consultation and dialog are valued per se.

In sum, the "conflict styles" approach to understanding traits is useful for identifying some masculine tendencies. But it isn't very helpful from a "diversity" perspective. It's a poor way of modeling how relationship-oriented people are predisposed to approach conflicts. Furthermore, by leading people to think purely in terms of the two axes used in game theory models, the conflict-styles model provides poor guidance for dealing with the kinds of conflict situations people most often get involved in. These are Type I negotiations in which there are commonwealth interests rather than individualistic interests at stake.

Resistance Points

Figure 6-9 showed that the feasible set of outcomes is limited by the Pareto-optimal frontier and the resistance-point utilities (x_{alt} and y_{alt}). Economists say that any outcomes that have less utility than the parties' resistance points aren't feasible because rational people wouldn't accept those deals. The resistance point represents the utility of the best deal you can get outside of the present negotiations—such as what you can get from going to court, dealing with someone else instead, or going on strike.

These alternatives to a negotiated settlement—fallback options—involve either abandoning the relationship, at least temporarily, or seriously damaging it. As a result, factoring in the alternative makes sense only if a person is transaction-oriented, not worried about implementation or future interactions, and indifferent to the relationship.

Thus, a model that uses resistance points to guide negotiator decision-making is applicable to transaction-oriented people engaged in Type II laboratory negotiations, but not far beyond. Now, at least half the people who engage in negotiations are relationship-oriented rather than transaction-oriented. All of them engage in Type I negotiations more often than Type II negotiations. And all participate in negotiations that are more complex than those we simulate in the laboratory. So *the gender bias that leads scholars and writers to emphasize resistance points can lead to bad advice to real managers engaged in real negotiations on and off the job.*

Just think about it. In Type I negotiations involving someone with whom you have a long-term relationship, what are your realistic alternatives? Common sense says you shouldn't be suing, striking, or walking away from the relationship just because you're not getting as much as you want. Maybe the real alternative is to spend *more time* negotiating. That's what Quakers do. So do diplomats, whose alternative is war. So do couples who invest time in marriage counseling. And so do effective managers.

Another alternative is to have *other people* do the talking for a while, to see if they can make better progress. This is useful, for example, when you have technical experts who can "talk shop." They don't have role relationships that get in the way—unlike purchasing agents and sales representatives.

There are additional alternatives to choose from. Negotiators can bring in a neutral *third party*—a mediator, arbitrator, or other facilitator. They can use *conflict-resolution* techniques to remove the blocks and reframe the issues. Yet another alternative—preferred by many women—is to resolve differences *communally.* This involves engaging in dialog with the broader circle of friends, to establish what is the wisest course of action given the circumstances.

In sum, there are a lot of alternatives to walking away, suing, or striking—even in Type II transactions. But the emphasis on resistance points arising from the masculine-biased old-paradigm theory doesn't help you see these better alternatives.

Ironically, many of the simplistic books and training courses on negotiation are advertised as a means of building skill. How much skill does it take to pick up your things and walk away from a negotiation? I've seen 3-year-olds do it quite effectively. It takes skill to hang in there and work out a settlement when it's not easy to get what you want.

Now, I'm not implying that you should *never* have a resistance point. Sometimes you should, and you should use it as a negotiation tool. Most of the time, however, you won't need it because *there isn't* a next-best alternative to a negotiated solution. So it shouldn't be highlighted in negotiation models: all it really tells you is what you can hope for if you *fail.*

Rationality and Emotion

The old-paradigm approach to negotiation emphasizes masculine rationality—the self-interested optimization of utility, logical argument, and economic goal orientation. If someone is upset, and is expressing feelings without couching these in cold, linear logic, the person risks being dismissed by stereotypical males.

This isn't really fair. Nor is it wise. And it certainly isn't inclusive. We've noted that Western masculine rationality is only one kind of rationality. We've also noted that all people are naturally communal and emotional. Men, however, are trained to suppress these aspects of their nature. When other people—particularly women—don't suppress this side of their nature, men look down on them as being irrational, which is equated with being inferior.[9]

When you think about it, this makes no sense at all. Negotiation occurs only when there's a conflict: if there were no conflict, there'd be nothing to negotiate. Conflicts are emotional events, involving anxiety, hope, disappointment, fear, relief, anger, resentment, excitement, pity, remorse, and many other emotions. The old-paradigm, transaction-oriented approach emphasizes making unemotional decisions. Any emotions that crop up are treated as extraneous events that, if unchecked, detract from negotiation effectiveness.

It's certainly useful to train people to function in organizations dominated by men, and run according to traditional Western white male norms. People need to learn about masculine rationality, even though it doesn't exactly fit human nature. But it's going too far when we imply that this particular approach to rationality is the *only* approach or the *best* approach. Scholars do everyone a disservice when they take masculine-oriented rationality as "a given," and treat other ways of approaching situations as deviations (in a negative sense) from this. If people are being judged against white, Western, masculine standards, how is this different from discrimination?

Separating People from Problems

An offshoot of masculine rationality is the notion that problems are distinct from the people involved in them. To see why this approach doesn't really work, look at the process by which disagreements escalate from "philosophical differences" (emotionless differences of opinion) to conflicts that strain relationships and need to be dealt with. People react to what issues *mean* to them. The meanings they ascribe depend on the relationship context. If a good friend says something that hurts your feelings, you'll figure that he or she was being clumsy in dealing with you. If an enemy says the very same words, you'll figure that he or she was attacking you and wanted to hurt you.

You can't understand meanings without understanding relationships; therefore, you can't separate people from problems. The people involved give rise to the relationships, and the people supply, experience, and react to the meanings they ascribe to actions. The people, therefore, *are* the problem in conflicts.

In fact, the more you understand about the nature of conflicts, the more you wonder how anyone could have thought separating people from problems is a good idea. Women reading this may easily conclude, "It's a guy thing." And they'd be right. Masculine upbringing emphasizes separation and individuation.[10] This leads to a concept of the self as a detached entity. From there it's not much of an extension to imagine that the self can be detached from problems—even interpersonal problems.

This notion pervades Western legal thinking. The law is a realm of rights and rules that has been male-dominated for centuries, and shows it. Issues are treated as if they're objective, then lawyers argue about which rules apply. The people are treated as largely irrelevant: an issue is an issue, and the law is an entity unto itself. But this doesn't mirror people's experience, how they interact, how they negotiate, and how they manage. Thus, in reality, you *can't* separate people from problems.

THE IMPLICATIONS FOR MANAGERS

We're near the end of this last chapter, so let's take stock of where we are. In Chapter 8, we looked at traits that arise from socialization experiences that begin in early childhood. We saw significant differences in the traditional way Western girls and boys are trained to deal with other people. It became fairly obvious that each personality type has strengths and weaknesses, depending on the circumstances. Transaction-oriented managers fare better in some situations, while relationship-oriented managers fare better in others. Remember Joe and Josephine, in Chapter 1?

The problem is that the academic world—like the management

world—has been dominated by men: in the West, it has been dominated by white men with European ethnic roots. *They* devised all the theory that underlies our "knowledge" of management. As a result, we have some excellent theory, research, and teaching methods that reinforce the skills of stereotypical Western white men. But no matter how good this knowledge is, it only tells part of the story. It doesn't tell us much about how stereotypical Western women—and anyone else who's relationship-oriented[11]—manage relationships. We illustrated the problem by showing how the gender bias in negotiation theory limits its applicability to the real world.

This chapter has attempted to make readers *informed consumers* of management education. You should be able to spot the biases in what you read and what you're taught, and then compensate for them. You should not be dismissing what has been written, because even biased work can have good insights. But you'll need to go beyond what you read in order to maximize your effectiveness as a manager. Management is no longer the private reserve of Western white men.

The Knowledge Needed to Be Effective

This book aspires to provide you with an update in knowledge, to prepare you for life in organizations of the new era. This chapter has raised the question, what *is* knowledge? In practical terms, knowledge is what *you* understand about managing that currently guides your choices.

We're at a crossroads. Management thought has been evolving in one direction since the start of the Industrial Revolution. But during the past few decades, organizations have begun to evolve in a new direction, due to a number of factors, including globalization, deregulation, increasing diversity, and rapid changes in technology. Young people going into management are increasingly rejecting old-paradigm organizations. They prefer the excitement, inclusion, challenge, and freedom of start-ups—commonwealth organizations that are run the way people have been running organizations for thousands of years. It's a mistake to assume that the only allure of these organizations is the opportunity to become a millionaire when the company becomes publicly traded. That may be part of the attraction, but the preference is still strong when gaining equity in the company is not an option. There's something else going on in start-up organizations. Something very important to human nature.

It'll take researchers and writers a while to catch up and develop a new science of management, one that gives business relationships the attention they deserve. The reason for the lag is not that scientists are unintelligent— or oblivious to what's going on in the world around them—it's that they're conservative. They stick to an old paradigm long after a better way of think- ing has emerged.[12] This is fine for people in an ivory tower, whose prosper- ity and career success are not dependent on the choices they make each day in a merciless business environment. But managers' fortunes rise and fall on the quality of the relationships they form and manage, so the update in their knowledge can't wait for scholarly consensus to emerge.

As you read, listen to experts, and study management practice, you'll encounter the voices of oldthink and newthink. You'll have to decide for yourself what ways of thinking are useful in the new-era organization. You won't be able to trust "the weight of scientific evidence" alone, because much scientific inquiry is biased and out-of-date. Instead, you'll have to become a sophisticated consumer of what's being presented to you.

Remember that not so long ago, the weight of scientific evidence showed that the earth was flat and the sun and planets rotated around it. . . .

NOTES

1. The foundational theory of business and economics was primarily written in the earlier part of the twentieth century. Almost all of the influential writers in this era were Western-educated white men. The few women who became sig- nificant contributors were educated in—and writing about—a world domi- nated by Western white men. The demographic mix in academia is changing rapidly, but the foundations will be slow to evolve. Therefore, male-dominated paradigms will be hard to change in the short run.

2. For example, if I'm a research subject, and you ask me how I'd respond to a trading scenario *if* I were engaged in a simple exchange relationship with a complete stranger, I could tell you. That doesn't mean that I normally get into simple exchange relationships with strangers. And it doesn't tell you anything about what I actually do in other relationships—especially long-term business relationships. So even though the resulting research is technically adequate in addressing the questions *being posed*, it may not be addressing the most important questions to which managers need answers. So be very wary of authors who tell you to manage or negotiate a particular way because "the research shows. . . ."

3. The gender-biased vocabulary is in the videotape.

4. Old-paradigm thinkers refer to "claiming value" in a transaction. But think about this for a moment. The basis of any *claim* is some rights. How could you

claim anything unless you had a right to do so? Sometimes rights are a genuine focal point of negotiation, such as when you're one of the heirs to an estate. But most of the time, thinking about your rights isn't a useful way to approach negotiation. You need to be thinking instead about crafting a strong agreement and nurturing the ongoing relationship. Thus, writers who focus on "claiming value" as a key construct keep you locked into the egoistic viewpoint that pervades traditional masculine socialization.

5. This can also be modeled as a three-person (as distinct from three-party) commonwealth negotiation between Anne, Nathan, and Sandra. I chose not to illustrate this because it would take up a lot of space.

6. It will also depict Type III and Type IV negotiations if we insist, but there isn't much point in portraying them graphically.

7. For alternative versions of this general idea, see R. Blake and J. Mouton, *The Managerial Grid* (Houston: Gulf, 1964); M. A. Rahim, *Rahim Organizational Conflict Inventory II* (Palo Alto: Consulting Psychologists Press, 1983); and K. W. Thomas and R. H. Kilmann, *Thomas-Kilmann Conflict Mode Survey* (Tuxedo, NY: Xicom, 1974).

8. I think this is a metaphor that comes from baseball. It implies a lack of courage, or an unwillingness to do one's part for the team.

9. For example, women often experience a sense of personal failure if they cry in the workplace. Their "failure" is, in fact, nothing more than not living up to the masculine standard. Yet the masculine standard of emotional suppression, if you think about it, makes no sense. Anyone—male or female—who's spent a significant amount of time in the workplace has encountered situations that evoke strong emotional responses. But Western masculine culture requires that people maintain a pleasant but otherwise almost deadpan expression, all day every day.

10. Let's not forget where this notion of separation comes from. It is rooted in the incest taboo. Even primitive societies don't want boys to be too close to their mothers as they mature sexually. But to derive negotiation "principles" from the incest taboo is preposterous.

11. Many cultures are more communal than the United States, and several subcultures within the United States are more communal than white workers with European roots. In the twenty-first century, Western white men will not be the majority of the workforce, like they were fifty years ago. Thus, workforce diversity calls for theory and knowledge that is more inclusive.

12. This tendency is well documented. See, for example, the classic work by Thomas Kuhn, *The Structure of Scientific Revolutions* (Chicago: University of Chicago Press, 1962).

INDEX

ABOUT THE AUTHOR

Leonard Greenhalgh is professor of management at the Amos Tuck School of Business Administration at Dartmouth College—the world's oldest graduate school of business. Born in Great Britain and educated broadly in the United States, he brings a variety of perspectives to bear on the managerial challenges of the new era. Moreover, he brings a practical perspective, having founded and run two small corporations, served as a purchasing manager in a large multinational, and worked as a management consultant. At the Tuck School, he teaches popular electives involving the management of business relationships and negotiation. He has also been involved in teaching at Stanford, MIT, Oxford, Duke, and Cornell. As well, he consults with and conducts executive programs in a wide variety of global corporations, providing the opportunity for him to apply the insights of twenty-five years of academic research to the experience of today's managers.